HISTORY
LAID
BARE

* * * * * * * * *

HISTORY
LAID
BARE

Love, Sex, and Perversity
from the Ancient Etruscans
to Warren G. Harding

Richard Zacks

HarperPerennial
A Division of HarperCollins*Publishers*

The Library of Congress has catalogued the hardcover edition as follows:

Zacks, Richard.
    History laid bare : love, sex, and perversity from the ancient Etruscans to Warren
  G. Harding / by Richard Zacks. — 1st ed.
      p.   cm.
    Includes index.
    ISBN 0-06-016953-2
    1. Sex—History—Anecdotes. 2. Sex customs—History—Anecdotes. I. Title.
  HQ12.Z3 1994
  306.7′09—dc20   93-36636

ISBN 0-06-092599-X (pbk.)

95 96 97 98 99 ❖/HC 10 9 8 7 6 5 4 3 2 1

This book is dedicated to H.Z. and L.Z.

A thousand kisses to your neck, your breasts, and lower down,
much lower down, that little black forest I love so well.

—NAPOLEON, IN A LETTER TO JOSEPHINE

God grant me the strength to be chaste, just not yet.

—ST. AUGUSTINE

Contents

3 The Middle Ages   57

4 The Renaissance   129

5 The Seventeenth Century   183

6 The Eighteenth Century   209

7 The Nineteenth Century 291

8 Early Twentieth Century   427

Lawrence of Arabia is Captured, 1917
President Harding in the White House Coat Closet, 1921

Introduction

When Joan of Arc was tried for witchcraft at Rouen, her virginity was tested at least twice. Physically tested. And a priest swore under oath that her enemy the duke of Bedford peeped at her through a hole bored in the wall.

Abraham Lincoln shared a bed with a man for four years; Mark Twain gave a speech on masturbation; Leonardo da Vinci scribbled a dirty joke in the margin of one of his notebooks.

I don't know about you, but I don't remember any of these stories included in *my* history books. Economic theory behind peasant rebellions, yes. Clothes, food, military strategy, yes, but sex was strictly left out. It's as though great men and women were never naked and never lusted.

This book aims to put SEX back in history. Where it always was until the Victorians and other prudish scholars took it out.

The ancients didn't sanitize their past. Suetonius writes of Nero dressing up in animal skins to claw at the genitals of male and female prisoners tied to stakes. Tiberius loved to watch threesomes. Herodotus writes of Egyptians enacting a law to prevent embalmers from raping female corpses. The Renaissance diary of the master of ceremonies for Pope Alexander VI graphically describes an orgy attended by the pope on October 30, 1501, in which naked prostitutes crawled on all fours gathering chestnuts. These scenes vivify history more than any political theory; they color the cold white marble statues.

When I first started this project—combing obscure books in English, French, Italian, Greek, Latin (thanks, Dad, for a wildly impractical education)—to discover these censored moments, I was focusing mainly on larger-than-life figures, like Lincoln and St. Augustine. But the more I delved, the more I discovered extraordinarily revealing accounts from the not so famous. Letters, court cases, doctor's reports, and diaries, which when piled end-to-end form an anecdotal time line of human sexuality—sometimes frightening, sometimes hilarious. The sheer creativity and diversity of horizontal (and not so horizontal) amusements is astounding.

I consider myself well read, but I had no idea that in 1012 a medieval German priest named Burchard of Worms catalogued close to two hundred different sexual sins and their punishments. He describes the penance required when a woman smears herself with honey, rolls in flour, and bakes a loaf of aphrodisiac bread, or when a man masturbates into a hollowed wooden device.

I was also amazed to find the confession of a Scottish witch named Isabel Gowdie, who in 1662 gave a detailed description of sex with the devil, right down to his ice-water sperm. There's also the long-overlooked diary of an American Civil War prostitute: "The praying general was brought in today by Preacher H. He is rough and brutal. After I serviced him, he dropped to his knees and asked God to forgive *me* for my sins!"

This is not fiction, it is contemporary reporting, very often from eyewitnesses. Joan of Arc's story is from her trial records, written in Latin. Flaubert filled his travel notebooks with tales of belly dancers. Lewis Carroll wrote letters requesting young nude models.

One warning, though: Don't expect a methodical history of sex here. This book is a collection of very revealing stories, fragments, vignettes—a kind of album of lewd snapshots, one that packs quite a few surprising insights. I always thought blockhead man hadn't a clue about the geography of a woman's genitals until the mid-twentieth century, that the search for the clitoris was like the search for the source of the Nile. Not true. Hippocrates describes the clitoris four hundred years before Christ. And as for woman's orgasms, influential ancient and medieval doctors (such as Galen and Albert the Great) believed that a woman's orgasm was necessary for conception, which means that millions of men through the ages thought the only way they could become fathers was by satisfying their wives. No doubt that misconception brought untold hours of enjoyment to lots of medieval women.

Regarding the wording in this book, I have tried to be straightforward about sexual terms but, unfortunately, the English language when dealing with body parts and sex acts tends to be either clinical or crude. There's rarely a "healthy" middle ground. In light of that, I've tried my best to find translations that are accurate and readable but not squeamish. In many cases, I've done my own, especially from French and ancient Greek.

This book aims to amuse, enlighten, and to fill a gap. Put it by your bedside and dip into it every night. Or read it cover to cover and see the changes in attitudes about sex. However you read it, I hope it will put flesh and blood on the bare bones of history, and I hope you enjoy reading these as much as I have enjoyed finding them.

Text Note

This book marches forward chronologically from the ancient Assyrians (1450 B.C.) to Warren Harding (1921), but every so often I've veered from following a strict time line to group together, say, a few items about the Crusades or flagellation. I did that for continuity and coherence and also to spare the curious reader from having to leapfrog from reference to reference.

As for the text, anything *not* from the original sources, such as my own comments, has been put into *italics*.

Finally, regarding a scholarly apparatus, it has been mostly dismantled. The stories and wisecracks should be the stars, not the footnotes. Anyone wanting to consult the originals can find the citations under the sections titled "Copyright Acknowledgments" and "Sources."

The
Ancient
World

Assyrian Law Tablet, 1450 B.C.

The eye-for-an-eye law code of the Old Testament shares common roots with other laws prevailing in the Near East, such as these found on a fifteenth-century B.C. tablet in Assyria:

If a citizen has kissed the wife of another citizen, they shall draw his lower lip along the edge of the blade of an ax and cut it off.

If a woman has a miscarriage by her own act [*i.e., an abortion*], when they have prosecuted her and convicted her, they shall impale her on stakes without burying her. If she died having the miscarriage, they shall [*still*] impale her on stakes without burying her.

When a married man raped a virgin in Assyria, who was punished the most?

If a citizen took the virgin by force and ravished her, either in the midst of the city or in the open country, at night in the street or in a granary or at a city festival, the father of the virgin shall take the rapist's wife and give her to be ravished; he shall not return her to her husband but take her. The father may give his own daughter to the ravisher in marriage.

—ASSYRIAN LAW TABLET

Hittites: Fine Points in Early Bestiality Laws, 1400 B.C.

The ancient Hittites perceived quite a few gray areas regarding fornication with the four-footed. Remember, the Hittites used to ride out on horseback on long, lonely raiding missions.

If a man does evil with a head of cattle, it is a capital crime and he shall be killed.
If a man does evil with a sheep, it is a capital crime and he shall be killed.
If anyone does evil with a pig, he shall die.
If a man does evil with a horse or mule, there shall be no punishment.
If an ox "leaps at" [*i.e., attempts to mount*] a man, the ox shall die, but the man shall not die. A sheep may be proferred in the man's stead and they shall kill that.
If a pig leaps at a man, there shall be no punishment.

—HITTITE LAW TABLET

Spoils of Egyptian War: Not Scalps, 1300 B.C.

Rape has long provided a vicious sexual means of humiliating the enemy, but the Egyptian king Menephta added another twist in his war against the Libyans. Here is an inscription found on a victory monument:

Phalluses of Libyan generals: 6
Phalluses cut off Libyans: 6,359
Sicilians killed, phalluses cut off: 222
Etruscans killed, phalluses cut off: 542
Greeks killed, phalluses given to the king: 6,111

Ancient Greece: A Roundup

The Golden Age of Greece—Socrates, Sophocles, the Parthenon, democracy—was a phenomenally creative period for Western civilization. It was also a great time sexually to be a man. As Demosthenes put it: "Men have 'hetairai' [*courtesans*] for erotic pleasures, female slaves to serve their daily physical needs, and wives to bear legitimate children and maintain a household."

And that doesn't include bisexual or homosexual recreation, both of which appear to have been fairly common, especially between men and teenage boys. A man could take advantage of a kind of mentor system, whereby the man taught the boy various subjects and the boy was sometimes skewered by more than the fellow's wit.

As for girls, their sex lives were very restricted. They were expected to be virgin brides. If they were not virgins when they married, it meant dishonor for their fathers. For most of their adult lives, "respectable" Greek women were kept secluded in the women's quarters and were never allowed at dinner parties, where geniuses like Plato entertained. Wives were probably undersexed by their husbands, if historian Xenophon got it right when he wrote: "By law, a couple lacking a legitimate heir is required to have sex three times a month."

Adultery became such a problem that it led Solon—the most famous early lawgiver—to set up state-run brothels. The world's first democracy had legalized prostitution. Foreign slaves—men and women—were imported to stock the brothels.

Unquestionably, the best chance a poor woman had in Ancient Athens for pursuing the arts and earning a few drachmai was by becoming a hetaira (or high-class courtesan).

Nudity in the Courts

Phryne the courtesan was so beautiful that she posed for several of antiquity's most famous statues of Aphrodite, including one at Delphi. A travel book dubbed it a "monument to Greek lust."

Phryne was brought to trial accused of a crime that called for the death penalty. . . . When her lawyer Hypereides realized he was losing the case, and that the judges meant to convict her, he summoned her to the center of the courtroom; then he tore off her skimpy tunic and revealed her naked breasts for all to see. And he started wailing hysterically at the sight of her spectacular beauty. The judges were flustered and awestruck by this handmaiden of Aphrodite and, feeling merciful, they didn't put her to death.

But once they acquitted her, a decree was passed that no lawyer may ever wail hysterically during a plea, and that no accused man or woman may ever be stripped in the courtroom.

—ATHENAEUS

Prostitution: Better than Adultery, and Safer

In the sixth century B.C., Solon imported girls from Asia Minor. The brothels paid taxes, and the world's first democratic government fixed prices very low to ensure that men could easily afford them.

The young men in Athens are doing absolutely shocking things [*like committing adultery*], and there's no excuse for it. For there are very fine-looking girls available at the brothels. And you can see them standing there outside, breasts bared in the bright sunshine, almost naked and lined up conveniently one after another. From these, anybody can pick out a favorite: skinny or fat; curvy, lanky, or bent over; young or old; firm or lush. You have no need to prop a ladder to climb in secretly [*to a married woman*] and you don't have to crawl in through the smoke hole or be smuggled in under a pile of straw. No way! These girls just about drag you in, calling the old men "Daddy," and the younger ones "Lover Boy." And you can have her, cheap and without any risk, available day and evening—and any way you want her.

But with married women, you can never see them clearly, and you're always skittish and afraid, risking your life. Oh, Aphrodite, how can men try to go after married women once they know the laws?

—XENARCHUS

Early Example of Creative Advertising

A pair of sandals owned by a Greek prostitute have survived, and embossed on the soles in raised letters, which would leave an impression wherever she walked, were two words:

Follow me!

Advice to Prostitutes:
Not a Padded Bra, But . . .

In ancient Greece, the most prized part of the female anatomy was not a woman's breasts.

What if a girl has no backside? She slips some padding underneath her shift, so that anyone catching sight of her cries out: What a great ass!

—ALEXIS

There was even a Temple of Aphrodite Kallipygiea (i.e., Aphrodite of the Great Ass). This was no fringe cult; this was part of the state religion.

Boy-Love

Although mature Greek men often played mentor to adolescent males and sometimes had sex with them, Athenian law clearly opposed anyone seducing prepubescent boys:

Boy-love is a forbidden pleasure, because it causes shame and fear. The man needs a plausible excuse for approaching young and beautiful boys, so he professes friendship and virtue. He covers himself with the sand of the wrestling floor, takes cold baths, arches his brows and calls himself a philosopher and shows himself disciplined—all because of the law.

But once night falls, and it's quiet: "Sweet is the harvest when the guard has gone away."

—PLUTARCH

Rules for the Ritual Rape of Cretan Teenage Boys

Strabo (63 B.C.–A.D. 21), the ancient world's most famous geographer, wrote that the world was a sphere. He also described homosexual customs in Crete:

Their custom in love affairs is quite unusual for the men gain their lovers not by persuasion but by [*ritual*] kidnapping. The lover warns the friends of the teenage boy three or more days in advance that he's going to kidnap him. For them to hide the boy or keep him from taking the designated road would be a severe disgrace because that would mark the boy as unworthy of such a lover. When the two meet, if the kidnapper is of equal or higher status, the boy's companions chase after him and grab him lightly—just to act out the ritual. They then happily hand the boy over to him, to the man's charge. If, however, the kidnapper is unworthy, they grab the boy back.

They only chase the kidnapper as far as his home. The Cretans consider the finest boy not the handsomest but the manliest and best behaved. The lover then gives the boy a gift and then leads him off to anywhere he likes in the countryside. And the witnesses to the kidnapping follow after them. They all feast and hunt for two months; it's not permitted to keep the boy any longer, then they return to the city. Before the boy goes away, he receives the gifts required by law: a military uniform, an ox, a drinking cup, and many other expensive presents. His friends chip in as well.

The boy sacrifices the ox, and throws a feast for his friends. Perhaps he'll share some details of his sexual relations with his lover, whether he enjoyed himself or not. The law gives him that privilege, so that, if force was applied during the kidnapping, he can avenge himself and be rid of his lover.

It's disgraceful for boys who are handsome or have famous ancestors not to have lovers, because it must mean their character's to blame.

—STRABO

Nude Olympics

Public nudity in ancient Greece was never the giddy frolic of both sexes in the buff that some people imagine. Young men did exercise naked or wearing only a string tying off their foreskin, but they did so in an all-male gymnasium. (The word "gymnasium" comes from the Greek "gymnos," or naked.)

In the public baths, naked men and women were strictly segregated. As for the Olympics, an all-male crowd, wearing clothes, watched male athletes compete naked. At least that was the plan.

As you go along the road to Olympia from the direction of Scillus, just before you cross the Alpheius, you find Mount Typaeum with high steep cliffs. It is the law there that any women caught at the Olympic Games . . . on those days forbidden to women must be thrown off the cliffs. However, it's said that no woman has been caught except the widow, Callipateira. . . . She disguised herself as a gymnastic trainer and escorted her son, Peisirodus, to compete at Olympia. He was victorious, and when she was jumping over the fence to leave the trainers' area, she [*accidentally*] showed herself naked. Immediately they knew she was a woman. However, they let her leave unpunished, showing respect to her father, her brothers, and her son—all Olympic champions. But they enacted a law that in the future, all trainers must strip naked before coming into the arena.

—PAUSANIUS

The Night Before the Track Meet

I observed one of the smarter coaches placing a lead plaster on the genitals of an athlete to prevent wet dreams.

—GALEN

The Father of Medicine, on Orgasms, 400 B.C.

Hippocrates (460–377 B.C.) was the most famous doctor of antiquity (his Hippocratic Oath is still often required to be taken by medical students today; the original Greek version of the oath though, also forbade abortion and the seduction of patients). Hippocrates devised many theories, such as this one on sexual pleasure, which involves some very convenient timing for the male:

During intercourse, once a woman's genitals are vigorously

rubbed and her womb titillated, a lustfulness [*an itch*] overwhelms her down there, and the feeling of pleasure and warmth pools out through the rest of her body. A woman also has an ejaculation, furnished by her body, occurring at the same time inside the womb, which has become wet, as well as on the outside because the womb is now gaping wide open.

A woman feels pleasure right from the start of intercourse, through the entire time of it, right up until the moment when the man pulls out; if she feels an orgasm coming on, she ejaculates with him, and then she no longer feels pleasure. But if she feels no oncoming orgasm, her pleasure stops when his does. It's like when one throws cold water onto boiling water, the boiling ceases immediately. The same with the man's sperm falling into the womb, it extinguishes the warmth and pleasure of the woman.

Her pleasure and warmth, though, surge the moment the sperm descends in the womb, then it fades. Just as when wine is poured on a flame, it gives a spurt before it goes out for good.

—HIPPOCRATES

Around the Mediterranean

Ancient travelers had a knack for coming back with tales of strange sexual customs. Herodotus (circa *484–425 B.C.) found necrophilia in Egypt; Theopompus* (b. circa *380 B.C.) found a sexual utopia in western Italy; Lucian* (circa *A.D. 120–200) found ecstatic self-emasculation in Syria.*

Is There Sex After Death?

[*In Egypt*] when the wives of high-ranking men die, the husbands do not deliver them right away to be embalmed, nor do they immediately hand over very beautiful or famous women but wait till the third or fourth day after death. They do this so that the embalmers may not have sexual intercourse with these women. For word has it that one was caught mounted upon a fresh female corpse, and was exposed by a fellow worker.

—HERODOTUS

Temple Prostitution (or, The Long Wait)

The most shameful law among the Babylonians is this: every woman once in her lifetime is required to sit down in the courtyard of the temple of Aphrodite and have sexual intercourse with a stranger. Many wealthy women disdain to mingle with the riffraff and travel to the temple gates in closed carriages, with many handmaidens following them. But most just walk in and seat themselves in the sacred plot of Aphrodite wearing a garland of rope round their heads. There's always a great hubbub, with some women arriving, some leaving.

Pathways are marked out in all directions among the women so that strangers can conveniently pass among them and make their choices. Once a woman has become seated, she may not return home until one of the strangers has tossed a coin in her lap and has had sexual intercourse with her outside the temple. When he casts the coin, he must say: "I invite you in the name of the goddess Mylitta ('Mylitta' is what the Assyrians call Aphrodite). It doesn't matter how little money he gives because he won't be rejected, for that would be a sin, since the money belongs to the temple. She follows the first man who tosses a coin and she never rejects anyone. Once she's finished having sex, she has fulfilled her vow to the goddess and can go home. Afterwards no gift, no matter how generous, will buy her.

Beautiful and shapely women are, of course, claimed quickly and can go home, but the ugly ones must often wait a long time because they can't fulfill the law—some of them stay three or four years.

—HERODOTUS

Sexual Utopia: Uncommonly Beautiful Common Wives

The Etruscans belonged to the first sophisticated culture on Italian soil, and they laid the groundwork for Rome. They also allowed their women greater freedom than did the Greeks.

Among the Etruscans, who are self-indulgent and love luxury, slave girls wait on their masters naked.

Etruscan law calls for the sharing of all women; the women take great care of their bodies and often do gymnastic exercises naked with the men, and sometimes among themselves. For it is not considered shameful for women to be seen naked. Also, they eat dinner, not just with their own husbands but with any men who chance to stop by, and they drink toasts to anyone they choose. And they love to drink and they are very beautiful.

The Etruscans bring up all babies in common, without ever

knowing who the father is. These children in turn live just like their relatives, drinking a lot and screwing around with any woman.

The Etruscans also don't consider it shameful to have sex openly with other males, either in an active or a passive role, for that's a custom in their country. They feel so little shame about it that if the master of the house is being screwed [*i.e., playing the woman's role*], and anyone comes asking for him, the servant says quite matter-of-factly that he's undergoing this or that, crudely specifying the act by name.

When they get together with friends or relatives, this is how they act: After they've finished drinking and are ready for bed (but while the lamps are still burning), the servants lead in to them courtesans, very beautiful boys or their wives.

Once the husbands have enjoyed any of these, the servants then fetch lusty young men, who also fool around with these courtesans, boys or wives. They adore sex, and have intercourse sometimes with others watching; but most of the time, they surround their beds with screens of cloth stretched over lattice. They enjoy sex with women but they much prefer it with boys and gay young men. For among the Etruscans, these gay youngsters are exceptionally beautiful because they're pampered and take great care of their bodies. In fact, all the Barbarians [*i.e., non-Greeks*] who live in the West remove all their body hair with pitch plasters. Among the Etruscans, there are many boutiques for this purpose with well-trained attendants, just as we have barber shops. People enter these places and contort their limbs and don't give a rat's ass about rubber-necking passers-by.

—THEOPOMPUS

A Bloody Fertility Rite

At the beginning of spring, when multitudes thronged to the sanctuary from Syria, . . . the flutes played, the drums beat, and the eunuch priests slashed themselves with knives, the religious excitement spread like a wave among the crowd of onlookers, and many a one did that which he little thought to do when he came as a holiday spectator to the festival. For man after man, his veins throbbing with the music, his eyes fascinated by the sight of streaming blood, flung his garments from him, leapt forth with a shout, and seizing one of the swords which stood ready for the purpose, castrated himself on the spot. Then he ran through the city, holding the bloody pieces in his hand till he threw them in to one of the houses he passed in his mad dash. The household thus honored had to furnish him with a suit of female attire and female adornments, which he wore the rest of his life.

—LUCIAN

Ancient Rome

Try to imagine the role models set by the emperors after Augustus (A.D. 14): Nero castrated and married a boy; Tiberius liked to watch three-in-a-row anal intercourse; Caligula deified his sex-partner/sister, Drusilla.

While an emperor could do almost anything—sex-wise or any-wise—to anyone, a rich Roman in turn could do almost anything to a slave. The Jewish historian Josephus tells us there were about a million slaves in Rome around A.D. 90. One noble Roman, Vedius Pollio, used to keep a pond filled with giant lamprey eels, and any slave who misbehaved he simply tossed in and watched the fish pick at his bones.

The power and cruelty boggles the mind. Around the Colosseum and Circus Maximus, prostitutes trawled the alleyways enticing the blood-crazed citizens exiting the gladiator shows.

In addition, bisexuality and homosexuality—often receiving the royal stamp of approval—flourished. Men spent long hours in the steamy baths inspecting and cavorting with other men, which gave rise to epigrams like this one from Martial:

When you hear clapping in the baths,
You know some moron with a giant dick has arrived.

The heyday of the Roman Empire also marked more freedom for women, at least wealthy women, to play. Unlike in ancient Greece, married Roman women could attend banquets; they could easily divorce their husbands; they had more property rights. And with the power came a reputation for rampant sexuality. How much is truth and how much the fiction of moralistic writers is hard to tell.

Empress Messalina, the Wife of "I, Claudius," A.D. 45

Once [*Messalina*] sensed that [*Emperor Claudius*] was asleep, this royal whore was brazen enough to prefer a common mat to her marriage bed in the palace, and she slipped on a night-cowl, and departed accompanied by only one female slave. She hid her black hair beneath a blond wig, and entered a brothel dank from old bedspreads, heading

straight to her own empty little cell. With her nipples exposed
and gilded, she prostituted herself under the alias of Lycisca,
and she displayed the womb that bore you, O high-born
Britannicus!

Here she passionately took on all comers and demanded the
coins due from each, and when finally the brothel-keeper sent
his girls home, she went away depressed—the last to close her
cell. Lust still flared in her throbbing loins.

Exhausted by men but not satisfied, her cheeks darkened
from the smoke of the lamps, Messalina carried the stink of
the brothel back to the imperial bed.

—JUVENAL

See-through Blouses

I see silk clothes, if these qualify as "clothes," which do
nothing to hide the body, not even the genitals. Women
wearing them can barely swear in good conscience they're not
naked. These clothes are imported from far-off countries and
cost a fortune, and the end result? Our women have nothing
left to show their lovers in the bedroom that they haven't
already revealed on the street.

—SENECA (*CIRCA* 4 B.C.–A.D. 65)

Roman Wives Find a Loophole, A.D. 19

*Married women were very creative in finding ways around strict
Roman adultery laws, which forbade them from having sex with
anyone other than their husbands and punished them with exile and
property loss:*

Married women from well-known families were registering as prostitutes, and were escaping punishment for their adulteries by renouncing the privileges of their rank in society.

—SUETONIUS

The Senate—male, of course—and Emperor Tiberius weren't thrilled:

In [A.D. 19], the Senate ruled that no woman—whose father, grandfather, or husband had been a Roman knight—could sell her body. For Vistilia, the daughter of a Praetorian family, out of sheer lust, had registered on the Aedile's List as a prostitute—the standard procedure set up by our ancestors who thought the shame of such an action would be punishment and prevention enough. Her husband, Titidius Labeo, also had to explain why, despite his wife's obvious guilt, he had not imposed the penalty of the law. Although he pleaded that his sixty-day deliberation period had not yet expired, it was deemed the right time to pass judgment on Vistilia. She was deported to the [barren] island of Seriphos.

—TACITUS

Married men, meanwhile, could legally have sex with slaves, prostitutes, divorcees, widows, virtually everyone but a Roman virgin or a Roman wife. Adultery was defined as sex with a married woman, not with a married man.

The Proper Position for Women, 60 B.C.

This Roman philosopher was clear about the differences between wives (breeding/family) and prostitutes (pleasure):

The sexual position is also important. For wives who imitate the manner of wild beasts and quadrupeds—that is, breast down, haunches up—are generally thought to conceive better, since the semen can more easily reach the proper place.

And it is absolutely NOT necessary for wives to move at all. For a women prevents and battles pregnancy if in her joy, she answers the man's lovemaking with her buttocks, and her soft breasts billow forward and back; for she diverts the ploughshare out of the furrow and makes the seed miss its mark. Whores practice such movements for their own reasons, to avoid conception and pregnancy, and also to make the lovemaking more enjoyable for men, which obviously isn't necessary for our wives.

—LUCRETIUS (*CIRCA* 96–55 B.C.)

Priapeia

In ancient Rome, statues of Priapus boasting a humongous erect phallus were set up in gardens as mock scarecrows to ward off thieves and maybe provide a laugh. Inscribed on them were very brief, very crude jingles, written in the voice of the phallus guard. Here are some examples:

Steal once, I'll give it to you in the rear.
Try it again, I'll overflow your mouth.
And if you steal a third time,
You'll suffer both punishments at once:
Mouth and rear packed beyond the limit.

✳

Hey, thief, you think it's funny standing there
Laughing at me, insulting me, giving me the finger.
I know, I know: although my member looks

Terrifyingly huge, it's only made of wood.
But, hold on, lemme call my horny master.
As a favor to me, he'll give you something to gag on.

✳

When you get the urge for a fig,
And are about to reach out to steal one,
Stare long and hard at me
And try to guess what shitting
A twenty-pound, two foot-long turd would feel like.

Wise Proverb

If you've run out of luck, it doesn't matter how long your penis is.

—JUVENAL

Beheaded in the Name of Love

Lucius Quintus was a Roman senator, at least for a while.

Lucius kept a pretty youngster, right from boyhood, as his lover; [*the older man*] always had him around, even took him on military expeditions, and gave him more respect and power than his closest friends and relatives.

One time Lucius was handling the affairs of his consular province, and at a certain dinner party, this youngster was lounging by his side and began to flatter the man, who, once he started drinking wine, was easily manipulated. "I love you so much," said the youngster, "that one time when I attended my very first gladiator show, I rushed away early to meet you although I wanted very badly to see a man get slaughtered."

Lucius immediately tried to placate the boy. "Now, don't just lie there," he said, "and hold it against me. I'll make it up to you."

Then he ordered a condemned man brought directly to the dinner party, and had an officer with an axe stand alongside him. Lucius asked his young lover if he wanted to see the man killed. The youngster said he would like that very much and Lucius ordered the man's head cut off.

—PLUTARCH

Lucius Quintus was expelled from the Senate for that display of love.

Eyewitness in the Baths

You pluck the hair from your breast, legs, and arms; you keep your penis cropped and ringed with short hair; all this, we know you do for your mistress' sake, Labienus. For whom do you depilate your ass?

—MARTIAL (*CIRCA* A.D. 40–102)

Chrestus, you appear with your parts all shaven,
So your penis looks a vulture's neck.

—MARTIAL

All those statues of women with no pubic hair? It wasn't artistic censorship, they just mirrored the prevailing fashion, which called for women's bodies to be completely depilated.

As for men, heterosexuals clipped some areas but it was homosexuals who mowed the underbrush of their nether regions to facilitate entry. Historians such as Suetonius and Lampridius loved to use this hygiene detail as a coy way to identify veteran homosexuals.

The Conquests of Caesar, *circa* 50 B.C.

Julius Caesar (100–44 B.C.), a tall Lothario with piercing brown eyes, was noted for his active libido, especially in the pages of Suetonius, the scandal-minded biographer of a dozen emperors:

[*Julius Caesar*] was something of a dandy, always keeping his head carefully trimmed and shaved; and he has been accused of having certain other hairy parts of his body depilated with tweezers. (*Roman readers—reading between the lines—would immediately know that the hairy part in question was Caesar's ass.*)

The only specific charge of unnatural practices ever brought against him was that he had been King Nicomedes' bedfellow—always a dark stain on his reputation and frequently quoted by his enemies. . . . Dolabella called him "the Queen's rival and inner partner of the royal bed."

And Marcus Brutus recorded that, about the same time, one Octavius, a scatterbrained creature who would say the first thing that popped into his head, walked into a packed assembly where he saluted Pompey as "King" and Caesar as "Queen."

Despite this one charge, Caesar was generally pegged as an almost insatiable heterosexual. Near the end of the Gallic Wars, his soldiers made up a little song about him:

Home we bring our bald whoremonger;
Romans, lock your wives away!
All the bags of gold you lent him
Went his Gallic tarts to pay.

For the good of the state . . . :
A tribune of the people named Helvius Cinna had informed
a number of people that, following instructions, he had drawn
up a bill for the commons to pass during Caesar's absence
from Rome, legitimizing his marriage with any woman or
women he pleased "for the procreation of children."

Despite all the conquests, Caesar was still insecure.
His baldness was a disfigurement that his enemies harped
upon, much to his exasperation; but he used to comb the thin
strands of hair forward from his poll, and of all the honors
voted him by the Senate and the people, none pleased him so
much as the privilege of wearing a laurel wreath on all
occasions—he constantly took advantage of it.

—SUETONIUS, *LIVES OF THE CAESARS*

Cleopatra Seduces Marc Antony, 42 B.C.

*Cleopatra (69–30 B.C.) apparently looked more like Olive
Oyl than Elizabeth Taylor. Contemporary medallions show her
to have a gaunt face with a long, beaked nose.*

*But what ancient historians stress is that she was very clever
and very sexy. Twice she seduced the invading conqueror to save
her kingdom. At twenty, she won over the most powerful man in
the world, the balding, lecherous, fifty-two-year-old Julius Caesar.*

Then, in 42 B.C., at age twenty-six, with Rome threatening again and with local enemies conspiring, she traveled to Tarsus in Asia Minor to meet general Marc Antony.

Cleopatra was an immensely wealthy, multilingual young woman of Greek ancestry on a diplomatic mission—doing it her way.

In preparation for leaving, Cleopatra prepared elaborate gifts, lots of gold and ornaments befitting the ruler of a prosperous land. But when she departed, she placed her greatest trust in her own self and in her ability to bewitch.

Despite many urgent letters from Marc Antony himself and his colleagues demanding her presence, she chose to toy with the man from the very start. She sailed slowly up the river Cydnus in a boat with a gilded prow, and sails of deep purple. Her rowers dipped silver oars to the cadence of flutes and guitars.

Cleopatra herself lolled beneath a canopy splashed with gold, posed like Venus in a painting, while boys handsome as Eros gently fanned her. Her most beautiful handmaidens, resembling river goddesses and Graces, were artfully placed about the ship. Beguiling perfumes billowing from incense burners engulfed the river banks. Local citizens from far and wide came to gawk. [*In Tarsus*] so many crowds flocked from the marketplace to the river until finally Marc Antony found himself alone, seated upon his throne.

Word spread that Aphrodite had arrived to sport with Dionysus for the good of Asia.

Antony sent a messenger to invite Cleopatra to dinner; she, however, preferred that he should come to her. And Antony, wanting to show goodwill and a cavalier attitude, agreed and went.

When he arrived, he was completely bedazzled by the magnificent display, especially by the lights. Pointing this way, arching that way, the lights carved out mesmerizing patterns: rectangles, circles, one of the most beautiful sights ever seen.

The next day, Antony aimed to outdo Cleopatra with an even more luxurious banquet but he failed and was the first to complain about the crassness of his own fare.

Cleopatra noted in Antony's crude humor much of the soldier and workingman. So, she quickly chameleoned herself to drop any airs and boldly play along.

For we've been told that her beauty was by no means flawless, nor even remarkable upon first meeting, but anyone listening to her but a moment sensed her irresistible charm. She had presence. Her voice was beguilingly rich and sweet. And she used her tongue like a many-stringed musical instrument. As for talking to foreigners, she rarely needed an interpreter, but answered them all, whether Ethiopians, Troglodytes, Hebrews, Arabians, Syrians, Medes, or Parthians. She knew many foreign languages, although many previous Egyptian kings [of Greek descent] never bothered to learn even the local dialect.

. . . Cleopatra flattered Antony, always dreaming up some fresh delight, careful never to let him stray from her either day or night. She rolled dice with him, drank with him, hunted with him, and faithfully watched him exercise and play war games. And even when he scrambled about the city hiding in doorways and windows, taunting and teasing complete strangers, she went along. For Antony liked to disguise himself as a servant and on occasion wound up cursed and sometimes beaten, although the majority of people probably recognized him.

Nonetheless, Alexandrians enjoyed his crude jokes, and joined in his pranks in their own elegant and cultured way.

Cleopatra's Little Joke

Now, to describe one jest: He [*Marc Antony*] was fishing and pulling up absolutely nothing and was annoyed that Cleopatra was there to see it. So he directed a servant secretly to swim with some freshly caught fish and attach them to his hook. He hauled up two or three. Even after the Egyptian queen figured out the ruse, she kept fawning over her lover's fishing skills. She then invited a vast number of guests to come watch the next day's fishing.

Then, with a large crowd looking on in boats, Antony felt a tug on his line and pulled out . . . a dried salted old herring. Amid the laughter, Cleopatra showed her cunning. "O Conqueror," she said, "give your fishing pole to the men of Pharos and Canopus; your sport is the hunting of cities and kingdoms and continents."

—PLUTARCH, *LIFE OF MARC ANTONY*

Marc Antony Defends His Sex Life

Marc Antony and Cleopatra teamed up over the following years to challenge Rome itself. In 34 B.C., Antony announced that Cleopatra's thirteen-year-old son by Julius Caesar, named Caesarion, was the rightful heir in Rome. Augustus Caesar fought back on many fronts, including the rumor mill, bidding his lackeys spread smutty stories about Antony and Cleopatra's sex life. Antony fired back an angry, slangy letter:

Why have you changed towards me? Because I screw a queen? She is my wife. Did I just start this now or have I been with her for nine years? Do you screw only Livy? My sincere compliments, if, when this letter arrives, you haven't been fooling around with Tertulla, Terentilla, Rufilla, or Salvia Titisenia, or all of them. Really, what's the big deal where or in whom you get a hard-on?

—SUETONIUS, *LIVES OF THE CAESARS*

Later, in 30 B.C., with troops routed, Marc Antony was informed of Cleopatra's death. He immediately stabbed himself. Only it turned out the report was wrong, so Antony had himself carried to Cleopatra's hiding place, where he died in her arms. Cleopatra killed herself soon after. Legend has it that the doctor who inspected her body found only two tiny marks on her arm, the puncture wounds from the fangs of an asp.

Magnifying Mirrors: A Sex Toy in Ancient Rome, A.D. 10

Seneca (4 B.C.–A.D. 65) wrote a serious book, in which he tried to explain natural phenomena such as earthquakes and tides. When the respected philosopher hit the subject of mirrors, he took a sudden detour:

Now, I want to tell you a story so that you may learn how a

lusty man never rejects any instrument for arousing pleasure and how ingenious he can be about it.

Take Hostius Quadra. His sex life was so notorious that it was featured in a stage play. He was a rich miser and when he was killed by his own slaves, the emperor Augustus regarded him as unworthy of vengeance.

Hostius' lewd behavior wasn't limited to one gender; he lusted after both men and women. He ordered mirrors made that magnified reflections so that a finger appeared greater in length and thickness than an arm. These mirrors were then placed so when he was surrendering himself to a man, he could watch all the thrusts of the young stallion behind him, and thrill to the false size of his partner's penis, as though it were really so huge.

In all the public baths, he would hold an informal draft and openly measure men as he selected them, but still his insatiable lust delighted in further enhancement.

Now tell me the mirror was invented just for checking hair and makeup!

. . . Those secret acts (the ones that, if accused of, every man denies), he experienced them not only in his mouth but with his eyes. . . . And he wasn't satisfied with just simply watching, he surrounded himself with mirrors strategically placed so he could divide up his sordid deeds and rearrange them.

For instance, since he could not scrutinize the goings-on closely enough when, while ridden from behind, his head dipped down and locked onto another partner's genitals, he delivered his own work back to himself through reflections. He used to admire the obscene artistry of his own mouth, and contemplate himself absorbing men at every orifice.

Sometimes sandwiched between a man and a woman with his whole body exposed serving both of them, he was able to witness his most deviant behavior. He was no fan of darkness. Far from fearing daylight, he craved it for his monstrous copulations and was proud to have them well lit. He even wanted to have his portrait painted in these positions.

Even prostitutes hide their subservience in the brothel . . . , but he wanted to turn his obscenities into a spectacle.

. . . "Yes," he said, "I play the passive partner to a man and a woman at the same time [*i.e., anal sex and cunnilingus*]; but nonetheless with my body part left free, I violate another man. Thus all my organs are occupied in lechery. Let my eyes too share in the nasty fun and be witnesses and judges of it. By means of mirrors, let even those acts be seen which the contortions of our bodies hide from sight, so that no one can claim I don't know exactly what I'm doing."

. . . "Let me, in my lust, see organs larger than they are and marvel at what I'm able to handle!"

—SENECA

The Active Retirement of Emperor Tiberius, *circa* A.D. 32

Tiberius (40 B.C.–A.D. 37) lived a very long life for a Roman emperor, thus gaining a rare opportunity among his peers: to become a dirty old man. Although he ruled for twenty-three years, he spent much of the last decade of his life in semiseclusion on the isle of Capri.

On retiring to Capreae, he made himself a private sportinghouse, where sexual extravagances were practiced for his secret pleasure. Bevies of girls and young men, collected from all over the empire as adepts in unnatural practices and known as "spintriae" [or "sphincterites"], would copulate before him in groups of three, to excite his waning passions.

A number of small rooms were furnished with the most indecent pictures and statuaries obtainable, also certain erotic manuals from Elephantis in Egypt; the inmates of the establishment would know from these exactly what was expected of them. He furthermore devised little nooks of lechery in the woods and glades of the island, and had boys and girls dressed up as Pans and nymphs prostituting themselves in front of caverns or grottoes; so that the island was now openly and generally called "Caprineum" [a pun suggesting "The Old Goat's Resort"].

His Minnows in the Pool

Some aspects of his [Tiberius'] criminal obscenity are almost too vile to discuss, much less believe. Imagine training little boys, whom he called his "minnows," to chase him while he went swimming and get between his legs to lick and nibble him. Or letting babies not yet weaned from their mother's breast suck at his breast or groin, such a filthy old man he had become! Then there was a painting by Parrhasius, which had been bequeathed to him on the condition that, if he did not like the subject, he could have ten thousand gold pieces instead. Tiberius not only preferred to keep the painting but hung it in his bedroom. It showed Atalanta performing fellatio with Meleager.

The story goes that once, while sacrificing, he took an erotic fancy to an acolyte who carried the incense casket, and could hardly wait for the ceremony to end before hurrying him and his brother, the sacred trumpeter, out of the temple and indecently assaulting them both. When they jointly protested at this disgusting behavior, he had their legs broken.

What nasty tricks he used to play on women, even those of high rank, is clearly seen in the case of Mallonia, whom he summoned to his bed. When she showed such an invincible repugnance to complying with his lusts, he set informers on her track and during her very trial continued to shout: "Are you sorry?" Finally she left the court and went home; there she stabbed herself to death after a violent tirade against that "filthy-mouthed, hairy, stinking old man."

—SUETONIUS, *LIVES OF THE CAESARS*

Cruel Caligula, *circa* A.D. 25–40

Caligula (A.D.12–42) was tall, spindly, bald, weak chinned, and pale. This didn't stop him from being cruel:

It was his habit to commit incest with each of his three sisters and, at large banquets, when his wife reclined above him, placed them all in turn below him. They say that he ravished his sister Drusilla before he came of age; their grandmother Antonia, at whose house they were both staying, caught them in bed together. Later, he took Drusilla from her husband, the former Consul Lucius Cassius Longinus, openly treating her as his lawfully married wife; and when he fell dangerously ill he left Drusilla all his property, and the Empire too. At her death, he made it a capital offense to laugh, to bathe, or to dine with one's parents, wives, or children while the period of public mourning lasted; and was so crazed from grief that he suddenly rushed from Rome by night, drove through Campania, took ship to Syracuse, and returned just as impetuously without having shaved or cut his hair in the meantime. Afterwards, whenever he had to take an important oath, he swore by Drusilla's divinity, even at a public assembly or an army parade. He showed no such extreme love or respect for the two surviving sisters, and often indeed let his boyfriends sleep with them.

. . . He had not the slightest regard for chastity, either his own or others', and was accused of homosexual relations, both active and passive, with Marcus Lepidus, also Mnester the comedian and various foreign hostages; moreover, a young man of consular family, Valerius Catullus, revealed publicly that he had buggered the Emperor, and quite worn himself out in the process.

Besides incest with his sisters, and a notorious passion for the prostitute Pyrallis, he made advances to almost every woman of rank in Rome; after inviting a selection of them to a dinner party with their husbands, he would slowly and carefully examine each in turn while they passed his couch, as a purchaser might assess the value of a slave, and even stretch out his hand and lift up the chin of any woman who kept her eyes modestly cast down. Then, whenever he felt so inclined, he would send for whoever pleased him best, and leave the banquet in her company. A little later he would return, showing obvious signs of what he had been about, and openly discuss his bedfellow in detail, dwelling on her good and bad physical points and commenting on her sexual performance. To some of these unfortunates, he issued and publicly registered divorces in the names of their absent husbands.

. . . Because of his baldness and [bodily] hairiness, he

announced that it was a capital offense for anyone either to look down on him as he passed or to mention goats in any context.

—SUETONIUS, *LIVES OF THE CAESARS*

Caligula ruled for three years, ten months, and eight days before being murdered by his friends. He was twenty-nine.

The Marriage of Nero, *circa* A.D. 60

Nero (A.D. 37–68) didn't fiddle while Rome burned, he put on a costume and sang a song: "The Fall of Troy." This pale and pudgy man was an enthusiastic bisexual:

Having tried to turn the boy Sporus into a girl by castration, he went through a wedding ceremony with him—dowry, bridal veil, and all—took him to his palace with a great crowd in attendance, and treated him as a wife. A rather amusing joke is still going the rounds: the world would have been a happier place had Nero's father, Domitius, married that sort of wife. He dressed Sporus in fine clothes normally worn by an empress, and took him in his own litter not only to every Greek assize and fair but actually through the Street of the Sigillaria at Rome, kissing him amorously now and then.

The lecherous passion he felt for his mother, Agrippina, was notorious, but her enemies would not let him consummate it, fearing that if he did she would become even more powerful and ruthless than hitherto. So he found a new mistress, who was said to be her spitting image; some say that he did in fact commit incest with Agrippina every time they rode in the same litter—the stains on his clothes when he emerged proved it.

Nero practiced every kind of obscenity, and after defiling almost every part of his body finally invented a novel game: He was released from a cage dressed in the skins of wild animals, and attacked the private parts of men and women who stood bound to stakes. After working up sufficient excitement by this means, he was dispatched—shall we say?— by his freedman Doryphorus. Doryphorus now married him— just as he himself had married Sporus. And on the wedding night, [*Nero*] imitated the screams and moans of a girl being deflowered.

According to my informants he was convinced that nobody could remain chaste or pure in any part of his body, but that most people concealed their secret vices; hence if anyone confessed to obscene practices, Nero forgave him all his other crimes.

—SUETONIUS, *LIVES OF THE CAESARS*

Nero, declared a public enemy by the Senate, committed suicide on June 9, 68. He overcame his jitters with the knife when informed that the Senate intended to thrust his head onto a wooden fork, then flog his naked body to death. One of the last things he said was: "What a great artist dies with me."

A Second-Century Gynecologist

Soranos, a highly respected doctor, was born in Ephesus (a Greek metropolis in Asia Minor) and later practiced medicine in Rome around the year 100. He wrote more than a dozen scholarly books, including four on women's illnesses. Here are some of his contributions to medical lexicography:

The vagina of a woman is described as follows: The visible

external parts of this organ are called the "wings," constituting the so-called "lips" of the vagina; they are thick and fleshy. Downward, they end at the thighs and are separated from each other by a slit; towards the top, they reach up to what's called the clitoris. This latter, which stands right at the start of the two lips, consists of a fleshy little button, which resembles the masculine organ.

It's called the clitoris [*Greek: "nympha"*], because it's hidden away just as newlywed brides [*Greek: "nymphae"*] are hidden away behind their veils.

Soranos was amazingly clearheaded in his understanding of the subject of birth control, and his discussion of abortion sounds very contemporary:

A contraceptive device differs from an abortion. The first prevents conception, the latter destroys that which has already been conceived. Let us be clear in distinguishing between that which destroys and that which prevents conception.

Now, as for abortives, some people call them "expulsives" and do not include any special drugs among them, but rather consider only physical actions such as violent movements or jumping up and down. Hippocrates, in his "On the Nature of the Child," mentions jumping combined with a hard spanking using the hand and fingernails to facilitate expulsion.

On the other hand, some doctors reject abortion entirely, quoting another line of Hippocrates: "I have never given a single abortive to one single woman." Supporters of that belief add that the role of medicine is to protect and safeguard that which Nature gives life to.

Still other doctors introduce a distinction: They refuse to

give an abortion to women wanting one as a result of adultery or to preserve their beauty, but they will authorize it when it provides a way to eliminate a health risk during pregnancy. Perhaps the womb is too small to handle going to full term or fistulas block the mouth of the vagina; or some other illness ravages the woman. These doctors say, though, they prefer contraceptives, since it's less dangerous to prevent pregnancy than it is to induce abortion.

For contraception, Soranos recommends avoiding sex during fertile times of the month; he advises inserting a wool tampon or a mixture of oil, honey, and resin. Under abortion methods, he lists taking bumpy wagon rides, lugging heavy weights, and taking hot baths and harsh enemas. But there is one approach he absolutely forbids:

One should never detach the embryo with a sharp instrument. There's too much risk of wounding the surrounding regions.

—SORANOS

Seduction in the Temple, *circa* A.D. 200

In ancient Greece and Rome, the gods had many human traits. They could be horny like Zeus; well hung like Hermes; jealous like Hephaistos; have a great ass like Aphrodite. And people believed that the gods physically came down and raped or seduced humans, like Leda and the swan. This could provide a setup for a scam.

A priest of Saturn, named Tyrannus, told the husbands of many beautiful women that Saturn himself had requested that their wives spend a night in the temple. The women, feeling honored, would arrive all dressed up and carrying gifts for the god.

In the sight of all, the matron was closed within the temple. Tyrannus would shut the doors, hand over the keys, and depart. Then, when silence ensued, he would go through hidden passages and underground approaches and creep into the statue of Saturn itself, by means of chambers that led into it. (The statue was hollowed out at the back and set up carefully against the wall.) And as the candles burned within the temple, he would suddenly speak to the woman, intent in prayer, through the statue of hollow bronze; and the poor woman would tremble with fear and joy thinking she had been found worthy to be addressed by so great a divinity.

After this base divinity had said what he pleased, either to cause great consternation or to incite lustfulness, the curtains were somehow drawn and all the candles were suddenly extinguished. Then he came down and by his godless deceits brought the stain of adultery upon the confused and dismayed woman.

When this had been happening for a long time to all the wives of the unhappy men, it came to pass that one woman of chaste disposition recoiled at the outrage; marking the voice more closely, she recognized that it was the voice of Tyrannus. Returning home, she told her husband of the criminal deceit. Passionately aroused by the wrong done to his wife, or rather to himself, he accused Tyrannus and had him led off to torture. When Tyrannus was convicted, and when he confessed, and the dark deceit stood exposed, all shame and dishonor pervaded the homes of the Pagans, since mothers had been found adulterous, fathers defiled, and children illegitimate.

—EUSEBIUS

This wasn't the only period during which temple seductions occurred. The historian Tacitus reports that in A.D. *19, two priests of Isis and a woman accomplice were all crucified in Rome for helping a young Roman knight impersonate a god so that he could seduce a very virtuous married woman, named Paulina; Jewish historian Josephus confirms the story.*

The Hygiene of Emperors, A.D. 220

In 218, the Roman army in Syria chose a fourteen-year-old Roman-born Syrian religious fanatic as emperor. He dubbed himself sun god, Heliogabalus (204–222), and was regal enough to empty his bowels only into gold cups.

Heliogabalus used to go all the time to the baths with his women, and he would rub a depilatory called psilothrum all over them [*remember, Roman women were depilated everywhere*], and he would also use some to lather up his own beard. Now, what I'm ashamed to repeat, is he used the very same stuff on them and on himself, and at the very same time. Also, he shaved the genital areas of his male lovers with his own hand, and used the same razor to shave his own beard.

. . . At Rome [*Heliogabalus'*] only care was to send agents everywhere to search out well-hung young men and bring them to court. He once staged a performance of the comedy "Paris" at the palace; he played the part of Venus himself and, suddenly dropping his clothes, he stood naked with one hand on his chest, the other on his genitals. He then knelt down and presented his raised buttocks to his young lover. He always painted his face like Venus, and made sure his entire body was perfectly polished, rating his highest priority the pursuit of new creative ways to satisfy his lust.

—LAMPRIDIUS

After a four-year reign, Heliogabalus was murdered and tossed into the Tiber.

2

Late Classical
and Early
Middle Ages

Chastity and the Early Christian Church

With paganism fading and Christianity piling up new converts, the early Christian leaders (including many future saints) had to define broad rules of personal conduct because Jesus left no written legacy.

And they came down like an Ice Age on sex. As St. Paul had observed earlier: "He who cannot control his lust may take a wife. I say this by way of indulgence, not command." *It was hardly a ringing endorsement. Sex was basically a necessary evil to procreate more Christians.*

In the fourth century, chastity was held in such high regard that a controversy erupted over whether castration was the ultimate show of love for God. The heretic (and self-castrator) Origen started a cult. (It didn't survive.)

The early Christian fathers—with St. Jerome, St. Basil, Tertullian, and others leading the way—hammered at pagan licentiousness and laid the groundwork for Catholic intolerance of homosexuality, extramarital sex, and most forms of marital sex other than what would one day be known as the "missionary position."

One clue to why these attitudes developed: In 325, the Council of Nicaea decreed that priests were not allowed to marry, which in effect meant that sex-forbidden (if not sex-deprived) bachelors would be determining rules for everyone else.

Advice to Monks, circa 370 A.D.

When sharing three to a bed, always have an old man sleep in the middle.

—St. Basil

Timing

Men ought to keep away from [*menstruous*] wives because thus is a deformed, blind, lame, leprous offspring conceived: so that those parents who are not ashamed to come together in sexual intercourse have their sin made obvious to all.

—St. Jerome

One priest tried an unusual dodge to keep his lover:

Leontius, for example, accused of flouting the rules and living openly with a young woman named Eustolia, castrated himself in order to be able to live with her unpunished. But instead of washing away all suspicion, that action, given the priest's reputation, hastened his defrocking.

—St. Athanasias

Scuthin's Experiment

Scuthin was an Irish holy man under investigation around the year 550 for trying an experiment, one that would be attempted a thousand-plus years later by Mahatma Gandhi:

Now two round-breasted virgins used to lie with Scuthin every night that the battle against lust might be greater. That practice caused him to be accused of living sinfully. So Brendan the Navigator came to test him. And Scuthin said: "Let Brendan lie in my bed tonight, and you maidens, lie alongside him."

Now when bedtime arrived, the maidens came into the house where Brendan was. They entered each carrying a lapful of warm glowing embers in the folds of their robes, and they spilled them before Brendan, then got into bed with him. "What is this?" asked Brendan.

"This is what we do every night," answered the maidens. They lay down with Brendan, and in no way could he sleep because of lustful longings.

"This isn't right," said the maidens. "He who is here every night doesn't feel a thing. Maybe you should go jump in a tub of cold water, o cleric, if that will make it easier for you, for sometimes even Scuthin must do that."

"Well, then," replied Brendan, "it is unjust for us to accuse this man for he is a holier man than we are."

Brendan and Scuthin made their union and covenant and parted friends.

—MARTYROLOGY OF AENGUS

Both men went on to sainthood.

Sinful Alexandria, circa 200

Clement of Alexandria (circa 150–220), a pagan converted to Christianity, was appalled by the seaside pleasure capital in which he lived. In Pedagogus, *he paints quite a picture:*

Beside the women standing in the brothels, offering their flesh for hire, stand the boys, taught to deny their sex and act the part of women.

. . . Men play the part of women, and women that of men, contrary to nature; women are at once wives and husbands; no orifice is closed against libidinousness.

Clement was especially intolerant of effeminate men:

For a man to comb himself and shave himself with a razor, for vanity's sake, to arrange his hair at a mirror, to shave his cheeks, pluck hairs out of them, smooth them, how womanly! And in truth unless you saw them naked, you would suppose them to be women.

For although not allowed to wear gold, yet out of effeminate desire they enwreathe their clasps and fringes with leaves of gold, or they wear the little balls of gold hanging from their ankles or their necks. This is a device of enervated men, who are dragged to the women's apartments, amphibious and lecherous beasts.

. . . For God wished women to be smooth, and rejoice in their locks alone growing spontaneously like a horse's mane; but has adorned man, like the lions, with a beard and endowed him, as an attribute of manhood, with shaggy breasts—a sign of his strength and rule.

. . . But using pitch to pluck out hair (I shrink from even mentioning the shamelessness connected with this process), consider how much they must bend over and bend back and contort their limbs. The outrage! And then to go like that amid young people or in the gymnasium, is this not the most extreme form of sin? For will not anyone who will act this shamefully in public not sin even worse in private?

For he who by daylight denies his manhood will prove himself by night manifestly a woman.

—CLEMENT OF ALEXANDRIA

Clement is not so subtly accusing men of being on the receiving end of sexual intercourse.

St. Augustine Observes Roman Sex Gods, *circa* 380

Augustine (354–430), born in what would be modern-day Libya, pioneered the "mea culpa" style of "Confessions" and was the first to recount his own personal battle against temptation. As a young man, he went to prostitutes, lived with women out of wedlock, fathered an illegitimate son at eighteen. When finally in his early thirties he set his sights on converting to Christianity, he summed up his battle with these immortal words: God grant me the strength to be chaste, just not yet.

Augustine turned out to be a great theologian, more tolerant and humane than most of his colleagues, and certainly equipped with a better sense of humor. He spent four years in Rome and Milan and had a good chance to observe the local customs:

When a man and woman get married, the god Jugatinus is invited along; that alone might be bearable. But there's also Domidicus to guide the bride home, Domitius to keep her there, and don't forget Manturna to make her stay with her husband. Isn't that enough? The gods should stop abusing people's modesty. Just let the longings of flesh and blood finish off the rest in private.

Why do a crowd of gods cram into the marriage bedroom, even after the guests have left? This imaginary horde of gods isn't supposed to make everyone embarrassed but rather to guarantee that the bride—though naturally weak due to her gender and as scared as any first-timer might be—will lose her virginity, thanks to their help.

The goddess Virginensis is there and the Father Subigus, the god, and the mother goddess Prema, and the goddess Pertunda, and Venus and Priapus. What's going on? If a man struggling at this task requires help from the gods, wouldn't perhaps one god or goddess be enough? Couldn't Venus do it alone? Isn't she supposed to get her name from the fact that a woman can't lose her maidenhead without some violence?

If humans have any sense of shame (which the gods obviously lack), and since the couple believes so many gods of both sexes are in the room staring at their lovemaking, wouldn't they become so inhibited that he would become less aroused and she more reluctant? And certainly if the goddess Virginensis is there to remove her maidenly underthings, if the god Subigus is there to position her for her husband, if the goddess Prema is there to hold her down so that she won't move once she's put in the right position, then what's left for the goddess Pertunda to do? Maybe she should just blush and exit the room. Leave something for the husband to do! It would be despicable for someone other than the husband to do what's implied by her name [*Latin "pertundo": to drill a hole*]. What if she were thought masculine and called "Pertundus"? The husband would need more help defending his wife's honor against the god than he will later protecting the baby from Sylvanus.

But what am I talking about? Priapus is already there and he's certainly all male. Newlywed brides used to be commanded to sit on his enormous and ugly phallus. And wasn't that by way of obeying a very honorable and sacred custom of the Roman matrons?

Augustine seems a bit fascinated by the Roman marriage custom that involved bringing virgin brides to a temple with a statue of a god with a giant, erect penis. The rite is confirmed by other ancient writers, such as Lacantius and Arnobius. Now, some scholars, including Sir Richard Burton and Mirabeau, have interpreted these passages to mean that the girl was physically deflowered on the marble phallus. But when Augustine mentions it again later in The City of God, *he gives a bit more of a clue:*

During the wedding celebration, the new bride used to be invited to sit on the post of Priapus. . . . The modesty of the new bride is disgraced but her fertility isn't stolen away, nor even her virginity.

—ST. AUGUSTINE

So perhaps the rod of Priapus was more a ritual sit-down than a bloody puncturing.

The Lewd Childhood of Empress Theodora,
circa 515

When Rome fell in 476, the eastern portion of the Roman territories survived and became a Christian theocracy called the Byzantine Empire, which lasted almost a thousand years, until the Turks captured Constantinople in 1453.

Court historian Procopius devoted his life to portraying his patrons, Emperor Justinian (483–565) and Empress Theodora (circa 500–548), as a couple of Christian saints, bringing kindness and justice to a vast empire. (Justinian's law codes are credited with laying the groundwork for much of Western jurisprudence.) But long after Procopius' death, the Secret History *of Procopius surfaced. If Procopius did in fact write it, call it* The Flack's Revenge *because he savages his former bosses. For Empress Theodora, he paints an astoundingly sleazy childhood. You start to wonder: What did she ever do to him?*

Procopius describes Theodora as one of three children, brought up by her poor widowed mother and her stepfather, who worked in the circus:

As soon as each of these children became old enough, their mother put them at once on the stage there—since they were very pretty.

Now, the oldest sister, Comito, had already become notorious among the courtesans; and Theodora, the next oldest, wearing a skimpy short-sleeved tunic fit for a slave, would trundle after her, taking care of various chores and in particular always toting on her shoulders the stool on which her sister was accustomed to sit in the clusters of men.

Now, since Theodora was immature at the time, she could not have sexual intercourse with a man, and she certainly could not copulate like a grown woman. Yet she did engage in masculine types of sex [*anal, oral, and manual*] with the wretches, the slaves who accompanied their masters to the theater. They took advantage of their spare time to negotiate these foul services. She spent much of her time in the brothel, performing these unnatural acts with her body. But as soon as she grew up a bit and reached maturity, she joined the women of the theater, and immediately became a courtesan, the type that men in the old days used to call "infantry" [*catering to the lowest-rank soldier*].

For she was neither a flute girl nor a harp player, nor had she yet developed as a dancer, but she sold her youth to anybody who wandered in, trafficking in just about her entire body.

Later on, she joined the actors on the stage, . . . and she clowned around, anything for a laugh. And she became well known for cleverness and her jokes. For she was shameless. . . . She would exhibit herself naked front and behind to anyone who happened to pass by, revealing those parts which good taste requires to be hidden from men.

She lazily kidded around with potential lovers, and by teasing them with inventions of new sexual techniques, she always succeeded in winning over the souls of the dirty-minded.

For she did not even expect the man meeting her to make the first move, but just the opposite, it was she laughing and grinding her hips wantonly who would lure all who passed by, especially beardless youngsters.

Still Hungry at Community Dinner

No one has ever been so unable to resist pleasure in all its forms; for often she would go to the community dinner with ten or more young men—all very well-muscled sexual professionals—and she would have an orgy with all of them all night long. When they were too exhausted from the work, then she would go with their servants, maybe thirty in number, and she would couple up with each one of them, yet still she hadn't drunk her fill of wantonness.

And once, she came to the home of a leading citizen right as his dinner party entered the time for drinking, and they say she climbed up amid their feet on the part of the couch that juts out, and she hoisted up her clothes and waggled her booty.

And though she took advantage of three orifices, she still cursed Nature, furious that her nipples didn't have holes big enough to allow her another orifice for copulation. Though she wound up pregnant many times, she was always able straightaway to secure an abortion.

Geese

And often in the theater before the eyes of the entire local population, she did a striptease and moved around naked, wearing only cotton drawers over her crotch and ass, not that she was embarrassed to show off these parts too to the crowds, but it was forbidden to appear naked on stage without drawers. In this scanty attire, she lay on her back on the ground and spread her legs far apart. And some slaves, who had but this job to do, sprinkled grains of barley over her private parts, and geese, provided for just this purpose, pecked them up one by one with their beaks and ate them. Not only didn't she blush when she stood up, but she strutted about, as though quite proud of the stunt. For she wasn't only trashy herself but she inspired trashy behavior in others. Often, she would strip and stand naked on the stage surrounded by actors, and she would arch her body backwards trying to poke the rear ends of those who had had her, and those who hadn't, sashaying through her own personal brand of wrestling exercises.

Deep Throat Joke, circa A.D. 520

And she seemed to have her sex organs not in Nature's intended location like other women, but rather in her face.

In 527 the former prostitute, standing alongside Justinian in the magnificent church of Hagia Sophia, was crowned empress. And Procopius, true to form, has very little nice to say in Secret History *about her behavior as ruler of a vast empire.*

Retirement Home for Prostitutes, A.D. 534

Here you can see two versions of the same "good deed" by Theodora. First, Procopius delivers the official version in a work called Buildings; *then Procopius hammers her in his* Secret History.

The Official Version

In Byzantium, there used to be a swarm of women who were sexually active in the brothels, not by their own choice but almost as slaves to men's lust. For these destitute women housed by brothel owners were forced to have sex at all times, pairing off with the very next stranger to happen along. Because, for a long time, a whole colony of pimps here have been packaging their merchandise of lust in the brothels, and selling off someone else's youth in the public marketplace.

But Emperor Justinian and Empress Theodora (who shared righteousness in all they did) masterminded the following: They purged the nation of the filth of whore houses, banning the very name of brothel owner [*"porno-boskos": literally, whore herder*]. They freed these poor exhausted women from their round-the-clock sexual drudgery fit only for a slave by making them financially independent and thus reviving their virtue. They accomplished it this way:

On the right as you sail towards the Euxine Sea stood a palace. They converted it into a magnificent convent, to serve as a refuge for women who repented of their former lives. Here, these women, by filling their minds with God and worship, could achieve catharsis and rid themselves of the sins of the brothel. They named this dwelling for women "Repentance," to match its purpose. And the emperor and empress have funded this convent with a large annual income, and have added on many lavish and lovely buildings to serve as a consolation to the women, so they should never again be forced to leave the path of righteousness, for any reason whatsoever.

—PROCOPIUS, *BUILDINGS*

Secret History

Theodora also meddled in devising punishments for those who had sinned with their bodies. For instance, she gathered together more than five hundred whores, the ones who sell themselves cheap in the marketplace for three obols—just enough to survive—and she ferried them to the opposite shore and locked them up in a convent called "Repentance," trying to force them to change their life-style. And some of the women were so desperate to escape the forced salvation that they threw themselves off the cliffs at night.

—PROCOPIUS

A Pregnant Pope? A.D. 855

Bartolomeo Platina, in his authoritative Lives of the Popes *(1479), reported that many people believed the following story and regarded it as the reason that the cardinals began requiring all papal nominees to have their testicles felt (and confirmed) before being installed as the new pope.*

John VIII, of English stock though born at Mentz, is said to have become pope [*in 855*] through magical arts. Although a woman, she disguised herself when young as a man and traveled with her lover, a scholar, to Athens. There, she advanced so far in her studies that when she later reached Rome, she met with few that could match or exceed her, even in the knowledge of Scriptures. And by her learned and brilliant readings and disputations, she gained such great respect and authority that upon the death of Leo, as Martin says, she was chosen pope by common consent in his room.

But later she allowed one of her servants to lie with her. She hid her big belly for quite a while until one day when she was going to the Lateran Church, between the Colosseum and St. Clement's, her labor came upon her, and she died upon the spot. She had presided two years, one month, and four days, and was buried there without any pomp.

. . . Some say, to prevent a similar error, when any pope is first seated in the porphyry chair, the youngest deacon reaches up through a hole in the chair's seat and touches the pope's genitals. . . . [*But*] I think the practice is done so that the pope may be reminded that he is not a God but a man, and is subject to the calls of Nature. That's why the chair is dubbed "Sedes Stercoraria," or "Fecal Throne."

—BARTOLOMEO PLATINA

In The History of Milan *(1510), Renaissance author Bernadino Corio matter-of-factly mentions the same rite for Pope Alexander VI in 1492:*

Finally, he was furnished with the remaining rituals in the Sancta Sanctorum, his testicles were intimately touched and he was given the benediction, then he returned to the palace.

Sexual Sacrifice at a Viking Chief's Funeral, A.D. 922

Ibn Fadlan, a representative of the Caliph of Baghdad, observed the Scandinavian merchants along the Volga:

I was told that the least of what they do for their chiefs when they die is to consume them with fire. When I was finally informed of the death of one of their magnates, I sought to witness what befell. First they laid him in his grave—over which a roof was erected, and for the space of ten days, until they had completed the cutting and sewing of his clothes. . . . To the use of wine they abandon themselves in mad fashion, drinking it day and night; and not seldom does one die with a cup in his hand.

When one of their chiefs dies, his family asks his girls and pages, "Which one of you will die with him?" Then one of them answers, "I." From the time that he utters this word, he is no longer free. Should he wish to draw back, he is not permitted. For the most part, however, it is the girls that offer themselves. So, when the man of whom I spoke had died, they asked his girls, "Who will die with him?" One of them answered, "I." She was then committed to two girls, who were to keep watch over her, accompany her wherever she went, and even, on occasion, wash her feet. The people now began to occupy themselves with the dead man—to cut out the clothes for him, and to prepare whatever else was needful. During the whole of this period, the girl gave herself over to drinking and singing, and was cheerful and gay.

When the day was now come that the dead man and the girl were to be committed to the flames, I went to the river in which his ship lay, but found that it had already been drawn ashore. Four cornerblocks of birch and other woods had been placed in position for it, while around were stationed large wooden figures in the semblance of human beings. Thereupon the ship was brought up, and placed on the timbers above mentioned.

. . . When they came to the grave, they removed the earth from the wooden roof, set the latter aside, and drew out the dead man in the loose wrapper in which he had died. Then I saw that he had turned quite black. . . . They now clothed him in drawers, leggings, boots, and a *kurtak* and a *chaftan* of cloth of gold, with golden buttons, placing on his head a cap made of cloth of gold, trimmed with sable. Then they carried him into a tent placed in the ship, seated him on the wadded and quilted covering, supported him with the pillows, and, bringing strong drinks, fruits, and basil, placed them all beside him. Then they brought a dog, which they cut in two, and threw into the ship; laid all his weapons beside him; and led up two horses, which they chased until they were dripping with sweat, whereupon they cut them in pieces with their swords, and threw the flesh into the ship. Two oxen were then brought forward, cut in pieces, and flung into the ship. Finally, they brought a cock and a hen, killed them, and threw them in also.

The girl who had devoted herself to death meanwhile walked to and fro, entering one after another of the tents which they had there. The occupant of each tent lay with her, saying, "Tell your master, 'I did this only for love of you.'"

. . . Then they lifted her into the ship. . . . Now men came up with shields and staves, and handed her a cup of strong drink. This she took, sang over it, and emptied it. "With this," so the interpreter told me, "she is taking leave of those who are dear to her." Then another cup was handed her, which she also took and began a lengthy song.

. . . At this point the men began to beat upon their shields with the staves, in order to drown out the noise of her outcries, which might have terrified the other girls and deterred them from seeking death with their masters in the future. Then six men followed into the tent, and each and every one had carnal companionship with her. Then they laid her down by her master's side, while two of the men seized her by the feet, and two by the hands. The old woman known as the angel of death now knotted a rope around her neck, and handed the ends to two of the men to pull. Then with a broad-bladed dagger she smote her between the ribs, and drew the blade forth, while the two men strangled her with the rope till she died.

The next of kin to the dead man now drew near, and, taking a piece of wood, lighted it, and walked backwards towards the ship, holding the stick in one hand, with the other hand placed upon his buttocks (he being naked), until the wood which had been piled under the ship was ignited. Then the others came up with staves and firewood, each one carrying a stick already lighted at the upper end, and threw it on the pyre. The pile was soon aflame, then the ship, finally the tent, the man, and the girl, and everything else in the ship. A terrible storm began to blow up, and this intensified the flames, and gave wings to the blaze.

—IBN FADLAN

* * * **3** * * *

The
Middle
Ages

Sex and Penance

When it came to Church-sanctioned sex during the Middle Ages, the straight and narrow path was extremely straight and extremely narrow. The only sex practice deemed proper for Christians was for a man to marry a virgin with her father's permission, then have procreative "missionary position" intercourse with her—except not naked, not in daylight, and not on Sundays, holidays, or menstrual days or during pregnancy.

That meant that a lot of activity required punishment. Influential theologians started writing "Penitentials"— basically, handbooks for priests hearing confession. In them, they outlined the exact type of penance that priests should require their parishioners to perform to gain forgiveness for various types of sins (and retain a shot at going to heaven). Usually, the penance involved a certain number of days or years of special prayers or fasting.

Burchard's Medieval Sexual Menu, 1012

The following is unquestionably the longest and kinkiest list of medieval sexual practices still in existence, and much of it has never before been translated into English from the original Latin.

In 1012, a German bishop with the unlikely name of Burchard of Worms wrote his Penitential. Most of Burchard's twenty-volume tome covers the usual lying, cheating, stealing, and so on. But in volume 19, chapter 5, he runs down an astoundingly varied menu of 194 different sexual sins. Burchard combines Teutonic thoroughness with a vivid imagination:

Questions for Men

Nuns

Have you committed fornication with a nun, that is to say, a bride of Christ? If you have done this, you shall do penance for forty days on bread and water, which they call a "carina," and [*repeat it*] for the next seven years; and as long as you live, you shall observe all six holy days on bread and water.

"Retro, Canino"

Have you had sex with your wife or with another woman from behind, doggy style? [*Latin: "retro canino"*] If you have done this, you shall do penance for ten days on bread and water.

Sunday

Have you had sex with your wife on a Sunday? You shall do penance for four days on bread and water.

Sister-in-law

If in your wife's absence, without your or your wife's knowledge, your wife's sister entered your bed and you thought that she was your wife and you had sex with her, if you have done this, then if you complete the penance, you can keep your lawful wife, but the adulterous sister must suffer the appropriate punishment and be deprived of a husband for all time.

Stepdaughter

Have you fornicated with your stepdaughter? If you have done this, you shall have neither mother nor daughter, nor shall you take a wife, nor shall she take a husband, but you shall do penance until death. But your wife, if she only learnt afterwards that you committed adultery with her daughter, shall not sleep with you but marry again in the Lord if she wishes.

Son's Fiancée

Have you fornicated with your son's fiancée, and afterwards, your son took her to wife? If you have done this, because you concealed the crime from your son, you shall do penance until death and remain without hope of marriage. But your son, because he was ignorant of your sin, if he wishes, may take another wife.

Mother

Have you fornicated with your mother? If you have done this, you shall do penance for fifteen years on the legitimate holy days, and one of these [*years*] on bread and water, and you shall remain without hope of marriage, and you shall never be without penitence. But your mother, if she was not consenting, shall do penance according to the decision of the priest; and if she cannot live chastely may marry in the Lord.

Sodomy

Have you fornicated as the Sodomites did, such that you inserted your penis into the rear of a man and into his posterior, and thus had intercourse with him in the Sodomite manner? If you had a wife and did this only once or twice, you should do penance for ten years on the legitimate holy days, and for one of these on bread and water. If you did this as a manner of habit, then you should do penance for twelve years on the legitimate holy days. If you committed this sin with your brother, you should do penance for fifteen years on the legitimate holy days.

Interfemoral

Have you fornicated with a man, as some are accustomed to do, between the thighs, that is to say, you inserted your member between the thighs of another and by thus moving it about ejaculated semen? If you did this, you shall do penance for forty days on bread and water.

Homosexual Mutual Masturbation

Have you fornicated, as some are accustomed to do, such that you took another's penis in your hand, while he took yours in his and thus in turn you moved each other's penises in your hands with the result that by this enjoyment you ejaculated semen? If you have done this, you shall do penance for thirty days on bread and water.

Masturbation

Have you fornicated with yourself alone, as some are accustomed to do, that is to say, you yourself took your penis in your hands and thus held your foreskin and moved it with your own hand so that by this enjoyment you ejaculated semen? If you have done this, you shall do penance for twenty days on bread and water.

Masturbation with Sex Aid

Have you fornicated, as some are accustomed to do, such that you inserted your penis into a hollowed-out piece of wood or some such device, so that by this movement and enjoyment you ejaculated semen? If you have done this, you shall do penance for twenty days on bread and water.

Kiss

Have you kissed some woman due to foul desire and thus polluted yourself? If you have done this, you shall do penance for three days on bread and water. But if this happened in a church, you shall do penance for twenty days on bread and water.

Bestiality

Have you fornicated against Nature, that is, you have had intercourse with animals, that is, with a horse or a cow or a donkey or with some other animal? If you did this only once or twice, and if you had no wife, so that you could to relieve your lust, you must do penance for forty days on bread and water, which is called a "carina," as well as [*repeating it*] for the seven following years, and never be without penitence. If, however, you had a wife, you must do penance for ten years on legitimate holy days; and if you were in the habit of this crime, you must do penance for fifteen years on the legitimate holy days. If, however, this occurred during your childhood, you must do penance on bread and water for one hundred days.

Questions for Women

Lesbians with Sex Aids

Have you done what certain women are accustomed to do, that is, to make some sort of device or implement in the shape of the male member, of a size to match your desire, and you have fastened it to the area of your genitals or those of another with some form of fastenings and you have fornicated with other women or others have done with a similar instrument or another sort with you? If you have done this, you shall do penance for five years on legitimate holy days.

Female Masturbation with Sex Aid

Have you done what certain women are accustomed to do, that is, you have fornicated with yourself with the aforementioned device or some other device? If you have done this, you shall do penance for one year on legitimate holy days.

Mother with Son

Have you done what certain women are accustomed to do, that is, have you fornicated with your young son, that is to say, placed your son above your "indecency" and thus imitated fornication? If you have done this, you must do penance for two years on legitimate holy days.

Bestiality

Have you done what certain women are accustomed to do, that is, you have lain with an animal and incited that animal to coitus by whatever ability you possess so that it will thus have intercourse with you? If you have done this, you shall do penance for one "carina," along with [each of] the seven following years, and you shall never be without penitence.

Aphrodisiacs and Superstitious Practices

Semen Swallowing

Have you tasted your husband's semen in the hope that because of your diabolical deed he might burn the more with love for you. If you have done this, you should do penance for seven years on the legitimate holy days.

Live Fish and Childbirth

Have you done what certain women are accustomed to do? They take a live fish and place it in their afterbirth and hold it there until it dies, and then after boiling and roasting it, they give it to their husbands to eat in the hope that they will burn all the more with love for them. If you have done this, you shall do penance for two years on the legitimate holy days.

Bread and Buttocks

Have you done what certain women are accustomed to do? They prostrate themselves face-down and uncover their buttocks, then they order that bread be prepared on their naked buttocks; when it's baked, they give it to their husbands to eat so they will burn more for love of them. If you have done this, you shall do penance for two years on legitimate holy days.

Menstrual Blood

Have you done what certain women are accustomed to do? They take their menstrual blood and mix it into food or drink and give it to their husbands to eat or drink so that they might be more attentive to them. If you have done this, you shall do penance for five years on legitimate holy days.

Selective Impotency Spell

Have you done what some adulterous women are accustomed to do? When they first find out that their lovers want to take legitimate wives, they then by some trick of magic extinguish the man's lust, so that they are impotent and cannot consummate their marriage with their legitimate wives. If you have done this or taught others to do this, you should do penance for forty days on bread and water.

Aphrodisiac Loaf?

Have you done what certain women are accustomed to do? They take off their clothes and smear honey all over their naked body and then lay down their honey-drenched body onto some wheat scattered upon a linen on the ground; they then roll around a lot this way and that, and then carefully collect all the grains of wheat which stick to their wet body, and place them in a mill and make the mill go backwards against the sun and grind it to flour; and they make bread from the flour and then give it to their husbands to eat that they may become feeble and waste away. If you have done this, you shall do penance for forty days on bread and water.

—BURCHARD OF WORMS

Over the years, the nature of penance changed away from being exclusively prayer and fasting. Many of Europe's glorious medieval cathedrals were built by peasants sweating off their sins through public works. And for the rich, gaining absolution became easier. By the mid-1200s, churchmen with the pope's blessing were selling "indulgences." A sinner with a bankroll could try out a smorgasbord of Burchard's sins and, if caught, simply buy forgiveness, and another shot at heaven.

Medieval Doctors on Sex

Many people have this image of mankind discovering the female orgasm in the 1950s, right along with the women's movement. Totally false.

Not only has mankind clearly known about women's orgasms for at least the past twenty-five hundred years but it was widely believed throughout much of recorded history that a woman's orgasm was ABSOLUTELY necessary for procreation to occur.

Two of the most influential medieval doctors—the famed Moslem physician Avicenna (980–1037) and the Christian saint Albert the Great (1193–1280)—both following the lead of Hippocrates and Galen, believed that a woman emitted sperm and that her sperm mingled with a man's in order to conceive a child.

Think about the implications. Any man who wanted to be a father had to make certain that both he and his wife had an orgasm. And there's little doubt that misconception led men to deliver hours of added attention to millions of medieval women. The belief persisted all the way past the time of Casanova, who mentions it in his memoirs, written in the 1790s.

It wasn't until the Victorians that medical science proved that a woman's orgasm wasn't needed for procreation, and certain prudes used the discovery to downplay the importance of woman's sexuality.

(For a great handling of the topic of female orgasm in this period, see Sexuality and Medicine in the Middle Ages, by Danielle Jacquart and Claude Thomasset [Princeton University Press, 1988].)

There is no shame in the doctor speaking about the increase in the size of the penis, or the narrowing of the receptive organs, or of the woman's pleasure, since these are factors that play a part in reproduction. For the small size of the penis is often a hindrance to climax and emission in the woman. And when the woman does not emit any sperm, conception cannot take place.

—AVICENNA

Men should take their time playing with healthy women. They should caress their breasts and pubis, and enfold their partners in their arms without really performing the act. And when their desire is fully roused, they should unite with the woman, rubbing the area between the anus and the vulva, for this is the seat of pleasure. They should watch out for the moment when the woman clings more tightly, when her eyes start to go red, her breathing becomes more rapid, and she starts to stammer.

—AVICENNA

Unfortunately for Christian women (and men), the foreplay mentioned by Avicenna was technically a sin, as was any oral sex or divergence from the missionary position:

The slightest deviation [*from the blameless path*] is the side position, then comes the sitting position, then standing, and, finally, the greatest sin is "retrorsum," like mares. That's why certain people have said this position constitutes a mortal sin, but that's not my opinion.

—ALBERT THE GREAT

Medieval doctors—besides their misconception about conception—also were a bit confused about the cause of a man's erection. Remember, back then doctors believed the body was controlled by forces, such as humors, wind, heat, cold, dryness, and wetness.

The mental picture of the opposite sex imagined in the mind of the lover is an important prerequisite to human mating. . . . When the semen descends to the seminal receptacles, the concomitant heat transforms part of the humor into a vaporous form, which expands the sexual organs. . . . The man's penis becomes erect and swollen.

—ALBERT THE GREAT

Basically, he was saying: pump it up.

In different monasteries and religious places, one comes across numerous men who, sworn to chastity, are often tempted by the Devil; the principle cause is that every day they eat food that leads to flatulence. This increases their desire for coitus and stiffens their member.

—Arnauld de Villanova

St. Albert also had theories about desire:
Before coitus a man is not afraid to go after the wife of another man, even in the latter's presence, for he is subject to the powerful motion of the spirits; but after the act, because of the debilitation he suffers, he becomes afraid and runs away at the mere sight of a rat or a cat.

—Albert the Great

Right up to the mid-twentieth century, most Western cultures at least, in theory demanded virgin brides. If the bride was not a virgin, the dowry could be forfeited and the marriage could be annulled. Here's a formula attributed to St. Albert for restoring virginity:
Take a half ounce of Venetian turpentine, a little of the milky sap of asparagus leaves, a quarter ounce of rock-alum steeped in lemon juice or the juice of green apples, the white of a fresh egg, and a little oatmeal. Mix these ingredients and roll into a ball of good consistency, which you will then insert into the vagina of the deflowered girl, after having syringed the part with goat's milk and rubbed it with an ointment of mature white wine. You will not have applied this secret preparation more than four or five times before the girl

returns to a state which would deceive even the matron who might examine her.

A Medieval Female Gynecologist, *circa* 1075

Trotula was an eleventh-century English doctor who excelled at the medical school of Salerno and wrote one of the earliest (surviving) health manuals ever written by a woman. Perhaps it's not surprising that it included advice on suppressing—as well as inciting—male passion, along with tips on hygiene.

Vervain carried or drunk will not permit the penis to go stiff until it is laid aside, and vervain placed under the pillow makes an erection impossible for seven days, which prescription if you wish to test, give to a cock mixed with bran and the cock will not mount the hen. . . . Likewise, anoint the shoelaces with the juice of vervain and wear them against the flesh, and you will be effeminate; and if a man touches anyone he will be inept for such things because it weakens the pleasure of touching.

Hygiene

Whenever a woman is going to sleep with someone, let her wash out the inside of her pudenda, inserting her fingers wrapped in dry wool . . . then let her carefully wipe inside and out with a very clean cloth. Next, she should bind her legs so that all the wetness may flow out from her insides and then, inserting a cloth, she should vigorously dry her genitalia; then let her take some powder in her mouth, and chew, and rub her hands, chest, and nipples; let her sprinkle rose water on

her pubis, genitals, and face. Thus nicely made up, let her
approach the man.

—TROTULA

Fiery Crusade against Homosexuality, 1048

*Pietro Damiani led a hell-for-leather effort to convince the
Church to be much tougher on homosexuality. In his* Book of
Gomorrah *(1048), he dwells on gruesome penalties. Damiani
quotes the "Rules for the Monastery of Compludo," then builds
to a fury:*

"A cleric or monk who seduces youths or young boys or is
found kissing or in any other impure situations is to be
publicly flogged and lose his tonsure. When his hair has been
shorn, his face is to be foully besmeared with spit and he is to
be bound in iron chains. For six months he will languish in
prisonlike confinement and on three days of the week shall
fast on barley bread in the evening. After this he will spend
another six months under the custodial care of a spiritual
elder, remaining in a segregated cell, giving himself to manual
work and prayers, subject to vigils and prayers. He may go for
walks but always under the custodial care of two spiritual
brethren, and he shall never again associate with youths in
private conversation nor in counseling them." *[Rule 16]*

. . . To punish this crime, this enormous crime, is it not
enough to be whipped in public, to lose his tonsure, to be
shamefully shaven, to be smeared with spit, to be cruelly
imprisoned for a long time and to be bound in iron chains
besides? Yet finally he is also ordered to be struck with a fast
of barley bread since it is right that whoever acts like a horse

and a mule not eat the food of men but is to feed on the grain of mules.

—PIETRO DAMIANI

The Original Lady Godiva, 1057

The first mention of the famous-maned streaker was in Roger of Wendover's Flowers of History. *But there's a key element missing from the story. Can you tell what it is?*

Countess Godiva, who was devoted to God's mother, longed to free the town of Coventry from the oppression of heavy taxes. With urgent prayers, she often begged [*her husband, Leofric, Earl of Chester*] that with fealty to Christ and his mother, he should free the town from such heavy taxes and other burdens. The earl railed at her for foolishly requesting something that would hurt him, and forbade her from ever bringing up the subject again. But she, with a woman's stubbornness, didn't stop pestering her husband about the matter until he at last snapped at her: "Mount your horse, ride naked before all the people through the market of the town, from one end to the other, and on your return you shall have your request."

To which Godiva replied: "But will you give me permission if I'm willing to do it?"

"I will," said he. Whereupon the countess, beloved of God, loosed her hair and let down her tresses, which covered the whole of her body like a veil, and then mounting her horse, and attended by two knights, she rode through the marketplace, without being seen, except her fair legs. Having completed the journey, she happily returned to her astonished husband, and obtained of him what she had asked. For Earl Leofric freed the town of Coventry from the taxes, and confirmed what he had done by a charter.

—ROGER OF WENDOVER

So what's missing? There's no mention of Peeping Tom; he doesn't appear for another hundred years or so.

A Wife's Most Prized Possession, *circa* 1058

During the reign of Henry the 1st of France [*1031–1060*], in the wars between the Greeks and the Duke of Benevento, the Greeks treated the duke very ill. Theobald, Marquis of Spoleto, his ally, came to his assistance and took several Greeks prisoner, whom he commanded to be castrated and then sent back in that condition to the Greek general. He added they should tell him that he did it to oblige the emperor who he knew had a very particular love for eunuchs, and that he would try very speedily to make him a present of a greater number. The Marquis resolved to keep his word, and one day when he took several other prisoners was preparing to execute that fatal resolution when a woman, whose husband was one of them, came running through the camp, and crying most pitifully, begging to speak to Theobald. . . . "My Lord," says she, "I am astonished to think such a hero as you should amuse yourself in making war with poor women, now that the men are in no condition to resist you."

Theobald replied, "Since the time of the Amazons, no one, as I ever heard, has made war with women."

"My Lord," says the Greek, "can you wage a more cruel war against us than to deprive our husbands of that which gives us health, pleasure, and children? When you can do thus, you make us, not them, into eunuchs; for several days now when you have taken away from us baggage and cattle, I have never made any complaint, but (and then she looked very intently at the marquis) the loss of those goods you have taken away from a great many women of my acquaintance being irreparable, I could not help coming to implore the compassion of a conqueror."

This honest speech of the poor woman so well pleased the whole army that they not only gave her back her husband, but everything else that had been taken from her. But as she was going away, the Marquis asked her what she would consent should be done to her husband in case he was found again, armed and fighting. "He has eyes (says she very hastily), a nose, hands, and feet, these are his goods, and you may take them away from him if he deserves it, but if you please let that alone which belongs to me."

—MEDIEVAL CHRONICLE, QUOTED IN CHARLES ANCILLON'S
EUNUCHISM DISPLAY'D, 1718

Horny Wives Endanger the Norman Conquest, 1068

In 1066, William the Conqueror led his fighting men from native Normandy into southern England in the Norman Conquest. The victorious troops spent the next two years carving up turf and putting down rebellions. Then they ran into an unexpected problem:

At this time, certain Norman women, consumed by fierce

lust, sent message after message to their husbands, urging them to return at once, and adding that unless they did so with all speed, they would take other husbands for themselves. For they dared not join their men themselves, being unaccustomed to the sea-crossing and afraid of seeking them out in England, where they were engaging in armed forays every day and blood flowed freely on both sides. The king, with so much fighting on his hands, was most anxious to keep all his knights about him, and made them a friendly offer of lands and revenues and great authority, promising them more when he had rid the kingdom of all his enemies. His loyal barons and stalwart fighting men were gravely perturbed, for they saw that continual uprisings threatened the king and their brothers, friends, and allies and feared that if they abandoned him they would openly be branded as traitors and cowardly deserters. On the other hand, what could honorable men do if their lascivious wives polluted their beds with adultery and brought indelible shame and dishonor on their offspring? As a result, Hugh of Grandmesnil, who was governor of Gewissae—that is, the region around Winchester—and his brother-in-law Humphrey of Tilleul, who had held the castle of Hastings from the day of its foundation, and many others departed from the country heavy at heart, and unwilling to go because they were deserting the king whilst he was struggling in a foreign land. They returned to Normandy to oblige their wanton wives; but neither they nor their heirs were ever able to recover the fiefs which they had held and chosen to abandon.

—ORDERICUS VITALIS, *ECCLESIASTICAL HISTORY*

Adultery and the Red-Hot-Iron Test, *circa* 1080

All that medieval warfare made for a lot of traveling husbands, wondering what was going on back home. A French knight fighting in England around 1080 suspected his wife of adultery, so he tried to get to the truth of the matter by using a typical medieval test on her accused lover: trial by red-hot iron.

Picture an iron bar roasting in a fire.

. . . Then the priest shall sprinkle holy water above the [*red-hot*] iron and shall say: "The blessing of God, the Father, the Son, and the Holy Ghost descend upon this iron for the discerning of the right judgment of God." And straightaway the accused shall carry the iron to a distance of nine feet. Finally, his hand shall be covered under seal for three days, and if festering blood be found in the wake of the iron, he shall be judged guilty. But if, however, he shall go forth uninjured, praise shall be rendered to God [*for his innocence*].

—*FORMULAE LITURGICAE*

After the trial, the knight-husband contacted the famous clergyman Yves of Chartres for advice. Here is Yves' reply:

You say your suspicions were confirmed when the knight you suspected of having an affair with your wife . . . was burned.

Yet no witness and no evidence besides this [*and calculating the conception date to be seven days before your last visit home*] exist to support your fears, which are therefore based solely on guesswork. And no ancient custom or law allows anyone to condemn another based solely on guesswork. . . .

The burn suffered by the knight is not a certain test, since by a secret judgment of God, we have often seen the guilty vindicated, while many innocents have been condemned by it. Such an ordeal is a challenge to God. Also, isn't it astonishing that Divine Help would abandon someone who willingly submitted to the test, without having been compelled by judges?

Yves also queried some housewives about the birth date:

I consulted with a few honest married women who told me with no hesitation that birth does not always follow an exact set number of days after conception. . . .

Yves—with a Dear Abbey flourish—ended in platitudes:

Mull all this over . . . control your anger. . . . You will never be able to undo this deed. . . . Be satisfied with the word of your wife, and the statements of honest people. . . . Adieu.

—YVES OF CHARTRES

It is surprising that when the Vatican addressed this issue of wives stuck home alone, it ruled in favor of the women. Pope Urban II, less than a year after he announced the First Crusade, wrote a letter in September 1096 urging that married men shouldn't "heedlessly" set out "without the consent of their wives," according to historian James Brundage. The reason? A distant husband cannot fulfill the marriage duty, guaranteed to both partners.

The Crusades, 1096–1270

Hundreds of thousands of Europeans during eight major Crusades swarmed to the Near East to try to recapture the Holy Land from the infidel Turks. And a man must work up a powerful lust while doing God's work, because thousands of prostitutes followed the crusaders. King Richard the Lion-hearted was furious at his troops for wasting much of his money; it got so bad that Pope Clement III in 1188 urged that no women accompany the soldiers except perhaps an unattractive laundress or two.

An Arab's View of the Crusaders' Prostitutes, 1180s

An Arab historian, Imad ad-Din, wrote a rococo account of Saladin's attempt to reconquer the Holy Land from the crusaders in the 1180s. Here's what ad-Din had to say about camp followers:

There arrived by ship three hundred lovely Frankish women, full of youth and beauty, assembled from beyond the sea and offering themselves for sin. They were expatriates come to help expatriates, ready to cheer the fallen and sustained in turn to give support and assistance, and they glowed with ardor for carnal intercourse. They were all licentious harlots, proud and scornful, who took and gave, foul-fleshed and sinful, singers and coquettes, appearing proudly in public, ardent and inflamed, tinted and painted, desirable and appetizing, exquisite and graceful, who ripped open and patched up, lacerated and mended, erred and ogled, urged and seduced, consoled and solicited, seductive and languid, desired and desiring, amused and amusing, versatile and cunning, like tipsy adolescents, making love and selling themselves for gold, bold and ardent, loving and passionate, pink-faced and unblushing, black-eyed and bullying, callipygian and graceful, with nasal voices and fleshy thighs, blue-eyed and grey-eyed, broken down little fools.

Each one trailed the train of her robe behind her and bewitched the beholder with her effulgence. She swayed like a sapling, revealed herself like a strong castle, quivered like a small branch, walked proudly with a cross on her breast, sold graces for gratitude, and longed to lose her robe and her honor. They arrived after consecrating their persons as if to works of piety, and offered and prostituted the most chaste and precious among them. They said they set out with the intention of consecrating their charms, and they did not intend to refuse themselves to bachelors, and they maintained they could make themselves acceptable to God by no better sacrifice than this. So they set themselves up each in a pavilion or tent erected for her use, together with other lovely young girls of their age, and opened the gates of pleasure.

They dedicated as a holy offering what they kept between their thighs; they were openly licentious and devoted themselves to relaxation; they removed every obstacle to making of themselves free offerings. They plied a brisk trade in dissoluteness, adorned the patched-up fissures, poured themselves into a spring of libertinage, shut themselves up in private under the amorous transports of men, offered their wares for enjoyment, invited the shameless into their embrace, mounted breasts on backs, bestowed their wares on the poor, brought their silver anklets up to touch their golden earrings, and were willingly spread out on the carpet of amorous sport. They made themselves targets for men's darts, they were permitted territory for forbidden acts, they offered themselves to the lances' blows and humiliated themselves to their lovers. They put the tent and loosed the girdle after agreement had been reached. They were the places where tent pegs are driven in, they invited swords to enter into their sheaths, they razed their terrain for planting, they made javelins rise towards their shields, excited the plough to plough, gave the birds a place to peck with their beaks, allowed heads to enter their antechambers and raced under whoever bestrode them at a spur's blow. They took the parched man's sinews to the well, fitted arrows to the bow's handle, cut off sword-belts, engraved coins, welcomed birds into the nest of their thighs, caught in their nets the horns of budding rams, removed the interdict from what is protected, withdrew the veil from what is hidden. They interwove leg with leg, slaked their lovers' thirsts, caught lizard after lizard in their holes, disregarded the wickedness of their intimacies, guided pens to inkwells, torrents to the valley bottom, streams to pools, swords to scabbards, gold ingots to crucibles, infidel girdles to women's zones, firewood to the stove, guilty men to low dungeons, money changers to dinar, necks to bellies, motes to eyes. They contested for tree trunks, wandered far and wide to collect fruit, and maintained that this was an act of piety without equal, especially to those who were far from home and wives. They mixed wine, and with an eye of sin, they begged for its hire.

The men of our army heard tell of them, and were at a loss to know how such women could perform acts of piety by abandoning all decency and shame. However, a few foolish mam-luks and ignorant wretches slipped away, under the fierce goad of lust, and followed the people of error.

—Imad ad-Din

A Crusader's Wife Gets Shaved
in a Turkish Bath, 1100s

*Moslems and Christians living together in parts of the Holy
Land led to some interesting situations. In many disciplines—
science, art, and medicine, to name a few—the Moslem
defenders were more sophisticated than the rough, self-
righteous Christian knights pouring down on them. Eyewitness
Usama ibn Munqidh, a cultured emir of the 1100s, packs his
autobiography with his often baffled impressions of "Frankish"
customs:*

I heard a similar case from a bath attendant called Salim
from Ma'arra, who worked in one of my father's bath houses.
This is his tale: I earned my living in Ma'arra by opening a bath
house. One day, a Frankish knight came in. They do not follow
our custom of wearing a cloth round their waist while they are
at the baths, and this fellow put out his hand and snatched off
my loincloth and threw it away. He saw at once that I had just
recently shaved my pubic hair. "Salim! It's magnificent! You
shall certainly do the same for me!" And he lay down flat on his
back. His hair there was as long as his beard. I shaved him, and
when he felt the place with his hand and found it agreeably
smooth, he said: "Salim, you must certainly do the same for my
dama. In their language, "dama" means lady, or wife. He sent
his valet to fetch his wife, and they arrived and the valet had
brought her in, she lay down on her back and he said to me:
"Do to her what you did to me." So I shaved her pubic hair,
while her husband stood by watching me. Then he thanked me
and paid me for my services.

You will observe a strange contradiction in their character:
They are without jealousy or a sense of honor, and yet at the

same time they have the courage that as a rule springs only from a sense of honor and a readiness to take offense.

—USAMA IBN MUNQIDH

Obviously, the sexual activity during the Crusades wasn't limited to prostitution and clean-shaven marital sex; battlefield rapes occurred. The Christian chroniclers liked to distinguish between how the Turks and the Christians treated women prisoners:

How the Turks Treated Women Prisoners

A high-born Christian lady was ambushed while playing dice with an archdeacon in an orchard:

The young lady was carried back still alive to the city, without having been beaten or wounded. But throughout the entire night and without the least show of mercy whatsoever, the Turks forced her to submit to all the excesses of their brutal orgy. Finally, after having physically abused her in the cruelest and most abominable ways, they dragged her onto the ramparts and condemned her to die. Then, they placed her head on one of their catapults, and flung it down from the walls.

—ALBERT OF AACHEN

How the Christians Treated Women Prisoners

Chronicler Fulcher of Chartres, commenting on the victory at Antioch, praises the chivalrous conduct of the crusaders (i.e., the Franks):

When the Franks found Saracen women in the tents, they did nothing evil to them—except run them through the belly with their lances.

Heretics' Orgies, 1114

Abbot Guibert of Nogent (1053–1124) describes in his autobiography the meetings of heretics near Soissons. He paints them as bisexual vegetarians:

They have their meetings in underground vaults or unfrequented cellars, without distinction of sex. After they have lighted candles, some loose woman lies down for all to watch and, so it is said, uncovers her buttocks, and they present their candles at her from behind; and as soon as the candles are put out, they shout "Chaos" from all sides and everyone fornicates with whatever woman comes first to hand.

If a woman becomes pregnant there, after the delivery the infant is taken back to the place. They light a great fire and those sitting around it toss the child from hand to hand through the flames until it is dead. Then it is reduced to ashes made into bread. To each person a portion is given as a sacrament, and once it has been received, hardly anyone recovers from that heresy.

—GUIBERT OF NOGENT

Heloise and Abelard: Tragic Love Affair, 1115

Among doomed couples and star-crossed lovers, Romeo and Juliet top the tip-of-the-tongue list, but during the Middles Ages it was Heloise and Abelard. Unlike Shakespeare's duo, there's nothing fictional about what happened to Heloise and Abelard; they even left extensive personal accounts of their tragedy.

In 1115, a fourteen-year-old orphan named Heloise (1101–1164), under the care of her doting uncle, was gaining a reputation around Paris for having a talent unheard of back then among young women: she was a promising scholar with a gift for classical languages. She was also pretty. That year, Peter Abelard (1079–1142)—mid-thirties, nationally known professor of philosophy with his own school—met Heloise, fell in love with her, and seduced her. And Abelard paid a price for it.

This is Abelard's version of events, from his Story of My Misfortunes, *written about 1132:*

There lived in Paris a maiden named Heloise, the niece of a canon named Fulbert, who from his deep love of her was eager to have her advanced in all literary pursuits possible. She was a lady of no mean appearance, while in literary excellence she was the first. And as gift of letters is rare among women, so it had gained favor for her and made her the most renowned woman in the whole kingdom.

I considered all the qualities which usually inspire lovers and decided she was just the one for me to join in love. I felt that this would be very easy to accomplish; I then enjoyed such renown and was so outstanding for my charm of youth that I feared no repulse by any woman whom I should deign to favor with my love. And I felt that this maiden would all the more readily yield to me as I knew she possessed and cherished a knowledge of letters. . . .

And so, all on fire with love for her, I sought opportunity to enable me to make her familiar with me by private and daily association, the more easily to win her over. To effect this, through the intervention of some friends, I arranged with her uncle to receive me at his own price into his home, which was near my school, on the pretext that the care of my household greatly interfered with my studies and proved too heavy a financial burden. He was a very avaricious man and also most anxious that his niece advance in her literary studies. Because of these two traits, I easily gained his assent and got what I desired, since he was all eager for the money and considered that his niece would profit from my teaching. On this latter point, he strongly urged me beyond my fondest hopes, acceding to my wishes and furthering my love. He put his niece entirely under my control that whenever I was free upon returning from school I might devote myself night and day to teaching her, telling me to punish her if I found her remiss. I was astonished at his simplicity in this matter and would have been no more astounded if he had been giving over a tender lamb to a ravenous wolf. For when he handed her over to me not only to teach but to discipline, what else was he doing but giving free rein to my designs, and an opportunity, even if I were not seeking it, easily to subdue her by threats and blows if flattery did not work? Two factors especially kept him from suspecting any wrongdoing—namely, his fondness for his niece and my own reputation in the past for chastity.

What was the result? We were first together in one house and then one in mind. Under the pretext of work we made ourselves entirely free for love and the pursuit of her studies provided the secret privacy which love desired. We opened our books but more words of love than of the lesson asserted themselves. There was more kissing than teaching; my hands found themselves at her breasts more often than on the book. Love brought us to gaze into each other's eyes more than reading kept them on the text. And the better to prevent suspicion, I sometimes struck her not through anger or vexation but from love and affection which were beyond the sweetness of every ointment. No sign of love was omitted by us in our ardor and whatever unusual love could devise, that was added too. And the more such delights were new to us, the more ardently we indulged in them, and the less did we experience satiety. And the more these pleasures engaged me, the less time I had for philosophy and the less attention I gave to my school. It became wearisome for me to go there and equally hard to stay when I was using nightly vigils for love and the days for study. I became negligent and indifferent in my lectures so that nothing I said stemmed from my talent but I repeated everything from rote. I came simply to say again what had been said long ago and, if I composed any verses the theme was of love and not of the secrets of philosophy. Many of these songs, as you yourself know, are still popular in various places and sung by people of like tastes. It is not easy even to realize the sadness, the expressed regrets and sorrows of my students when they saw the preoccupation and disturbance of my mind with such things.

Such a course could have escaped the notice of very few and of no one at all, I feel, except the man most disgraced by such base conduct, I mean the uncle of the maiden. When it was suggested to him at times by some, he could not believe on account of his extreme love of his niece noted above and of my well-known chastity in the past. For it is hard for us to suspect those we love. . . .

But Uncle Fulbert did eventually find out and immediately separated the lovers. It was too late: Heloise was pregnant. Abelard disguised her as a nun and smuggled her to his family's farm in Brittany.

There she stayed with my sister until she gave birth to a boy, whom she named Astralabe.

Upon his return, her uncle almost went mad and no one could appreciate except from experience the anguish which wrenched him or the shame he felt. He did not know what to do to me or by what plan he could waylay me. He was very much afraid that if he maimed or killed me, his dear niece would pay for it in my native place. He could not get hold of me and coerce me anywhere against my will, especially since I was very much on my guard. For I had no doubt that he would quickly attack if he could or dared to. After a while, I began to sympathize with him in his extreme anxiety and blamed myself for the deceit which love had wrought, which was, as it were, a base betrayal. I went to see him and, begging forgiveness, promised to make whatever amends he decided on. I told him that whoever had felt the force of love or recalled to what a crash women from the beginning have brought even the greatest men would not be surprised at my fall. And further to appease him, I made an offer beyond his fondest hopes to make satisfaction by marrying her whom I had defiled, provided this be done secretly so my reputation would not be damaged. *[Abelard was a clergyman and would be disgraced by marrying and possibly barred from teaching.]*

He agreed both by his own word and kiss of peace and by that of his backers. He thereby became on good terms with me, which was what I asked, but he did only the more easily to betray me.

. . . And so when the infant was born we entrusted it to my sister and returned secretly to Paris. After a few days, we spent a night in a secret vigil of prayer in a church and early on the following day we were joined by the nuptial blessing in the presence of her uncle and some of his and our friends. We straightaway separated and left secretly. After that we saw each other only rarely and then on the quiet, hiding by dissimulation what we had done.

But her uncle, seeking solace, and the members of his household, seeking solace for his disgrace, began to make our marriage public and thereby to break the word they had given regarding it. Heloise on her part cursed and swore that it was a lie. Her uncle became strongly aroused and kept heaping abuse upon her. When I found this out, I sent her to a convent of nuns in a town near Paris called Argenteuil, where as a young girl she had been brought up and received instruction. I had a religious habit, all except the veil, made for her and had her vested in it.

When her uncle and his kinsmen heard of this they considered that now I had fooled them and that by making her a nun I wanted easily to get rid of her. They became strongly incensed against me and formed a conspiracy. One night when I was sound asleep in an inner room of my lodgings, by bribing my attendant they wrought vengeance upon me in a cruel and shameful manner and one which the world with great astonishment abhorred—namely, they cut off the organs by which I had committed the deed which they deplored. They immediately fled but two of them were caught and had their eyes put out and were castrated; one of these was my servant already mentioned who while in my service was brought by greed to betray me.

When morning came, the whole city flocked to me and it is hard, yes impossible, to describe the astonishment which stunned them, the wailing they uttered, the shouting which irritated me and the moaning which upset me. The clerics and especially my students by their excessive lamentation and wailing pained me so that I endured more from their expressions of sympathy than from the suffering caused by the mutilation. I felt the embarrassment more than the wound, and the shame was harder to bear than the pain.

Heloise formally took vows as a nun; Abelard became a monk at St. Denis. Both of them continued their brilliant scholarly careers—Heloise excelling in Latin, Greek, and Hebrew. While Abelard, castrated, became calmly philosophical about their separation, proud of his new chaste love of God, Heloise suffered and still bitterly burned with passion for him.

Heloise's Oath of Love

Someone slipped Heloise a copy of Abelard's account quoted above and Heloise wrote a letter to him. The strength of her passion after more than a decade of no contact is almost eerie.

> . . . God is my witness that if Augustus, emperor of the whole world, thought fit to honor me with marriage and conferred all the earth on me to possess for ever, it would be dearer and more honorable to me to be called not his empress but your whore. . . .

Abelard wrote back, but mostly with pious advice for her to concentrate on love of God. Here's his tone right from the start:

> If since our conversion from the world to God I have not yet written to you any word of comfort or advice, it must

not be attributed to indifference on my part but to your own good sense, in which I always had such confidence that I did not think anything was needed; God's grace has bestowed on you all essentials to enable you to instruct the erring, comfort the weak, and encourage the faint-hearted.

Heloise found cold comfort in his words. She could not renounce their earthly love. She wrote back:

. . . In my case, the pleasures of lovers which we shared have been too sweet—they can never displease me, and can scarcely be banished from my thoughts. Wherever I turn they are always there before my eyes, bringing with them awakened longings and fantasies which will not even let me sleep. Even during the celebration of the Mass, when our prayers should be purer, lewd visions of those pleasures take such a hold upon my unhappy soul that my thoughts are on their wantonness instead of on prayers. I should be groaning over the sins I have committed, but I can only sigh for what I have lost. Everything we did and also the times and places are stamped on my heart along with your image, so that I live through it all again with you. Even in sleep I know no respite. Sometimes my thoughts are betrayed in a movement of my body, or they break out in an unguarded word. In my utter wretchedness, that cry from a suffering soul could well be mine: "Miserable creature that I am, who is there to rescue me out of the body doomed to this death?" [*Romans 7:24*] Would that in truth I could go on: "The grace of God through Jesus Christ our Lord." This grace, my dearest, came upon you unsought—a single wound of the body by freeing you from these torments has healed many wounds in your soul. Where God may seem to you an adversary He has in fact proved himself kind: like an honest doctor who does not shrink from giving pain if it will bring about a cure. But for me, youth and passion and experience of pleasures which were so delightful intensify the torments of the flesh and longings of desire, and the assault is the more overwhelming as the nature they attack is the weaker.

Men call me chaste; they do not know the hypocrite I am.

Nuns: Some Background

Joining a nunnery in the Middle Ages was rarely a voluntary decision by some devout young woman. Often, a girl's family would place (some might say "dump") a girl there who'd been seduced or one for whom they didn't want to spring for a dowry. A contribution would accompany the girl's arrival. By the time of the Renaissance, quite a few nunneries got a reputation for having lewd goings-on. So Hamlet's famous line, "Get thee to a nunnery," cuts both ways.

A Nun's Tale, 1165

This is the story of a medieval nun's disastrous love affair, as recorded by her abbot, Aelred of Rievaulx:

When Henry, whose memory is sacred and pious, was priest

at the Church of York (1147–1153), a girl of about four years old was received to be cared for in that same monastery. She, as soon as she had passed the age of infancy, acquired along with her girlish years a girlish licentiousness. She had no love for religious practice, no care for the order, no inclination towards fear of God. Her glance was forward, her talk vulgar, her walk wanton. She ventured out covered by the sacred veil, but she showed nothing worthy of such a habit in her actions. She was reproved with words, but not improved. She was set upon with whips but not set straight. She slipped away for hours from the eyes of her teachers, in order to enjoy leisure, to waste her time, to tell stories, or to persuade others to do something worthless. The discipline of the order was under siege, and she was forced unwillingly at least on the outside to preserve decency. She agreed to everything out of fear, nothing out of love. And already upon becoming pubescent, she preferred external things to those internal, frivolous pastimes to repose, games to serious matters.

The Handsome Gardener

One day the monastic brothers who took care of the grounds entered the woman's monastery to do some work. Noting their arrival, she drew close to them and stared rather too curiously at their faces and work. There was a youth among them who was more handsome and younger. The wretched girl glanced his way and he in fact was already looking at her. They looked at each other with too fawning an eye; and soon the twisting serpent, entering into each of their breasts, calls forth—with a hiss through all their vital organs—the poison which brings happiness. They start with nods but gestures follow nods. Finally, the silence is broken and they share talk about the deliciousness of love. They inflame each other in turn; on either side, they sow the seeds of pleasure, the inducements to lust. And while he was plotting to have illicit sex, she was thinking only about love, she later said.

Meanwhile, they grew closer. But in order that they might speak together more freely or perhaps enjoy themselves more fully, they agreed upon place and time. And so they preferred night; they fled from the public and they found a more secret place. That most impious scoundrel gave her a signal: the accursed boy would throw a stone onto either the wall or the roof of the room she usually stayed in, and she'd come out. Where, then, holy father, was your vigilance over your charges?

An interlude of topical prayers, then cut back to the action:

. . . Close your ears, maidens of Christ; open your eyes. A maiden of Christ is coming out, an adulteress beyond measure is about to go back in. She comes out, and like the dove . . . is soon snatched up by the talons of the hawk. She is thrown on her back, her mouth is covered lest she cry out and she, already corrupted in mind, is corrupted in flesh. The pleasure experienced prompted a repetition of the crime.

But the nuns began to wonder about the sound of the stones, and suspected a deception. She lay most open to suspicion whose character was suspected by all. The flight of the young man also increased suspicion. For when she had showed the adulterer [*N.B.: a nun is married to God*] that she was pregnant, he was afraid of being implicated, so he had left the monastery. . . . The senior nuns called the girl to a meeting. She, unable to hide it any longer, confesses his departure. Anyone who heard her story was amazed. Soon a zeal flared up in the nuns' bones and looking at each other in turns and clapping their hands together they rushed upon her, the veil snatched from her head; some thought she should have her heart torn out while still alive, others that she should be tied to a stake, with coals placed below her and burned. The senior sisters checked the fervor of the young ones. Nevertheless she was stripped, stretched out, and whipped without any pity. A jail was prepared, she was bound and thrown in; on each of her two feet, small shackles with small chains were placed, to which two heavier chains were attached, one nailed to a huge tree, the other drawn through a hole and locked to the door bolt outside. She survived on bread and water; she was scolded constantly. Meanwhile her uterus swelled and revealed her pregnant.

O how great was the mourning of everyone! Especially the lamentations of the holy virgins! They—afraid of her shame— are fearful that the crime of one will be cast upon all of them. They all already feel as though exposed to ridicule in the eyes of everyone, as though delivered up to be gnawed by the teeth of everyone! They all will weep; every single woman will weep! Inflamed with their outrageous pain again, they rush in to the prisoner. And if the senior sisters had not spared the fetus, they would scarcely in the end have ever stopped punishing her. She for her part patiently tolerates all these evils, and shouts that she is worthy of greater torments. But she believes the others will not suffer any evil on account of her unfaithfulness. They deliberate about what to do. If she were expelled, this would redound to the discredit of all of them, and no small danger would hang over all their souls if a pregnant mother were cast out to meet her death. If she is saved, they cried that the birth could not be hidden. Then one of them said: "It is best to entrust her to that vile youth—since she's his prostitute and pregnant with the adulterer's child— and she should be sent off to her partner in wickedness."

The unhappy girl replied: "If this [*plan*] can be a remedy for you, I know it will mean destruction for me. The youth will come to me as he promised on that night, that hour, in that secret place of our wickedness; then it will be up to you whether to hand me over to him. Let it happen according to heaven's will." Immediately they seize upon the word from her mouth. Again and again, swearing vengeance upon the youth, they ask of her the truth about everything. She confesses to them, affirming what she had said was true.

The Trap

The master of the congregation ordered that on that night one man, his head covered by a veil, should sit in the designated place and that the older monks would hide and pounce upon the man when he arrived, pummel him with clubs, tie him up, and hold him prisoner.

He said it and it happened just that way. The young man, ignorant of the girl's fate, entered, secular not only in mind but in clothing. And burning with lust, as soon as he spied the veil, like a mindless horse or a mule rushed towards the man whom he thought was a woman. But the brothers, beating him with sticks, extinguished his lust. The matter was referred to the nuns.

Some, zealous for God but not wise, wanting to avenge the insult to their virginity, soon asked the brothers to hand over the young man for a few moments, as though they wanted to question him. He was grabbed by them, thrown down, and held. The guilty nun was brought in for the spectacle; an instrument was placed in her hands, and she was forced against her will to cut off his manhood with her own hands. Then one of the onlookers picked up the parts of which he had been deprived and crammed them, still filthy with blood, into the mouth of the sinful young woman. . . .

I do not praise the deed but the zeal; I do not condone the spilling of blood but I do praise such impassioned efforts by the holy virgins against sin.

—AELRED OF RIEVAULX

The nuns chained her back up. When she gave birth, angels came down and took the baby away and her chains dropped off. These two "miracles," confirmed by the author, brought glory to the nunnery at Watton, instead of shame.

Art of Courtly Love, *circa* 1175

The popular image of courtly love features knights in armor galloping to win the affection of high-born ladies. What most people forget is that the knights were pursuing other men's wives. Courtly love was dreamed up by the troubadour poets of southern France, and it promoted extreme chastity and devotion (how romantic!), followed by adultery (how French!).

There were many rules for behavior, the most famous collection of them being The Art of Courtly Love, *written by a clergyman, Andreas Capellanus. His first rule was this:* Marriage is no excuse for not loving.

Love between Husband and Wife? Are You Mad?

The following was written as though a man were replying to a woman:

I am greatly surprised you wish to misapply the term "love" to that marital affection which husband and wife are expected to feel for each other after marriage. . . . They may be bound to each other by a great and immoderate affection, but their feeling cannot take the place of love, because it cannot fit under the true definition of love.

For what is love but the inordinate desire to receive passionately a furtive and hidden embrace? But what embrace between husband and wife can be furtive, I ask you, since they may be said to belong to each other and may satisfy each other's desires without fear that anybody will object?

But there is another reason why husband and wife cannot love each other, and that is the very substance of love, without which true love cannot exist: jealousy. A married couple should avoid it like the plague while lovers should always welcome it as the mother and nurse of love.

Capellanus, a chaplain himself, is rather tolerant:

A clergyman . . . ought not to devote himself to the works of love but is bound to renounce absolutely all the delights of the flesh. . . . But since hardly anyone lives without carnal sin, and since the life of the clergy is, because of the continual idleness and the great abundance of food, naturally more liable to temptations of the body than that of any other men, if any clergyman should wish to enter the lists of Love, let him speak and apply himself to Love's service in accordance with the rank or standing of his parents.

Advocating Rape?

If you should, by some chance, fall in a love with a peasant woman, be careful to puff her up with lots of praise and then, when you find a convenient opportunity, do not hold back but take your pleasure and embrace her by force. For you can hardly soften their outward inflexibility so far that they will grant you their embraces quietly or permit you to have the solaces you desire unless you first use a little compulsion as a convenient cure for their shyness. We do not say these things, however, because we want to persuade you to love such women, but only so that, if through lack of caution you should be driven to love them, you may know, in brief compass, what to do.

Maimonides' Letter of Sexual Advice, 1190

Moses Maimonides (1135–1204) was a world-famous Jewish theologian and doctor. As a personal favor to his patron, Saladin, long-time foe of the crusaders, he doled out some sexual advice to Saladin's aging nephew, the ruler of Hamat, Syria. At the time, Jews lived far more compatibly with Moslems than with Christians:

Thus speaks Moses, the son of the Lord's Servant, the Israelite from Cordova: the Reverend Master, may God make his glory eternal, has commanded me to instruct him in a regimen that is helpful in increasing his sexual potential, because he has said he has a weakness in that regard. . . . He wishes this regimen because of fear, due to the meagerness of his body. He desires these increases (in coital activities) because of the multitude of young maidens. He further requests I only mention in this regimen that which is easy to carry out and whose performance is pleasant.

. . . Among foods, medications, and other regimens of health, all that which moistens and warms to an intermediate degree is extremely beneficial to the entire body or to the organs of coitus in this regard. For example, happiness, delight, laughter, rest, and sleep that is not excessive are of value in this matter.

All in Your Head

It is known that this activity is not purely a natural function—that is, erection is not similar to nutritional or growth activities in which emotions play no part. Rather it is also an emotional process controlled by the psyche. As a result, various emotions can be greatly detrimental or beneficial (for coitus); i.e. sorrow, anxiety, and mourning, or the repulsiveness of the women with whom one intends to have sexual intercourse, are among the things that markedly weaken coitus. . . .

What to Avoid

Physicians have already mentioned that which especially weakens coitus: sexual intercourse with numerous maidens, elderly women, or a young girl who has not reached puberty, or a woman who for many years has not been intimate, or a menstruating or ill woman; even more than this is coitus with a repugnant woman who has passed the menopause.

Maimonides now launches into a very long list of foods helpful for potency, including lamb, pigeon, chicken brains, rooster testicles, dove's eggs, breast milk, turnips, asparagus, and pistachio nuts. He recommends warm massages on the lower back, and especially on the feet, but near the end, he shares a "wondrous secret":

Because there are many people who desire to prolong erection by not ejaculating, it seems appropriate that I mention the following remedy. It is a wondrous secret which no person has (heretofore) described: take one liter each of carrot oil and radish oil, one liter of mustard oil, combine it all and place therein one half liter of live saffron-colored ants. Set the oil in the sun for between four and seven days and afterwards utilize it. Massage the penis therein, for three hours or two hours before sexual intercourse. Then wash it with warm water, and it will remain in erection even after ejaculation. Nothing comparable has yet been prepared for this purpose.

. . . Let the Master choose this and that which is easy to carry out, and do it time after time. And may the Lord lengthen his days with pleasures.

—Maimonides

The Pope's Dirty Story, *circa* 1260

Franciscan monk Salimbene de Adam was an eyewitness to many of the events he describes in his Chronicle, *which was completed in 1288. He paints an astoundingly lusty, prank-filled, violent picture of religious life in the Middle Ages, a vision that seems right out of Chaucer.*

Once, Brother Bonaventure asked Pope Alexander IV [*reigned 1254–1261*] whether or not it pleased him that the

[*Franciscan*] Friars Minor heard confession, and the pope answered, "It pleaseth me very much. And I will give you a horrible example on the subject. There was a certain woman who confessed to the priest of her church. But this priest, wishing to know her carnally, began to solicit her sexually. And so in the very church itself behind the altar near the place where the Lord's body is kept, he sought to rape her. But the lady said to him, 'This is neither the time nor the place for the work of Venus. Let us seek a more convenient time when we can do this thing together.'

"She said this, however, merely in order to get away from him. Yet anticipating such future pleasure, the priest desisted from his actions and simply talked with her in a friendly fashion. As she was leaving, however, he said to her, 'Remember our bargain, keep in mind our tryst.' And she answered, 'Oh, I will remember well.'

"When she arrived home, however, she made a pie which appeared beautiful on the outside but which was filled with human excrement and sent it to the priest as a gift, along with a vase full of fine white wine. And this was the woman's only fault, she should have sent her own urine to the priest in the vase, just as she sent her own excrement in the pie.

"When the priest saw this fine pastry, he thought it would make a fine gift for his bishop, and so he sent it to him. Thus when the bishop was dining with his household, he ordered his servant to cut the pie and place it on the table before his guests. When the servant cut the pie in the other room, however, he discovered some excrement and was horrified. Then he set the pie aside to show the bishop later, and to the bishop's insistence that the pie be brought to the table, he said, 'You have enough for now. Another time, the Lord willing, you will have better.' What more can one say? When the bishop saw such a pie, he was 'exceedingly angry' [*Esther 5:9*] at the priest.

"He had the offender brought before him and said, 'Tell me, priest, where did you learn to send such fine pies to your bishop? In what way have I offended you? How have I earned such an insult from you? Why have you sent me a pie filled with human excrement?' When the priest heard this, he was stupefied, and he said to the bishop, 'Father, truly I did not make the pie myself. Such and such a lady sent it to me, and, thinking that such a fine gift was worthy only of you, I sent it to you in order to honor you, believing the whole time it was a splendid pie.'

"When the bishop heard this, 'he was satisfied' [*Leviticus 10:20*]. But after the priest left, the bishop sent for the lady in order to find out the truth of the matter. And she 'confessed, and did not deny' [*John 1:20*] that she was the one who made the pie, but that she did it to get back at the priest, who had attempted to seduce her during confession right in the church behind the altar. Then the bishop praised the lady highly for her deed, and punished the priest grievously."

—SALIMBENE DE ADAM

Monkish Humor

Friar Detesalve is a prime joker throughout the Chronicle:

On another occasion when Friar Detesalve was walking in Florence during the winter, he slipped on the ice and fell flat, upon which those great pranksters, the Florentines, gathered round him and began to laugh at his expense. And one of them derisively inquired whether he would not like something more underneath him, to which Detesalve retorted, "Yes, your wife."

Alberigo the Tyrant: Sexual Torture, circa 1250

Most of Italy in the mid-1200s was a checkerboard of petty tyrants under the shadow of the pope. Our monk Salimbene recounts the life of one of the cruelest ones, Alberigo da Romano, ruler of Treviso. Arbitrary executions weren't enough for him—he added an extra dose of sexual humiliation:

Alberigo had had twenty-five civic leaders of Treviso hanged on a single day and they had neither offended nor harmed him in any way. But because he was afraid that they would perhaps do him harm, he had them removed from his face and shamefully hanged. And he required thirty noble women—their mothers, wives, daughters, and sisters—to come and watch the execution. He also wanted to cut off the noses of these women, but by the happy intervention of a man who was falsely said to be Alberigo's bastard son, this was not done. Furthermore, he had their clothes cut off from the breasts down so that with bodies all nude they stood before the eyes of the men to be hanged. Moreover, he had the men hanged very near the ground and then forced the women to walk between their legs so that the men kicked them in the face as they were dying in great bitterness of spirit. And the women had to endure the horror and pain of such base mockery. To see such things was the greatest kind of misery and cruelty, the like of which has never been heard.

Then Alberigo had the women carried off beyond the river Sile to go wherever they could. And with the pieces of garment they had about their breasts, the women made coverings for their genitals (that is, their pudenda) and then walked the whole day for fifteen miles with bare feet and nude bodies through wild fields, bitten by flies and torn by thorns and briars and nettles and burrs and thistles. And they went weeping, for they had great cause for weeping, and they had nothing to eat. "O God, look upon the sorrow and pain! These troubled ones, these your children, are lost without You. Yours it is to help, Yours it is to help. . . ."

These women arrived late in the day at the Venetian lagoons, and, behold, suddenly they saw a lone fisherman in his little boat, and they called out to him. He was, however, terribly frightened, for he thought he was seeing demonic illusions, or phantasms, or at least sea monsters.

The fisherman eventually calmed down enough to transport the women to Venice, where the cardinal decided to help them.

All the citizens of Venice gathered together in the square of San Marco, and [*the cardinal*] Lord Ottavio recounted to them the entire story given above. And in order to anger the people more against Alberigo and to make them pity the ladies more, the cardinal also did the following: He had the women come forth in that same shameful and nude condition that the wicked Alberigo had reduced them to.

And when the Venetians had heard the entire story and looked upon the nude women, they cried out in loud voices, "Let him die, let that evil man die! Burn him and his wife alive! And destroy all his progeny from the face of the earth!"

. . . After this, by the will of the entire city, the cardinal preached a crusade against the accursed Alberigo: Whoever take up the cross and go to destroy him or send someone in his place, paying all expenses—would receive plenary indulgence for all his sins. *(Basically, an offer of one-size-fits-all forgiveness.)*

. . . These people then marched unanimously against Alberigo and did him great harm, although they did not totally destroy him. Only a short time after the cross was taken up against him, however, he was completely destroyed along with all his offspring, all of which he thoroughly deserved. For once, when he lost his falcon, he pulled down his pants and turned his arse up to the heavens in mockery and insult to God himself, thinking in this way to avenge himself on God for his loss. And when he got home he went into the church and defecated on the very altar itself, in the place where the body of the Lord is consecrated. Moreover, his wife called noble ladies and matrons "whores" and "prostitutes," and neither did her husband rebuke her at any time.

Salimbene describes the fate of Alberigo and his family:

For those who killed them pulled the arms and legs off the children while they were still alive in the presence of Alberigo and his wife and struck them in the mouth with these limbs. Then they tied mother and daughters to stakes and burned them. Yet these daughters were young and beautiful virgins, and were guilty of nothing. But their slayers showed no mercy to innocence and beauty on account of the great hatred they had for the mother and father. For they were horrible in their evil treatment of the people of Treviso. Thus in the public square of the city, they came at Alberigo with pincers and tore the flesh piecemeal from his body while he was still alive, and so they tore his body to pieces amid jeers and insults and heavy torments. For Alberigo had killed their kinsmen: their brothers and fathers and sons. And he had laid such heavy taxes and fines on the land that the citizens had to tear down their houses and send the materials of which they were constructed (along with such movables as chests, casks, and urns) on ships to sell in Ferrara in order to get the money to meet the obligations. I saw these things with my own eyes. . . .

Nose Saver Spared

It should be noted that the people of Treviso spared the man on whose insistence the noses of these ladies had been saved; they permitted him to live and indeed gave him many goods, of which he was well worthy. For he had often restrained Alberigo and his wife from many wicked deeds that they would otherwise have committed.

—SALIMBENE DE ADAM

Marco Polo's Sexual Travelogue, 1271–1292

Marco Polo (1254–1324), Venetian by birth, was certainly the greatest traveler of his day, zigzagging all over Asia, but what's usually forgotten is that Polo co-wrote his book with a professional romance writer, one Rustichello of Pisa. The more you read Travels, *the more you get the feel of a very observant merchant reciting facts to a TV producer who's trying to juice the whole thing up.*

Kublai Khan's Beauty Contest

Genghis Khan, with his fierce Mongolian hordes, conquered the largest empire in the history of mankind, stretching from

China to Europe. In the 1280s, Marco Polo met Genghis'
descendant, Kublai Khan, who then ruled much of the empire.
Here is what a man does when he is the most powerful being
on the entire planet, according to Marco and Rustichello:

Kublai, who is styled grand khan or lord of lords, is of
middle height, neither tall nor short; his limbs are well
formed, and his body well proportioned. His complexion is
fair, and occasionally suffused with red, like the bright tint of
the rose, which adds much grace to his countenance. His eyes
are black and handsome, his nose is well shaped and
prominent.

He has four wives of the first rank, who are esteemed
legitimate, and the eldest son born of any one of these
succeeds to the empire, upon the decease of the grand khan.
They bear equally the title of empress, and have their separate
courts. None of them have fewer than three hundred young
female attendants of great beauty, together with a multitude of
youths as pages, and other eunuchs, as well as ladies of the
bed chamber; so that the number of persons belonging to each
of their respective courts amounts to ten thousand. When his
majesty is desirous of the company of one of his empresses, he
either sends for her or goes himself to her palace.

[*Besides these,*] he has many concubines provided for his
use, from a province of Tartary, named Ungut, the inhabitants
of which are distinguished for beauty of features and fairness
of complexion. The grand khan sends his officers there every
second year, or oftener, as it may happen to be his pleasure,
who collect for him, to the number of four or five hundred, or
more, of the handsomest of the young women, according to
the estimation of beauty communicated to them in their
instructions.

The mode of their evaluation is as follows: Upon arriving, the commissioners give orders for assembling all the young women of the province and appoint qualified persons to examine them. They carefully inspect each of them, by category, that is to say, as to the hair, the countenance, the eyebrows, the mouth, the lips, and other features, as well as the symmetry of these with each, estimate their value at sixteen, seventeen, eighteen, or twenty or more carats [*i.e.*, *points*], according to the greater or less degree of beauty. Those who score more than standard set by the grand khan of twenty or twenty-one—depending on how many are required—are selected from the rest and they are conveyed to his court.

Upon their arrival in his presence, he causes a new examination to be made by a different set of inspectors and from among them a further selection takes place, when thirty or forty scoring highest are retained for his own chamber. These, in the first instance, are committed separately to the care of the wives of certain of the nobles, whose duty it is to observe them attentively during the course of the night, in order to ascertain that they have not any concealed imperfections, that they sleep tranquilly, do not snore, have sweet breath, and are free from any unpleasant scent in any part of the body. Having undergone this rigorous scrutiny, they are divided into groups of five, who attend during three days and three nights, in his majesty's interior apartment, where they are to perform every service that is required of them, and he does with them as he likes. When this term is completed, they are relieved by another group, and in this manner successively, until the whole number have taken their turn; when the first five recommence their attendance.

But while one party officiates in the inner chamber, another is stationed in the outer apartment; in order that if his majesty should have occasion for anything, such as drink or food, the former may signify his commands to the latter, who brings the required article immediately. And thus the duty of waiting upon his majesty's person is performed exclusively by these young females. The remainder of them, who have scored lower, are assigned to the different lords of the household, under whom they are instructed in cookery, in dressmaking, and other suitable works; and upon any person belonging to the court expressing an inclination to take a wife, the grand khan bestows upon him one of these damsels, with a handsome dowry. In this manner, he provides for them all among his nobility.

It may be asked whether the people of the province do not feel themselves aggrieved in having their daughters thus forcibly taken from them by the sovereign? Certainly not; but, on the contrary, they regard it as an honor done to them; and those who are fathers of handsome children feel highly gratified by his condescending to choose their daughters.

Travelers Help Tibetan Brides

This desolate country, [*of Tibet*], infested by dangerous wild beasts, extends for twenty days' journey, without shelter or food except perhaps every third or fourth day, when the traveler may find some habitation where he can renew his stock of provisions. Then he reaches a region with villages and hamlets in plenty and a few towns perched on precipitous crags. Here there prevails a marriage custom of which I will tell you. It is such that no man would ever on any account take a virgin to wife. For they say that a woman is worthless unless she has knowledge of many men. They argue that she must have displeased the gods, but if she enjoyed the favor of their idols then men would desire her and consort with her. So they deal with their womenfolk in this way. When it happens that men from a foreign land are passing through this country and have pitched their tents and made a camp, the matrons from neighboring villages and hamlets bring their daughters to these camps, to the number of twenty or forty, and beg the travelers to take them and lie with them. So these choose the girls who please them best, and the others return home disconsolate. So long as they remain, the visitors are free to take their pleasure with the women and use them as they will, but they are not allowed to carry them off anywhere else. When the men have worked their will and are ready to be gone, then it is the custom for every man to give the woman with whom he has lain some trinket or token so that she can show, when she comes to marry, that she has had a lover. In this way, custom requires every girl to wear more than a score of such tokens hung round her neck to show that she has had lovers in plenty and plenty of men have lain with her. And she who has most tokens and can show that she has had most lovers and that most men have lain with her is the most highly esteemed and the most acceptable as a wife; for they say she is the most favored by the gods. And when they have taken a wife, they prize her highly; and they account a grave offense for any man to touch another's wife, and they all strictly abstain from such an act. So much, then, for this marriage custom. Obviously the country is a fine one to visit for a lad from sixteen to twenty-four.

The Slow Walk of Chinese Virgins

In Cathay province:

When the contracts and covenants have been duly entered into and confirmed between the parties, the intended bride is conducted to the baths for her chastity to be put to the proof. Here the mothers and kinswomen of the betrothed pair will be waiting, and certain matrons specially deputed by both parties will test her virginity with a pigeon's egg. If the women of the bridegroom's party are not satisfied with this test, on the grounds that loss of virginity may be disguised by means of medicaments, one of the matrons, having wrapped one finger in fine white linen, will slightly bruise the <u>vena virginalis</u> [*i.e., the hymen*], so that the linen may be slightly stained with the virginal blood. For it is a distinctive property of this blood that its stain cannot be removed from cloth by any washing. So, if the stain is washed out, that is a sign that the blood is not that of an undefiled virgin. When the test has been carried out, if the bride is found to be a virgin, the marriage is valid. If not, it is invalid and the girl's father is obliged to pay a penalty specified in the contract. You must know that, to ensure this strict preservation of virginity, the maidens always walk so daintily that they never advance one foot more than a finger's breadth beyond the other, since physical integrity is often destroyed by a wanton gait.

The Catholic Inquisition: Some Background

Pope Lucius III authorized bishops in 1184 to conduct an inquisition to root out heretics. It's uncanny how often heretics were accused of "un-Christian" sexual practices. The inquisitors—doing God's work—needed a powerful weapon to get at the truth; so, from 1257 to 1816, the Vatican sanctioned torture as a means of eliciting confessions. One such was the Chambre Chauffee ("Heated Room") in which Sodomites were lowered onto the needle-sharp tip of a tall wide-based cone while heated braziers were held nearby.

The Inquisition Quizzes French Peasants on Their Sex Lives, *circa* 1320

Jacques Fournier, who later became Pope Benedict XII, headed an inquisition (1318–1325) into the Cathar heresy in Pamiers diocese in southern France and meticulously interrogated the peasants there. The resulting thousand-plus pages of testimony cast an unprecedented glimpse into the sex life of several small medieval villages, especially Montaillou. (For a further look, see the fine book Montaillou, *by E. Le Roy Ladurie.)*

Local Priest and Lost Virginity

Short, energetic, and charming, priest Pierre Clergue had dozens of lovers. He sometimes started off by saying, "I love you more than any woman in the world." If that didn't work, he might drop hints about his influence with the Inquisition.

In the year of our Lord 1320 on the 19th day of August, Grazide, the wife of Pierre Lizier of Montaillou, swore by evangelical saints that she would tell the truth. . . .

About seven years ago in the summer, the priest [*Pierre Clergue*] came to my mother's house during the harvest, and asked me to know him carnally. I was about fourteen or fifteen years old and I agreed. He deflowered me in the hay in the barn. However, he did not rape me. Afterwards, he knew me carnally on a frequent basis until January of the following year, and always in my mother's house, always in the daytime. My mother knew about it and consented.

Afterwards, the same priest married me to Pierre Lizier, my late husband, and over the next four years the priest continued to know me carnally with the knowledge and consent of my husband, right up until my husband's death. When my husband would ask me if the priest was up to anything, I would say "Yes" and then he would warn me to guard myself against all other men except the priest. However, the priest never knew me carnally when my husband was in the house. . . .

She was asked: Do you feel it was a sin that you slept with the priest and does such an act displease God? She answered: "I don't think it was a sin nor do I think it could displease God because Pierre and I both enjoyed it."

Contraception in Church

The attractive young widow Beatrice de Planissoles describes her first encounter with the randy priest:
Pierre Clergue, the priest of the church of Montaillou, who had come to see me, told me he would send his pupil John to me on the following night to ask whether I would sleep with him [*i.e., Pierre*]. I consented to all this. On the arranged night, just as people were drifting off to sleep, I was waiting in the house for the pupil. When he arrived, I followed him since the night was pitch-black, arrived at the church, entered and found Pierre Clergue, who had made up a bed in the church. I

asked the priest, "How can we do such a deed in the church of Saint Peter?" To which the priest replied, "Oh, what a pity for Saint Peter!"

With these words, we got into bed, and he knew me carnally. Afterwards, before dawn, he led me out of the church himself and took me as far as the gate of the cottage where I lived.

Before the priest had known me carnally for the first time, I asked him, "What shall I do if I become pregnant by you? I will be dishonored and lost." To which the priest replied, "I have a certain special herb. If a man carried it when he has intercourse with a woman, he would not be able to impregnate her nor can she conceive."

I asked, "What sort of herb is it? Is it the one cowherds put over their milk churns to keep the milk from curdling?"

He replied, "Don't bother about what herb it is."

But there is such an herb as he said and he had a supply of it.

From that moment whenever he wanted to know me carnally, he used to carry something wrapped up and fastened in a linen cloth, the weight and length of an ounce, about the size of the first joint of my pinkie. He also had a long cord which he used to place around my neck when he was having intercourse with me and the thing he called an herb hung from the cord and passed down between my breasts resting at the bottom of my stomach. He always positioned it this way when he wanted to know me carnally, and it remained around my neck until the priest wanted to get up. And, anytime he wanted to know me carnally twice or more, the priest would ask me, before we had sex, "Where are the herbs?" I would find them by the cord hanging around my neck and place them in his hand. The priest would then place them at the bottom of my stomach, with the cord running between my breasts, and so he would know me carnally and in no other way. *(The Latin wording on this is unclear; this could be herbal magic or a kind of pessary on a string to be inserted.)*

Once, I asked the priest to give me the herb, but he said, "No, I won't because then you would be able to have sex with another man without fear of pregnancy." For this reason, he did not want to give me the herb so I would refrain from having sex with another man out of fear of pregnancy. He did this because of his cousin, Raymond Clergue, my lover before him. They were very jealous over me.

He added that I need not confess to another priest the sins that I had committed with him but only to God alone, who knew the sins and who could absolve me of them, something which no man could do.

The Inquisition locked Beatrice up from March 8, 1321 to July 4, 1322. Pierre Clergue, sometime spy for the inquisitors, escaped punishment for years, but eventually died in prison.

First Homosexual Encounter

In the days before ID cards, pedophile Arnaud de Verniolles posed as a priest:

It must have been twenty years ago, when I was ten or twelve years old, that I was sent by my father to learn grammar in a schoolroom in Pamiers kept by Master Pons de Massabuc. Staying together with me in the room were Master Pons, Pierre Delille from Montégut, Barnard Balesse from Mercadal de

Paumiers, Arnaud Auréol, son of Knight Pierre Auréol from the area of Bastide de Sérou who was already shaving, and my late brother, Bernard de Verniolle. I can't remember any other names.

When I lived in that schoolroom, with those companions, I slept for a good six weeks in the same bed with Arnaud Auréol. When I had slept with Arnaud Auréol for two or three nights, Arnaud Auréol waited until he thought I was asleep, and he hugged me. He then positioned himself between my thighs, and placing his member between my thighs, by moving himself as though he were having his way with a woman, he ejaculated between my thighs. He continued to commit the sin thus almost every night as long as I slept with him. But because I was still a boy, although I didn't like it, I did not dare reveal the truth to anyone even though I had no desire to commit that sin because I did not yet possess such desires. After those six weeks, Master Pons, Arnaud Auréol, and my brother and a certain boy from Cintagabelle named Thibaud, who was shaving, moved from that building to a residence near the Pont de Lacledas. I slept with my brother and Master Pons, who sought no wicked acts with me.

Arnaud describes several homosexual encounters, and recalls what made him decide to be a pedophile:

It was back when they were burning lepers; I was living in Toulouse and went one day with a common whore. And after I had perpetrated this sin, my face swelled up. I was terrified that I had caught leprosy; I swore that from then on, I would never have sexual relations with a woman again; and in order to keep this solemn oath, I began to abuse little boys.

—Inquisition register of Jacques Fournier

Medieval Prostitution

Extensive brothel rules for London passed by Parliament in 1161 have survived and paint a relatively humane picture, aimed at stopping pimps from exploiting girls. For instance, no woman could be forced into prostitution; girls had to live and eat outside the brothel, could not be charged exorbitant room rents, and could not work there on Sundays or holidays. No diseased girls, nuns, or wives were allowed, and all sex trade had to be for overnight stays.

Cruel Haircuts for Pimps, 1300s

The White Book of the City of London *collected a huge array of civic documents dating up to 1419:*

In the first place, if any man shall be found to be a common whoremonger or bawd [*i.e., a pimp*], and shall of the same be attainted [*i.e., convicted*], first let all his head and beard be shaved, except a fringe on the head two inches in breadth; and let him be taken into the pillory, with minstrels, and set thereon for a certain time at the discretion of the Mayor and Aldermen.

Madames: Bowl Cut

Item, If any woman shall be found to be a common receiver of courtesans or bawd, and of the same shall be attainted, first let her be openly brought with minstrels, from prison unto the thew [*i.e., women's stocks*], and sat thereon for certain times at the discretion of the Mayor and Aldermen, and there let her hair be cut around.

Cokkeslane

Item, If any woman shall be found to be a common courtesan, and of the same shall be attainted, let her be taken from the prison unto Algate, with a hood of ray [*i.e.*, *striped cloth*], and a white wand in her hand; and from thence with minstrels unto the thew, and there let her cause be proclaimed, and from thence, through Chepe and Newgate to Cokkeslane, there to take up her abode.

As for Cokkeslane, a whorehouse district, it's a variant spelling of "Cock's Lane." In the Middle Ages, street names were much franker than they are today.

Medieval Prostitutes' Street Name, London, 1276

This one was notorious for brothels:
Gropecuntlane
By 1349, it was Grape Street; then it became Grub Street, an address for a long time popular with many publishing houses.

Medieval Prostitutes' Street Name, Near Paris

French: Rue du Poil au Con.
English Translation: Street of Cunt Hair

Prostitutes working there chose to disobey the city health ordinance requiring them to shave their pubes, according to Medieval Underworld, *by Andrew McCall.*

Today it's called Rue de Pélécan.

Queen Johanna Judges Her Husband by His Nose, 1343

Queen Johanna I of Naples (1326–1382) was quite optimistic when she consummated her marriage to Prince Andrew of Hungary in 1343:

[*Roman historian*] Lampridius describes big-nosed men as being more virile and well hung than others, and it was with these sorts of men that Queen Johanna of Naples, a woman of unbridled lust, most enjoyed having sexual intercourse. . . . The poor woman believed in the old saying, "Nasatorum peculio" [*crudely put: "Big nose, big hose"*], and she expected the magnitude of her husband's member to match the size of his nose, but she wound up very frustrated. "Oh nose," she cried, "how horribly you have deceived me!"

—HENRY SELMUTH, COMMENTARY TO GUIDO PANCIROLLI'S
MEMORY OF THINGS FORGOTTEN

Johanna, no cupcake, had Prince Andrew strangled, but she paid for her crime when Andrew's brother, King Louis of Hungary, drove her out of Naples. Joanna wisely diversified: On August 8, 1347, she opened Europe's most sumptuous brothel located on her family's property in Avignon. The following year, she sold the whorehouse—along with the rest

*of the city—to Pope Clement VI and he granted her absolution
for murdering her husband.*

Johanna's Brothel Rules of 1347

- The Queen desires that every Saturday the baillive
  [*brothel keeper*] and a barber [*doctor*] shall examine all
  the debauched girls at the brothel; if any of them has
  caught some illness from venery, then that girl shall be
  separated and lodged apart, so that no one may conjoin
  with her and that no young man may catch the disease.
- If any girl in the bordello gets pregnant, the baillive shall
  take care the baby isn't killed, and shall alert the consuls
  to provide for the child.
- The baillive shall not allow admittance to any Jew, and if
  by some trick a Jew has entered, and had carnal
  knowledge of any woman, he shall be imprisoned, and
  then whipped by everyone in the city.

*The Vatican kept the whorehouse open, and it thrived,
under the nickname "The Abbey."*

The Lusty Pope's Self-defense, 1350

*Clement VI (pope 1342–1352) declared a Jubilee year in
1350, offering forgiveness for all sins to all Christians coming
to Rome—one of the better travel package deals of all time.
Apparently, the pope committed a few sins of his own:*

Every night at vespertide Clement VI was accustomed, after

the cardinals' audience, to hold a public audience of all the wives and respectable women who wished to come. At last, some men speaking ill of him on this account began to stand by the palace doors and secretly count the number of women who went in and who came out. And when they had done it for many days, they realized always one fewer exited than had entered. When many scandals and rumors arose on this account, the confessor of the Lord Pope warned him frequently to desist from such conduct and to live chastely and more cautiously. But he ever made the same reply: "Thus have we been accustomed to do when we were young and what we do now we do by counsel of our physicians."

But when the pope was aware that his brethren the cardinals and his auditors and the rest of the court murmured and spoke ill of him on this account, one day he brought in his bosom a little black book wherein he had the names written of his diverse predecessors in the papal chair who were lecherous and incontinent; and he showed by the facts therein recorded that these had better ruled the Church, and done much more good than the other chaste popes.

—ABBOT THOMAS, *CHRONICLE OF MÉAUX*

An Organ Stuck in a Church

In the fourteenth century, Knight Geoffrey de la Tour-Landry wrote a book of pious instruction for young women, with many examples of what not to do:

It happened in a church on an evening of our lady, a man called Pers Lenard, who was sergeant of Candee, had carnal relations with a woman on an altar. God, in his great might to show them they did evil, tied them fast together that night and all the next day in the sight of the people that came to town. And all the people in the surrounding region came down to see them.

And they might never be separated but were fast like a dog and bitch together that night and the morrow all day until the time the people made a procession to pray to God that the horrible sight may cease and be hidden. At last at night, they were able to separate. And after the church was blessed. And they that did the deed were required to do penance to go naked after the procession three Sundays—beating themselves and announcing their sin before the people. So there's an example of why nobody should commit such filthy acts in a church but keep it clean and worship God there.

—GEOFFREY DE LA TOUR-LANDRY

The Virginity Tests of Joan of Arc, 1429–1431

It was simply unheard of for a teenage peasant girl, who wasn't a prostitute, to travel with a medieval army, much less lead one. Yet Joan of Arc (1412–1431)—a cross-dressing seventeen-year-old who heard heavenly "voices"—helped lead the French to several key victories in their attempts to oust the invading English.

She was known as La Pucelle ("The Virgin"), or the Maid of Orleans, so what better way for her enemies to discredit her than to prove she was not a maid?

Joan was captured in 1430 by the Burgundians and sold for £10,000 to the English, led by the Duke of Bedford.

From the court records of her trial:

I know well that her virginity was examined by women or midwives (by order of the Duchess of Bedford) and one of these was Anna Bavon, the other a woman but I can't remember her name. After the visit they reported she was a virgin and untouched. I heard these things reported by Anna herself. And it was because of this the Duchess of Bedford ordered the guards not to rape her.

—TESTIMONY OF JEAN MASSIEU, A PRIEST AT ST. CANDÉE LE VIEUX

I have heard that the Duchess of Bedford ordered that examination, and that the Duke of Bedford was hiding in a secret place so that he could see Joan being examined.

—TESTIMONY OF GUILLAUME COLLES, A SIXTY-SIX-YEAR-OLD PRIEST AND NOTARY

I remember that it was said at the time of her virginity exam that her nether regions were found to be scarred from horseback riding.

—JEAN MONNET, A FIFTY-YEAR-OLD THEOLOGIAN

A Knight Tries to Seduce

Throughout her various prison stays, Joan fought to defend her honor:

I first saw Joan when she was handed over to the dungeons in the Château de Beaurevoir. I saw her several times in the prison and spoke to her on several occasions. I often tried, while joking around with her, to touch her breast and place my hand into her bosom, but she would not put up with this and fought me off with all her strength.

—TESTIMONY OF A BURGUNDIAN KNIGHT, LORD HAIMOND,
FIFTY-SIX YEARS OLD

Joan's ecclesiastical trial was handled by Pierre Cochon, bishop of Beauvais, hardly impartial since he had been booted from his territory by King Charles.

Prison Rape and Dressing Like a Man

The church threatened Joan with heresy if she didn't stop dressing like a man (i.e., flouting the Bible's prohibition [Deuteronomy 22:5] against transvestitism):

The bishop and the Earl of Warwick were asking her why she would not wear women's clothing, and how it wasn't proper for a woman to wear a man's tunic, strongly fastened to her hose with many tight laces. It was then I heard Joan complain that she didn't dare remove the hose nor loosen the laces since the bishop and the earl knew full well that her guards had often tried to rape her. In fact, one time, when she was shouting for help, the earl himself came to her rescue, and if he hadn't arrived, those guards would have raped her.

. . . If the Lord's judges would put her in a safe place, where she would not be at risk, she was ready to wear women's clothes again and to continue her trial.

—TESTIMONY OF GUILLAUME MANCHON, PRIEST AND NOTARY,
ABOUT SIXTY YEARS OLD

An English Tailor

I heard it said of the tailor Jonathan Simon—whom the Duchess of Bedford had commissioned to make a woman's tunic for Joan—that when he was fitting the tunic on Joan, he softly touched her breast. She was indignant, and slapped the aforementioned Jonathan.

—TESTIMONY OF JEAN MARCEL, FIFTY-SIX-YEAR-OLD PARISIAN CITIZEN

Joan of Arc put on a dress and confessed, but when she found out she was not to be freed, she renounced her confession and returned to men's clothing. She was sentenced to die. On May 30, 1431, she was burned at the stake in the public square at Rouen as a heretic. She died a virgin. And her martyrdom helped unify France.

Gilles de Rais: Sex Crimes against Children, 1440

Gilles de Rais, one of the wealthiest men in France, fought bravely side by side with Joan of Arc to liberate Orleans in 1429. A decade later, his world suddenly crumbled. He stood accused of alchemy, brigandage, and some of the most heinous sex crimes ever recorded.

The following deposition of Henriet Griart, Gilles de Rais' servant and accomplice, was recorded in the ecclesiastical court records of his trial in Nantes.

October 17, 1440

Furthermore, the present witness testified and said that he, de Sillé, and Étienne Corrillaut, alias Poitou, brought to Gilles de

Rais' room and delivered to the accused very many male and female children—as many as forty, as it seemed to him—at Nantes, Machecoul, and Tiffauges, too. Gilles satisfied with them his libidinous passion contrary to the proper natural practice: first, holding his virile member in his hand, stretching, rubbing, and shaking it, then placing it between the thighs of the said children and rubbing it on their belly in this manner, he took such great pleasure from this and became so inflamed that his sperm criminally and improperly spurted upon the belly of these children.

Item, he said and testified that after Gilles had abused each of these children once or twice only, the children were murdered, sometimes by Gilles de Rais' own hand and at others by de Sillé, Corrillaut, alias Poitou, and the witness, who sometimes acted together and at others individually.

Having been asked how these children were murdered, he answers that sometimes their heads were cut off, at others their throats were slit, with the head remaining attached to the body, and at other times their necks were broken with blows from a club; and that after the veins in the neck or throat had been slit so that they died languishing as their blood was pouring out, then Gilles sometimes sat on the belly of these languishing children and took pleasure in this, and leaning over them, he watched them die.

Item, he said and testified that sometimes when Gilles wanted to perform his shameful abuse on these children, he hanged them or caused them to be hanged by the neck with a rope by this witness, Corrillaut and de Sillé, sometimes from a pole and at others from a hook in Gilles' room, so that thus having been frightened and debilitated they would not let out shouts or cries; that after they had been hurt and frightened by this hanging he soothed them, told them not to be afraid, and asserted that he had done this only to play with them; and that consequently he abused them, as said above.

Moreover, he testified and said that sometimes Gilles abused these children before murdering them or before beginning to murder them, at others after he had begun to murder them and while they were languishing and dying, and at yet others after they had been murdered and while they were still warm.

Having been asked what was done with their blood, he answers that it flowed and ran onto the floor and that it was wiped up afterward. . . .

Item, he testified that he heard Gilles say he took greater delight in murdering these children, in seeing their heads and other members cut off one after the other, in seeing them languish and also in looking at their blood than in possessing them carnally.

Item, he said that Gilles had a sword called a <u>braquemart</u> in French for amputating the heads of these children and for slaughtering them, and he often delighted in looking at the severed heads of these children and in showing them to the witness and Etienne Corrillaut, alias Poitou; that he used to ask which one of these heads was the most beautiful, the one he was showing then, or the one he had cut off yesterday or the day before that or at some other time; that he often used to kiss the heads or the faces of the severed heads which he found pleasing; and that he also took delight in this.

Item, he testified that Gilles abused girls and satisfied his lust with them in the same manner that he abused boys, and he spurned their sexual organ; and that the witness heard Gilles say that he found greater pleasure in debauching himself with girls in the aforesaid way than in using their proper sexual organ.

—DEPOSITION OF HENRIET GRIART

Confession?

The court record states that Gilles de Rais confessed "freely, voluntarily and with great sadness of heart" to the crimes described above. He was convicted and sentenced to die, along with Griart and another accomplice. On October 26, 1440, Gilles was lightly roasted on a pyre, then "mercifully" strangled to death.

There are, however, two things to bear in mind before placing Gilles at the top of the dung heap of sex fiends. Some modern scholars contend that Gilles was framed to steal his wealth. They point out that twelve days before Gilles' arrest, his archenemy, the Duke of Brittany, confiscated all Gilles' vast property. And heading the inquisition bringing charges against Gilles was the Bishop of Nantes, the duke's closest religious adviser. Also, testimony was routinely prompted by torture; court records were often altered after the trial; and the testimony of Gilles' two main accusers matched almost word for word.

Genital Bells, *circa* 1440

Travelers were still coming back from Asia with some pretty wild tales. Nicolo de Conti (1395–1469) observed this unusual sex aid in Arra in India:

There are some old women who earn their daily bread by selling little bells of gold, silver, and copper as small as little nut shells and made very cleverly. As soon as a man has reached the age when he can go with a woman, one of these little bells is attached to his member, between skin and flesh. Without them, he would be rejected. Either gold or silver bells are bought, according to the rank of the person. The same women who sell them also attach them. They loosen the skin at certain places, put the bells in and sew them up. After a few days, the wounds close. Many voluntarily attach a dozen or more. The men decorated in this fashion are held in high esteem by the women and, when they walk through the streets, believe it to be a mark of honor if the tinkling of bells is heard.

An unnamed European trader in India in the fifteenth century added the following, preserved in Hakluyt Society records:

When they are sewn under the skin of the man's member they cause a swelling of tremendous length of the entire genital parts. Hence they claim their males have greater endurance and give them far greater pleasure than we poor Europeans. It is true that when there are a number of natives about, the women will invariably choose the one with a titillating member. As soon as the boys reach puberty, they rush to have the bells sewn into their members, and constantly change them for larger sizes as they grow up.

4

The Renaissance

In Italy: Some Background

The sexual symbol of the Italian Renaissance could well be the bulging silk-and-jeweled codpiece, bursting with male arrogance. In art, a lush pagan nudity—especially delighting in the male body—was imposed onto Christian themes: St. Sodoma's muscles rippling. Artists served ambitious patrons, such as the Estes, the Sforzas, the Medicis, all in passionate pursuit of unique beauty and unique pleasure. And looming over all, often setting the tone, was a stupendously powerful and wealthy man, the pope.

The Pleasures of a Renaissance Pope, 1489–1501

Pope Alexander VI (1431–1503), who had many mistresses, once presided over a contest at an orgy. We know this because it's all documented in the diary of the pope's own master of ceremonies, Bishop Johann Burchard. In a way, the pope's behavior isn't surprising. Before he purchased the papacy, the man's name was Rodrigo Borgia; his offspring include the notorious Lucrezia and Cesare.

The Pope's Copulation Contest, 1501

October 30, 1501

On the last Sunday in October, Cesare Borgia invited to supper in his apartment at the apostolic palace fifty fine prostitutes, or courtesans, who after supper danced with the valets and other persons present, first in their clothes, then naked. And after this, the candelabra holding lighted candles were placed on the floor here and there and chestnuts were scattered about, which the courtesans collected, crawling naked on their hands and knees amid the candles. The pope, Cesare, and Lucrezia were all among the spectators. Finally, prizes were brought in—silk mantles, pairs of shoes, headdresses, and other objects to be given to those who had carnal knowledge with the greatest number of courtesans. The women were publicly enjoyed in that room there—as the onlookers acted as referees and awarded the prizes to the winners.

The pope had a taste for other sex shows as well:

November 11, 1501

A peasant entered Rome by the Porta Viridaria leading two mares loaded with wood. When they came to St. Peter's Square, some papal soldiers rushed over to them, slashed the horse's harness straps, flung down the saddles and the wood and led the mares inside the palace courtyard nearest the gate. Then four stallions were freed from their reins and let out of the palace. They raced over to the mares and began to struggle frantically among themselves, using their teeth and their hooves, raising a huge racket as they mounted and penetrated the mares—pounding and wounding them.

The pope and Lucrezia watched it all from a window above the palace gate; and the two laughed a lot and enjoyed themselves.

The diary also provides many glimpses into sexual attitudes at the time at the Vatican and in Rome.

Dying Young, 1489

Dominic the Florentine asked the pope's blessing to attend a funeral service for Ursino Lanfredini, the son of a powerful Florentine:

January 1489

The boy was about fifteen years old. On November 22nd past, he had too much sexual intercourse, then was struck with fever and died. Now, some people say that he knew a young girl seven times in one hour, while others say eleven times in one night.

Punishing a Transvestite Prostitute: Spanish Barbara, 1498

Burchard's diary provides here an unusual picture of Rome at the height of the Renaissance—of the pageant and barbarity:

April 1498

On the preceding days, a certain courtesan was imprisoned, that is, an out-and-out prostitute, named Cursetta, who had as a friend a Moorish man who dressed in the clothing and habit of a woman and called himself Spanish Barbara. Since they knew each other somehow, they were led together in disgrace through the city. She was wearing a full-length tiger skin that reached the ground with nothing to belt it shut, while the Moor was in his habit or clothing of a woman, with arms, high above the elbow, bound tightly behind his back and with all his clothing down to his linen undershirt pulled up as far as his belly button so that his testicles and genitalia might be seen by all and his trickery exposed. When they had completed a circle through the city, Cursetta was released.

The Moor, however, was put in prison and on the seventh day of the present month of April, he was led out from the cells of the Ninth Tower with two other thieves; preceding them was a deputy seated on a donkey and holding up two testicles (bound on the point of a stick), which had been cut off a Jew who had had sexual relations with a Christian woman. They were led to the Campo Flore and the two thieves were hung on crosses there. The Moor, however, was placed on a pile of wood and killed at the post of a "patibulum" [*a forked yoke*]. A cord was drawn around his neck, pulled behind the column, and twisted well and tightly with a stick. The pile of wood was set on fire so that it would blaze, but that didn't happen because of a recent rain; eventually his legs were burned, being closer to the fire.

Cure for Syphilis, 1498

Syphilis, which first appeared in Europe at Naples in 1494 (possibly spread by Columbus' returning sailors) was growing to epidemic proportions:

April 1498

This morning, six turbaned rustics who regularly sold oil throughout Rome were beaten with sticks through the city. Because, it was said, that certain people afflicted with the "French disease" [*i.e., syphilis*], hoping for some sort of cure, had paid them for a chance to bathe themselves in vessels filled with the rustics' oil. After the bath was finished, the men put the oil back in jars and sold it as good and clean to people throughout Rome.

—DIARY OF JOHANN BURCHARD

Sex Crimes in Renaissance Venice, *circa* 1450

In Venice around this time, the ruling families exerted the same intolerance as did the pope. (For more details, see Guido Ruggiero's excellent book, The Boundaries of Eros: Sex Crime and Sexuality in Renaissance Venice, *Oxford University Press, 1985.)*

Fornicating with a Jew, 1451

The senate passed a law in 1443 requiring Jews to wear yellow badges in Venice, and making fornication between Christian and Jew strictly forbidden. Nonetheless, one Jew, Josep, son of Cressoni, decided to take a flier:

One day in contempt of Catholic faith he entered a whore's room near the Rialto and began to have intercourse with her putting his member in her. But the other prostitutes outside, knowing that he was a Jew when he entered, called out saying this whore has a Jew in her room. The said whore then pulled away rapidly, not allowing the Jew to expel or project his semen.

Lucky for her that she was quick. In 1459 a girl named Silvestra was sentenced to twenty-five lashes for fornication with a Jew. Her mother also received the same punishment.

Doctors: Probing for Homosexuality, 1467

The Venetian ruling council passed the following regulation, requiring doctors to be an arm of the police (modern-day confidentiality rules would presumably prevent this kind of behavior):

To eliminate the vice of sodomy from this our city is worth every concern and as there are many women who consent to this vice and are broken in the rear parts and also many boys are so broken and all these are treated, yet still none are accused and their deeds go unpunished; therefore, because it is wise to honor God, just as blows with weapons are denounced to the Signori di Notte [*by medical practitioners*], so too those who are broken in those parts, be they boys or women, are to be denounced. . . . Thus it is ruled that it be added to the "matricula" of the surgeons and barbers and others who heal . . . that whoever treats any woman or boy with a break in the rear parts caused by a member . . . must give notice to the Lord Heads of the Ten or others of that council concerning the above injury that very same day or the next.

Several Venetian wives, perhaps not enjoying this form of sexual entertainment, alerted the authorities that their husbands were practicing it. In 1481, convicted of "frequent sodomy with his own wife," one fisherman, Giovanni Furlan, was beheaded and then his remains were burned.

Bestiality, with an Excuse

A craftsman named Simon was caught having intercourse with a goat. His excuse? He hadn't been able to ejaculate for three years because of an accident. A team of surgeons examined him:

The said Simon has a normal member to the extent that it can become erect, but he has a defect in his testicles which leaves him little sensation and as a result he can neither emit sperm nor be healed. Nonetheless he can have an erection.

The court decided more experts were needed.

The Signori di Notte had two prostitutes carry out many experiments to see if the said Simon could be corrupted [*i.e., have an orgasm*].

—STATE ARCHIVES

He couldn't. The Signori, therefore, decided to be merciful and waive the usual penalty for sodomy, which was burning alive. Instead, they cut off his right hand and had him branded and beaten.

Cruel and Unusual Punishment for Sodomy, 1574

In the mid-sixteenth century, throughout Europe the punishment for homosexual acts—at least those officially

stated in law books and by theologians—was quite severe.
However, there's much debate over how often these brutal
statutes, such as the following, were actually enforced.

Treviso, Italy, near Venice

If any person (leaving the natural use) has sexual relations
with another, that is, a man with a man if they are fourteen
years old or more, or a woman with a woman, if they are
twelve or more, by committing the vice of sodomy—popularly
known as "buzerones" or "fregatores"—and this has been
revealed to the city magistrates, the detected person, if a male,
must be stripped of all his clothes and fastened to a stake in
the Street of Locusts with a nail or rivet driven through his
male member, and shall remain there all day and all night
under a reliable guard, and the following day be burned
outside the city. If, however, a woman commits this vice or sin
against nature, she shall be fastened naked to a stake in the
Street of Locusts and shall remain there all day and night
under a reliable guard, and the following day shall be burned
outside the city.

—STATUTES OF TREVISO

Witchcraft: Some Background

On December 5, 1484, Pope Innocent VIII issued a papal
bull upgrading witchcraft from minor spell casting to a major
form of heresy and he ordered the Holy Inquisition to
concentrate on rooting it out. That pronouncement sounded
the death knell for thousands of young women. It's been
estimated that more than two hundred thousand people,

mostly women, were executed in Europe and America for the heresy of witchcraft between 1450 and 1750. And many, if not most, of them were questioned about their sex lives before they died.

Inquisitors—in the course of eliciting confessions—were encouraged to focus hard on witches' sex crimes, since all witches were thought to have frequent sex with the devil, but there was much debate over the details: Did the devil use the bodies of hanged men? Could he borrow sperm from wet dreams?

*The definitive handbook for witch hunters—*Malleus Maleficarum *(literally, "Hammer of the Witches") (1486)—was written by two German inquisitors, Heinrich Kramer and James Sprenger.*

A Witch Makes a Man's Penis Disappear, 1486

We have already shown that they can take away the male organ not indeed by actually despoiling the human body of it, but by concealing it with some glamour [*i.e., magic*]. And of this we shall instance a few examples.

In the town of Ratisbon a certain young man who had an intrigue with a girl, wishing to leave her, lost his member; that is to say, some glamour was cast over it so that he could see or touch nothing but his smooth body. In his worry over this he went to a tavern to drink wine; and after he had sat there for a while he got into a conversation with another woman who was there, and told her the cause of his sadness, explaining everything, and demonstrating in his body that it was so. The woman was astute, and asked whether he suspected anyone; and when he named such a one, unfolding the whole matter, she said: "If persuasion is not enough you must use some violence, to induce her to restore you to your health." So in the evening the young man watched the way by which the witch was in the habit of going, and finding her there, prayed her to restore him the health of his body. And when she maintained that she was innocent and knew nothing about it, he fell upon her and winding a towel tightly round her neck, choked her, saying: "Unless you give me back my health, you shall die at my hands." Then she, being unable to cry out, and with her face already swelling and growing black, said: "Let me go, and I will heal you." The young man then relaxed the pressure of the towel, and the witch touched him with her hand between the thighs, saying: "Now you have what you desire." And the young man plainly felt that his member had been restored to him by the mere touch of the witch. . . .

And what then is to be thought of those witches who sometimes collect male organs in great numbers, as many as twenty or thirty members together, and put them in a bird's nest, or shut them up in a box, where they move themselves like living members, and eat oats and corn, as has been seen by many and is a matter of common report? It is to be said that it all is done by the devil's work and illusion, for the senses of those who see them are deluded. For a certain man tells that, when he had lost his member, he approached a known witch to ask her to restore it to him. She told the afflicted man to climb a certain tree, and that he might select the member he liked out of a nest in which there were several members. And when he tried to take a big one, the witch said:

"You must not take that one because it belongs to a parish priest."

—HEINRICH KRAMER AND JAMES SPRENGER, *MALLEUS MALEFICARUM*

Witches Describe the Devil's Penis, 1595

Nicolas Rémy, a privy councilor, compiled the book Demonolatry, *based on the trial records of nine hundred persons executed for witchcraft from 1580 to 1595 in the region of Lorraine (modern-day France). With prudish fervor, he explores all manner of commingling with the devil:*

All female witches maintain that the so-called genital organs of their Demons are so huge and so excessively rigid that they cannot be admitted without the greatest pain. Alexée Drigie reported that her Demon's penis, even when only half in erection, was as long as some kitchen utensils, which she pointed to as she spoke; and that there were neither testicles nor scrotum attached to it. Claude Fellet said she had often felt it like a spindle swollen to an immense size so that it could be not contained by even the most capacious woman without great pain. This agrees with the complaint of Nicole Morèle that, after such miserable copulation, she always had to go straight to bed as if she had been tired out by some long and violent agitation. Didatia of Miremont also said that, although she had many years' experience of men, she was always so stretched by the huge swollen member of her demon that the sheets were drenched with blood. And nearly all witches protest that it is wholly against their will that they are embraced by Demons, but that it is useless for them to resist.

—NICOLAS RÉMY

Supporting Evidence

Pierre de l'Ancre published his book Picture of the Inconstancy of Bad Angels and Demons *in 1612. He says:*

The devil, whether he assumes the form of a man or whether he's like a goat, always has the member of a mule, having chosen the best-hung animal of all.

The member of the devil is about half a yard long, of medium thickness, red, dark and crooked, very rough and almost pointy.

—PIERRE DE L'ANCRE

(For more on the topic of demonic intercourse see "Eyewitness Account of Sex with the Devil, 1662" in chapter 5.)

Christopher Columbus' Unusual Gift, 1493

Michele de Cuneo, a childhood friend of Columbus, accompanied the explorer on his second voyage to the New World. (Columbus' dad had once bought a country house from de Cuneo's dad.)

It was November 1493; the buddies had just landed in Santa Crux (i.e., St. Croix, Virgin Islands). That de Cuneo reports Columbus' gift so matter-of-factly in a letter says volumes about the admiral's attitude toward the local inhabitants, and especially toward women.

One of those days while we were lying at anchor we saw coming from a cape a "canoe," that is to say a boat, which is how they call it in their language, going along with oars so that it looked like a well-manned "bergantino," on which there were three or four Carib men with two Carib women and two Indian slaves, of whom (that is the way the Caribs treat other neighbors in those other islands) they had recently cut the genital organ to the belly, so that they were still sore; and we having the flagship's boat ashore, when we saw that canoe coming, quickly jumped into the boat and gave chase to the canoe. While we were approaching her the Caribs began shooting at us with their bows in such manner that, had it not been for the shields, half of us would have been wounded. But I must tell you that to one of the seamen who had a shield in his hand came an arrow, which went through the shield and penetrated his chest three inches, so that he died in a few days. We captured the canoe with all the men, and one Carib was wounded with a spear in such a way that we thought he was dead, and cast him for dead into the sea, but instantly saw him swim. In so doing we caught him and with the grapple hauled him over the bulwarks of the ship where we cut his head with an axe.

The other Caribs, together with those slaves, we later sent to Spain. While I was in the boat I captured a very beautiful Carib woman, whom the said Lord Admiral [*i.e., Columbus*] gave to me, and with whom, having taken her into my cabin, I conceived desire to take pleasure. I wanted to put my desire into execution but she did not want it and treated me with her fingernails in such a manner that I wished I had never begun.

But seeing that (to tell you the end of it all), I took a rope and thrashed her well, for which she raised such unheard-of screams that you would not have believed your ears. Finally we came to an agreement in such a manner that I can tell you that she seemed to have been brought up in a school of harlots.

—MICHELE DE CUNEO

Amerigo Vespucci Discovers a Penis Enlarger, 1504

Vespucci, while in the New World, found time to explore the sexual customs of the local Indians, especially the ones eager to copulate with Christians. (Be warned, though: at least one scholar, J.T.L. Hitt, believes Vespucci's letters were juiced up by the world's first generation of printers, just learning their craft, free from any copyright laws.)

When the [*Indians*] evacuate their bowels, they do everything to avoid being seen; and just in this they are clean and modest, the more shameful and dirty they are in making water. Because even while talking to us, they let fly, without turning around or showing shame.

They do not practice marriage amongst themselves. Each one takes all the wives he pleases; and when he desires to repudiate them, he does repudiate them without it being considered a wrong on his part or a disgrace to the woman; for in this the woman has much liberty as the man. They are not very jealous and are libidinous beyond measure, and the women far more than the men; for I refrain out of decency from telling you the trick they play to satisfy their immoderate lust. [*See next item.*]

. . . They are women of pleasing person, very well proportioned, so that one does not see on their bodies any ill-formed feature or limb. And although they go about utterly naked they are fleshy women, and that part of their privies which he who has not seen them would think to see is invisible; for they cover all with their thighs, save that part for which nature made no provision, and which is, modestly speaking, the "mons veneris." In short, they are no more ashamed of their shameful parts than we are in displaying the nose and mouth. Only exceptionally will you see a woman with drooping breasts, or with belly shrunken through frequent parturition, or with other wrinkles; for they all look as though they had never given birth. They showed themselves very desirous of copulating with us Christians.

—VESPUCCI, LETTER TO PIERO SODERINI

The Trick

They have another custom, very shameful and beyond all human belief. For their women, being very lustful, cause the penis of their husbands to swell up to such an enormous size as to appear deformed and grotesque. This is accomplished through a certain trick, namely the bite of a poisonous lizard. By reason of this, many lose their virile organ, which burst through a lack of attention, and they remain eunuchs.

—VESPUCCI, LETTER TO LORENZO PIETRO DE' MEDICI, 1503

Leonardo da Vinci's Dirty Joke, 1493

*Designer of helicopters and submarines, painter of the
"Mona Lisa," Leonardo da Vinci (1452–1519) is sometimes
called the greatest genius who ever lived. He also found time to
scribble a dirty joke in the margin of one of his notebooks:*

A woman was washing clothes, and her feet were very red
with cold. A priest who was passing by asked her in
amazement whence came the redness and the woman replied
at once that it was the result of the fire she had burning below.
Then the priest seized that part of his being that was
responsible for his being a priest and not a nun and drawing
close to her, with a sweet and soft voice, begged her to be so
kind as to light his candle for him.

*Leonardo was smart not to quit his day job. Actually, the
great artist was quite uncomfortable with the topic of sex.
Maybe it stemmed from the following incident, which occurred
when he was younger. On April 8, 1476, someone dropped an
anonymous note in the "tamburo," or morals box, in Florence,
accusing a seventeen-year-old artist's model, old Jacopo
Saltarelli, of "sodomia" with four men, including Leonardo,
son of Piero da Vinci.*

*This was very traumatic for the twenty-four-year-old da
Vinci, who for two months was grilled by the police. His
notebooks show traces of preparing for all possibilities,
including designing a sort of pick-lock to escape prison, as well
as how to drill poison into a tree so it would yield poisoned
apples. Da Vinci was eventually acquitted, but the effects
lingered. Witness this notebook entry for 1510:*

The sexual act and the members employed therein are so

repulsive that were it not for the beauty of the faces and the
adornments of the actors and the pent-up impulse, nature
would lose the human species.

—LEONARDO DA VINCI

King Henry VII of England Investigates His Fiancée's Body, 1505

*Arranged marriages between monarchs often resembled
treaty negotiations—a kind of blood kinship insurance policy
tacked onto the uniting of empires—but not for Henry VII of
England. In 1505, he gave a twenty-four-part query to his
three ambassadors—Francis Marsin, James Braybroke, and
John Stile—to find out about his proposed bride, the twenty-
seven-year-old queen of Naples. Here are a few of the queries:*

Item: To mark her breasts and paps, whether they be big or
small.

Response: As to this article, the said queen's breasts be
somewhat great and fully, and inasmuch as that they were
trussed somewhat high, after the manner of the country, the
which causeth her grace for to seem much the fuller and her
neck to be the shorter.

Item: To mark whether there appear any hair about her lips or
not.

Response: As to this article, as far as that we can perceive and
see, the said queen hath no hair appearing about her lips or
mouth.

Item: That they endeavor to speak with the said queen fasting [*i.e., not eating*], and that she may tell unto them some matter at length, and to approach as near to her mouth as they honestly may, to the intent that they may feel the condition of her breath, whether it be sweet or not, and to mark at every time when they speak with her if they feel any savor of spices, rose water, or musk by the breath of her mouth or not.

Response: To this article, we could never come unto the speech of the said queen fasting, wherefore we could not nor might not attain to knowledge of that part of this article, notwithstanding at such other times as we have spoken and have had communication with the said queen, we have approached as nigh unto her visage as that conveniently we might do, and we could feel no savor of any spices or waters, we think verily by the favor of her visage and cleanness of her complexion and of her mouth that the said queen is like for to be of a sweet savor and well aired.

Item: To note the height of her stature and to inquire whether she wear any slippers and of what the slippers be, so they be not deceived in the very height and stature of her; and if they may come to the sight of her slippers, then to note the fashion of her foot.

Response: As to this article . . . , it is answered that we could not come by the perfect knowledge of her height, forasmuch as that her grace weareth slippers after the manner of the country, the width be of six fingers breadth, of height large and her foot after the proportion of the same is but small. . . . Also she of herself is somewhat round and well liking, which causeth her grace to seem lesser in height.

—AMBASSADORS' REPORT

Despite the favorable physical report on the queen, Henry VII never married her.

Martin Luther Schedules His Lovemaking, 1525

Martin Luther helped kidnap twelve nuns in a herring wagon—some say in the herring barrels—to free them from the Nimbschen convent so they could marry. And Luther himself married one of them, Katherine von Bora, on June 13, 1525. His marriage represented a slap in the face of the Catholic pope, who forbade monks to marry, but it was more than that. Catholic theologians generally regarded marriage as a necessary evil to further the human species, as a way to funnel man's reprehensible sexuality into one partner. Luther—powerful, influential rebel that he was—defied them; he celebrated marriage, called it a sacred duty, and marveled at the happiness it could bring.

Luther wrote this letter to his good friend Spalatin, who had also broken his monastic vows and married:

December 6 (St. Nick's Day), 1525
Grace and Peace in the Lord, and joy in your most sweet little wife. However displeasing your marriage is to your brothers the priests of Baal, so pleasing it is to me. Indeed, God has shown me nothing in you more wonderful than to see and hear you a husband. . . . I wish for you both great happiness and many offspring. . . .
Greet your wife most lovingly for me, and when you hold Catharina amid the pillows with sweetest embraces and kisses, think: "Ah, this person, the best little creation

of my God, my Christ has given her to me; let there be praise and glory to Him."

And on that same night—once I figure out the day on which you'll receive this letter—I also in just the same way will make love to my wife while thinking of you, and will make an equal exchange with you.

Even Mom and Dad Did It

Summer 1531

I find there's nothing but godliness in marriage. To be sure, when I consider marriage, only the flesh seems to be there. Yet my father must have slept with my mother and made love to her and they were nevertheless godly people. All the patriarchs and prophets did likewise. The longing of a man for a woman is God's creation—that is to say when nature's sound, not when it is corrupted as it is among the Italians and Turks. (*Luther was referring to homosexuality.*)

—LUTHER'S TABLE TALK, COLLECTED BY HIS COLLEAGUES

Wide Fundament

Luther loved his Katy, but let's not romanticize the attitudes of the sixteenth-century Bible-nurtured German monk:

Summer 1531

Men have broad shoulders and narrow hips, and accordingly they possess intelligence. Women have narrow shoulders and wide hips. Women ought to stay at home; the way they were created indicates this, for they have broad hips and a wide fundament to sit upon to keep house and bear and raise children.

—LUTHER'S TABLE TALK

Pietro Aretino and Sixteen Positions, 1524

The career break of Pietro Aretino (1492–1556) came when he wrote a mock last will and testament in 1516 for Pope Leo X's pet elephant, Hanno, complete with bequeathing the beast's genitals to one of the lustier cardinals. From then on, he became infamous in Italy as one of the lewdest and wittiest writers, the Renaissance mouth that roared.

In 1524, Aretino wrote sonnets to accompany the drawings of sixteen sexual positions by Giuliano Romano, Raphael's talented twenty-five-year-old pupil. Their collaboration produced one of history's most notorious works of erotic art.

Aretino dedicated the Sedici Modi *to a doctor friend, Battista Zatti of Brescia:*

I dedicate this lewd memorial to you, and let the hypocrites take a flying leap; I'm sick of their thieving justice and their filthy traditions that forbid the eyes to see what most delights them. What harm is there in seeing a man mounted atop a woman? Must beasts be more free than we are? It seems to me that the organ given us by Nature to perpetuate our race should be worn around the neck like a pendant or as a medallion on a hat, because it is the source that feeds the rivers of mankind. . . .

It has made you who ranks among the greatest living doctors.

It has created me, who is "better than bread" [*i.e.*, *good as gold*]. It has produced the Bembos, the Molzas, the Fortunios, the Francos, the Varchis, the Ugolino Martellis, the Lorenzo Lenzi, the Dolces, the Fra Bastianos, the Sansovinos, the Titians, the Michelangelos, and after them, the popes, the emperors, and the kings; it has fathered beautiful little children, and the most exquisite women with their "holy of holies."

Therefore we should set aside holidays for it and sacred vigils and feast days, and not just wrap it up in a bit of cloth or silk. The hands might be better hidden because they gamble, swear falsely, commit usury, give the finger, rip, yank, punch, wound, and murder. And what do you think of the mouth, which curses, spits in your face, overeats, gets drunk, and vomits? In sum, lawyers could win some honor for themselves if they would add a clause for it in their books, and I think they will. In the meantime, try to decide whether my verses have accurately captured the positions of the jousters.

Casanova in his memoirs mentions spending New Year's Eve 1753 with a nun doing Aretino's "straight tree" position, which he says featured the man standing and holding the woman upside-down for mutual oral sex.

Aretino barely escaped prison for his involvement in the Sixteen Positions, *but it certainly didn't teach him to mend his ways.*

Letter to a Baffling Unisexual

March 1548, Venice

To La Zufolina [*The Chatterbox*]:

Twice, good fortune has sent your beautiful person into my house: one time, as a woman dressed like a man; the other time, as a man dressed like a woman. You are a man for events behind you and a woman for those in front. . . .

It's undeniable that Nature has composed you of both sexes; that in one instant it shows you as a man, the next as a woman. And for absolutely no other reason did the Duke Alessandro [*de' Medici, of the famous Florentine family,*] want to have sex with you than to find out if you were really a hermaphrodite, or just playing at it. Your manner of speaking is like a lady, your manner of behaving is like a boy. So much so that anyone who didn't know you would judge you now the rider, now the mare; that is, now the nymph, now the shepherd; that is, the active and passive lover.

What's more? Even the clothes which tumble on and off your body don't clear up the mystery of whether the boy-prattler is a girl-prattler or the girl-prattler is a boy-prattler. . . .

I dreamt last night that I did that act with you, that I hung you on the hook, that I drilled your mixing spoon, but with a comedy of jest, with a farce of farts, with a pastoral of love-pinches, so that no lewd priest, no horny monk or concupiscent nun would not have traded in the love notes of their youth for the

conjugation of your old age and mine. However, our
dreams would make us look like goats, if we tried to
live out the pleasures of our visions.

Whatever, we all have to go to the gates of the
Inferno, and it won't matter a bit whether we have
worked the treadle more or less.

So come on up, and let's throw ourselves into it, and if
someone dies, let 'em die!

—PIETRO ARETINO

Sir Thomas More's Sneak Preview of His Daughter, 1521

*Sir Thomas More (1478–1535), as England's lord
chancellor, was adamantly opposed to allowing Henry VIII to
divorce Catherine of Aragon, and his religious views
eventually cost him his head. In his book* Utopia *(1516), More
describes the Utopians' unusual courtship practices.
Biographer John Aubrey shows how More actually practiced
what he preached:*

Utopian Courtship

In choosing a spouse, they use a method that would appear
to us very absurd and ridiculous, but it is constantly practiced
by them and considered wise.

Before marriage, some honorable older woman presents the
bride naked, whether she's a virgin or a widow, to the
bridegroom; and after that, some honorable older man
presents the bridegroom naked to the bride. We indeed both

laughed at this and condemned it as a very indecent thing. But they, on the other hand, wondered at the folly of the rest of men, who when they are about to buy a horse for a piddling price, are so cautious that they will examine every part of it, and take off both the saddle and all the other tackle that there should be no sore hidden anywhere. Yet in the choice of a marriage partner, which could decide their happiness or unhappiness for the rest of their lives, they venture forward upon trust, and see only about a hands breadth of the face, leaving the rest of the body covered, where there might be concealed something contagious, as well as hideous.

—SIR THOMAS MORE

Practicing What He Preaches

John Aubrey in Brief Lives *describes More's actions in regard to his own teenage daughters:*

In his *Utopia,* his law is that young people are to see each other stark naked before marriage. Sir William Roper, of Eltham, Kent, came one morning, pretty early to my lord, with a proposal to marry one of his daughters. My lord's daughters were then both together abed in a truckle-bed in their father's chamber asleep. He carries Sir William into the chamber and takes the sheet by the corner and suddenly whips it off. They lay on their backs, and their smocks up as high as their armpits. This awakened them, and immediately they turned on their bellies. Quoth Roper, "I have seen both sides," and so gave a pat on the buttock, he made choice of, saying, "Thou art mine." Here was all the trouble of wooing.

—JOHN AUBREY, *BRIEF LIVES*

Aubrey fails to mention whether More's sixteen-year-old daughter, Margaret, ever got a naked preview of her twenty-eight-year-old lawyer fiancé. In any case, they did, in fact, marry.

Anne Boleyn Cuckolds Henry VIII, 1536

After five years of waiting for a divorce, King Henry VIII (1491–1547) dared to defy the pope and risk eternal damnation to marry Anne Boleyn (1507–1536), a beautiful young handmaiden serving his wife, Catherine of Aragon. Henry appears at first to have been genuinely in love with Anne, and during their courtship he wrote her lovesick letters in schoolboy French, signed with his initials, "HR" (Henricus Rex), on either side of a heart containing her "AB." But, of course, it all soured.

Affair with a Monochord Player

In 1536, three and a half years (and no sons) later, Anne was accused of having an adulterous affair with Mark Smeeton, a handsome young musician described as "one of the prettiest monochord players and deftest dancers in the land."

An anonymous Spaniard wrote the following contemporary account, so it's wise to bear in mind that Anne had ousted a Spanish queen, Catherine of Aragon, from the throne:

One morning, when the queen was in bed, she sent for Mark to play whilst she lay in bed, and ordered her ladies to dance. They began dancing; and after a while when Anne saw they were becoming very merry, she ordered one of the ladies to play while the others danced. When she saw they were intoxicated with their dancing, she called Mark to her, and he fell on his knee by her bedside, and she had time to tell him that she was in love with him, whereupon he was much surprised; but being of a base sort, he gave ear to all the queen said to him, forgetting, the sinner, that only two months before he was a poor fellow, and that the king had given him a good income and might give him much more; so he answered, "Madam, I am your servant, you may command me." And the lady bade him keep it secret, and she would find means to compass her desires.

A few days later, the king left for Windsor, and Anne instructed a trusty old servant to help her:

One night, while all the ladies were dancing, the old woman called Mark and said to him gently, so that none should overhear, "You must come with me," and he, as he knew it was to the queen's chamber he had to go, was nothing loath. So she took him to an antechamber, where she and another lady slept, next to the queen's room, and in this antechamber there was a closet like a store room, where she kept sweetmeats, candied fruits, and other preserves which the queen sometimes asked for. To conceal him more perfectly, the old woman put him in this closet, and told him to stay there till she came for him, and to take great care lest he was heard. Then she shut him up and returned to the great hall where they were dancing, and made signs to the queen who understood her, and although it was not late, she pretended to be ill, and the dancing ceased. She then retired to her chamber with her ladies, while the old woman said to her, "Madam when you are in bed and all the ladies are asleep, you can call me and ask for some preserves, which I will bring, and Mark shall come with me, for he is in the closet now."

The Queen went to bed and ordered all her ladies to retire

to their respective beds, which were in an adjoining gallery like a refectory, and when they were all gone but the old lady and the lady who slept with her, she sent them off too. When she thought they would all be asleep, she called the old woman and said, "Margaret, bring me a little marmalade." She called it out very loudly, so that the ladies in the gallery might hear it as well as Mark, who was in the closet. The old woman went to the closet and made Mark undress, and took the marmalade to the queen, leading Mark by the hand. The lady who was in the old woman's bed did not see them when they went out of the closet, and the old woman left Mark behind the queen's bed, and said out loud, "Here is the marmalade, my lady." Then Anne said to the old woman, "Go along; go to bed."

As soon as the old woman had gone, Anne went round to the back of the bed and grasped the youth's arm, who was all trembling, and made him get into bed. He soon lost all bashfulness, and remained that night and many others, so that in a short time, this Mark flaunted out to such an extent that there was not a gentleman at court who was so fine, and Anne never dined without having Mark to serve her.

Henry VIII learned of the alleged affair, and Anne was locked up in the Tower of London, then sentenced to die. During their brief marriage, Anne never gave Henry VIII his male heir, but their little daughter grew up to be Queen Elizabeth, and to rule England for forty-five years.

Benvenuto Cellini Is Accused of Doing It the "Italian Way" in France, 1542

When it comes to deviant sex, people are only too happy to name the practice after some nation other than their own.

*Benvenuto Cellini (1500—1571), a world-renowned sculptor
and goldsmith, was in Paris working for King Francis I. He
went to a garden party, entrusting his household to a young
Florentine accountant named Pagolo Micceri. When he comes
back early, he is convinced he has caught his beautiful French
model and bed mate, Caterina, with Micceri:*

When I arrived, that girl's whore-mistress French mother
called out in a loud voice: "Pagolo, Caterina, the master is
home!"

I watched each of them come forward, terrified and dizzy,
without a clue as to what they were saying, acting like idiots,
not knowing where they were going; one could see clearly that
they had been sinning.

Overflowing with rage, I put my hand on my sword;
I resolved to kill them both. Pagolo ran away; she fell down
on her knees, wailing to high heaven for mercy. My first goal
was to take on the man, but I failed to nab him right away. By
the time I did finally capture him, I decided to kick them
both out instead, since killing them tacked onto my other
recent problems would make it tough for me to save my own
skin.

Therefore, I said to Pagolo: "If my eyes had seen what you,
rogue, make me believe happened, I would run you through
the guts ten times with this sword. Now get lost, and if you
ever say a 'Pater noster,' make it to St. Julian."

Then I brutally chased away the mother and rotten
daughter with both kicks and punches.

They thought to avenge themselves for my rough treatment,
and they consulted with a lawyer from Normandy, who
coached them to say that I had used Caterina in the Italian way
(by which they mean "against Nature," namely, "sodomy"). He

explained to them: "At the least, when this Italian hears of this and realizes what great risk he's in, he'll quickly fork over several hundred ducats to keep you silent, especially considering the extreme punishment we have here in France for such a crime."

So they made a pact. They officially accused me, and I was called to court. . . .

Cellini, after first deciding to flee, changes his mind and storms into court with ten armed men:

When I arrived in the presence of the criminal judges, I noticed Caterina and her mother, who the moment I passed them were laughing with their lawyer.

I walked straight in the court and impetuously hollered for the judge, who, looking bloated, oily, and fat, loomed above the others on his tribunal. This man, when he saw me, made a menacing gesture with his head, and said in a low voice: "Although your name is Benvenuto [*"Welcome"*], this time you will be Malvenuto [*"Unwelcome"*].

I heard him, and I repeated my request. "Quick, clue me in," I said. "Tell me what I've come here to do."

Then the judge turned to Caterina and said to her: "Caterina, tell everything that you were forced to do with Benvenuto." Caterina said that I had "used" her in the Italian way. The judge turned to me and said, "Do you hear what Caterina says, Benvenuto?"

Then I replied, "If I had used her in the Italian way, I would have done it only out of desire to have a son, just as you others do it."

Then the judge answered back, "She means that you used her outside of the vessel where sons are made."

To this I replied, "That is not the Italian way, perhaps it

must be the French way; she might know something about that but I don't. I want her to reveal exactly how I did it with her." Then that skanky whore viciously reported, in an open and clear fashion, the brutish method that she meant. I made her restate it three times, one after another, and then I said in a loud voice: "Respected Judge, deputy of his most Christian majesty, I demand justice from you, because I know the laws of the most Christian king for that crime guarantee burning at the stake for both the active and passive partner. That girl there confesses her crime; for my part, I have never had sex with her in any way whatsoever. Her bawd of a mother is here too, who for one crime or another deserves the bonfire. I demand justice from you."

I thundered these words over and over, constantly yelling that they should burn her and her mother at the stake. I warned the judge that if he didn't throw her in prison in my presence, I would rush to the king and tell him of the injustice perpetrated by one of his judicial officers. Because of the huge racket I made, they began to lower their voices; I just raised mine even louder. That rotten whore began to cry; so did her mother, and I kept shouting at the judge: "Roast them! Roast them!" That cowardly jerk, seeing that everything was not going according to plan, began with soft words to excuse the weaker sex. At this, I knew I had won a great battle; so grumbling and threatening, I eagerly rushed off. Actually I would have paid five hundred scudi to have never shown up in court in the first place. Having escaped that hell, with my whole heart thanking God, I happily returned with my young men to my castle.

—BENVENUTO CELLINI

Cellini found out later that Pagolo and Caterina were living together, mocking him; he surprised them, forced them at sword point to marry, then he began hiring Caterina for modeling sessions, posing her nude for hours in excruciating positions and topping it off by cuckolding her husband.

A Feud Fought Over a Statue's Genitals, 1544

Cellini, who had as much genius for feuding as for art, squared off against the king's all-powerful mistress, Madame d'Étampes. She felt Cellini had slighted her, so she was determined to spoil the unveiling of Cellini's much-heralded statue of Jupiter:

Madame d'Étampes said: "Look at that work, it won't look one thousandth as good by day as it does by night. Also, look, he put a veil across to hide his mistakes."

That was an extremely delicate veil that I placed with beautiful grace across Jupiter to further magnify his majesty. So, at her words, I took the veil and lifted it up, revealing the statue's impressive genitals, and then, obviously annoyed, I yanked it away entirely. She thought that I had uncovered the genitals to embarrass her. When the king saw that she was insulted and that I was enraged and was also about to speak, the wise king immediately said these exact words in his language: "Benvenuto, don't say anything; keep your mouth shut, I'll give you more treasure than you ever wanted, a thousand times more."

Forbidden to speak, I bridled my fury, which caused her to mutter even more insultingly. The king departed much sooner than he would have, but added, to bolster my spirits, that he had imported from Italy the greatest man ever born, a master of his art.

—BENVENUTO CELLINI

Maybe old Benvenuto didn't keep his mouth shut. Jules Alvarotto, the ambassador of Ferrara, wrote in a letter dated January 29, 1545, that Cellini—when he exposed the statue's manhood, which was duly enormous to suit a Roman god— said the following to d'Étampes:

"So, are they big enough for you?"

Renaissance Doctor Tackles Sex Problems, 1564

Sigmund Freud called Dr. Johann Weyer's On the Devil's Magic and Witches' Spells *(1583) one of the ten most significant books ever written. It's not hard to see why the father of psychiatry liked it. Weyer, though he believed in an all-powerful Devil, examined superstitious beliefs and looked for commonsense explanations based on human nature.*

The Gyrating Nuns at Cologne

Nuns sometimes complain of satanic sexual possession. Here's how one such later incident at Loudun was described: "She fell on the ground blaspheming in convulsions, lifting up her petticoat and chemise, displaying her privy parts without any shame, and uttering filthy words. Her gestures became so indecent that the audience averted its eyes. She cried out again and again, abusing herself with her hands: *"Come on, then, foutez-moi [screw me]!"*

In response to a similar case at Cologne, Dr. Weyer was brought in for expert consultation:

Some religious women cloistered in the convent of Nazareth at Cologne. . . . For years they had been harassed, tormented, and sent into spasms by the Devil in many and various ways; but during the year 1564, above and beyond this . . . , they were frequently thrown to the ground and their lower torso was made to thrust up and down in the way usually associated with sexual intercourse. During this time their eyes were shut, and later they opened them with shame, panting as though they had undergone a great labor. The occasion for this evil was provided by a woman named Gertrude who had been cloistered in the convent at the age of twenty-four; she was often subjected to these mocking illusions in bed with licentious laughter, even though she tried to use her consecrated stole to drive away the lover who would come to her almost every night. When a second nun, sleeping in the other bed (she had been put in that room so that her companion would be safer from the attacks of her lover), thought she heard this skirmishing, she trembled all over, and finally she too became an abode for the Devil, and she was torn by dreadful convulsions, sometimes becoming blind during the onset. Though she appeared to be of stable mind, she uttered various wildly inconsistent remarks verging on despair. Many other nuns were similarly afflicted, and the plague spread like a contagion, especially since they did not take refuge in legitimate counsels to begin with.

On May 25, 1565, I conducted an investigation at this religious community, in the presence of that most noble and prudent man, Master Constantin of Lyskerken, the most worthy Burgermeister Master Johann Altenanus, the former

Dean at Cleves Master Johann Echt, illustrious Doctor of Medicine, and my son Heinrich, Doctor of Philosophy and Medicine. I learned that the nun who was the object of the demon's love had written some frightful letters (later discovered) to her suitor. But there is no reason for anyone to doubt that they had been composed by her when she was in a state of possession and not in control of her senses.

While the Devil was still practicing this torture, some of these young women fell ill with the plague, and when they were in the throes of that disease, they experienced no harassment from the Devil, because of the singular kindness of the one true God who has set limits to Satan's torments in this age, limits beyond which he cannot go.

Now the beginning to this calamity was provided by some lascivious young men who took advantage of an adjacent ball court to strike up a friendship with one or two of the nuns and then secretly climbed into the convent and satisfied their lust. When the men were later excluded and the young women could no longer enjoy the reality of intercourse, the arch-contriver corrupted their minds with an image of the same, and presented to the eyes of those present the ignominious spectacle of such erotic movements. But in special letters sent to the convent, I explained at length how to deal with the tragedy in an appropriate and Christian manner.

Impotency Spells

So, too, in Italy, and especially at Rome, the most notorious and disgusting prostitutes believe they also render a man impotent if they secretly remove the front band of his underclothes and tie knots in it. By returning it they claim to free the man again from his impotence. The same effect is supposedly achieved by knotting or unknotting a wolf's penis in the name of some victim. Likewise, when a groom is lying in the bed chamber with his bride, if some ill-wisher merely knocks upon the door and calls out the groom's name while implanting a knife in the door, and if the groom responds, and if the malefactor breaks off the tip of the knife and leaves it in the wood and silently departs, they say that the groom will not be able to perform the sexual act during the night. But this is all nonsense.

One individual writes that a fellow countryman of his, a nobleman, swore that he had been bound in such a way that he could not have relations with women; he was cured by a clever stratagem whereby the writer attempted to confirm this belief of his by showing him Cleopatra's book on fashioning women's beauty, and by reading the passage in which she directed that the entire body of a man so bound should be relieved by an anointing with raven's gall mixed with sesame. When the nobleman heard this, he trusted the words of the book, followed the advice, and was quickly restored, with his sexual desire increased. It is plausible, and frequently observed in practice, that a man who is harmed by false credulity is also thus relieved by the same credulity.

To End a Love Affair

According to the physicians Nicola and Guilielmo Varignana, and the surgeon Pietro d'Argelata, the bridegroom should urinate through the wedding ring to be free from the evil eye and from sexual impotence. If anyone wishes a love to be dissolved, let the woman's feces be placed in the man's shoe, and the odor, when detected, will destroy their love. Certainly the cause of this power is abundantly clear there is no need to refer to it by tortuous reasoning to some hidden property.

Hanging Over the Altar

I would like to whisper into the ear of my many readers a most ridiculous and clearly pious cure. A woman named Katharina Loe (I know her children), upon being married to her husband, discovered at the outset that he was impotent. Therefore, acting upon the various advice that she had rashly sought, she hung a wax representation of a penis upon the altar of St. Anthony (at Everfeld in the Duchy of Berg where she lived), as a religious offering that her husband might be relieved of his misfortune. Unaware of this, the priest read the Canon of the Mass with his eyes lowered in the usual manner, and then looked up and to his surprise saw this waxen penis. "Get that demon out of here!" he exclaimed in an angry voice.

—DR. JOHANN WEYER

Naughty Tales at the French Court, 1500s

Seigneur de Brantôme (1540–1614) was a gossipy French writer who in his Lives of Fair and Gallant Ladies *tried to find an anecdote for every form of love and sex practiced around the courts of Europe. Although nominally appalled by the behavior he observed, Brantôme displayed an uncanny knack for unearthing the more unusual varieties:*

The Admiral Gets Soaked

I've heard it said of King Francis I [*1494–1547, Leonardo da Vinci's patron*], who long kept a very beautiful woman for his mistress, that one afternoon he decided to pay her a surprise visit for some sport. He knocked loudly on the door, since he was the master of the place. She—at that moment occupied with Admiral Bonnivet—didn't dare speak the words of the Roman courtesans: "Non si parla; la signora est accompagnata!" ("Don't say a word; the lady has company!") Rather, it was just a matter of choosing the safest hiding place.

Since it happened to be summer, when the French custom is to put branches and leaves in the unused fireplace, that's where she advised the admiral to hurl himself as quickly as possible.

After the king did the deed with his lady, he wanted to take a pee; and getting up, lacking any other handy spot, he did it in the fireplace. He really had to go, so much so that he soaked the poor lover more than if he had thrown a bucket of water at him. I will leave you to consider the discomfort of that gentleman since he dare not move, and what patience and control he showed as well. The king bid farewell to the lady and left the room. The lady closed the door behind him and called her servant to her bed, warmed him with her own fire, and made him borrow a white shirt.

A French Virgin!

Brantôme repeatedly defends France:

Next, I must mention an unfavorable opinion, still held to this day, about the court of French kings. Some men claim that the ladies of the court—both wives and maidens—indulge in sinful pleasures, and, moreover, do so often. But they're quite wrong about this because there are some very chaste, honorable, and virtuous women, maybe even more here than elsewhere. . . .

To cite just one example, I'll mention the case of the Madame grand duchess of Florence, originally of the house of Lorraine. She arrived in Florence the same night the grand duke was to marry her. And he wanted to bed her and deflower her right away. But first he had her pee in a beautiful "urinoir" [*chamber pot*] of crystal, the most elegant and transparent imaginable. He examined the urine, and he consulted with his doctor, a famous and wise expert, in order to find out whether she was a virgin or not. The doctor, after scrutinizing the contents, found she was in exactly the same state as when she exited the belly of her mother. The grand duke boldly leapt to business, and he didn't find the route the least bit open, tattered, or battered. He found her "honor" to be real and strong.

The next morning, he shouted in amazement: "Lo and behold, a miracle—the girl arrived a virgin from the court of France!"

Chastity Belts

In the time of King Henri [*Henri III, reigned 1574–1589*], there was a certain hustler who brought to market at St. Germain a dozen of these devices that bridle a woman. They were made of iron in the form of a girdle which was closed below and locked with a key, and so cleverly made that it was not possible for a woman, being once encased, to overcome them to enjoy a delightful pleasure, because all she had were a few small holes for pissing.

Lesbians and an Early Toilet

The "chaise percée" was a forerunner of the toilet: a chair with pierced seat and a chamber pot hidden below. Leave it to Brantôme to find two lesbians using it as a couch:

There were two servants: a widow and a married woman. And in honor of the big holiday, the married woman had decked herself out in an expensive dress of silver cloth. Since their mistress had gone to Vespers, they entered her room and on her "chaise percée" started to diddle each other so rudely and impetuously that the seat broke beneath them. The married woman, who was on the bottom, fell backwards in her beautiful silver dress smack on top of the ordure in the bowl. She stained and soiled it so badly that all she could manage to do was wipe at it, then take it off and rush to change her dress in her own room. Perhaps she wasn't seen; but more probably she was smelt.

The Wife Was Bait

Next there are yet another type of cuckold, entirely abominable and despicable. . . .

At Ferrara, there was a husband completely enthralled with a certain stunning young man [*who kept refusing him*]. So the older man persuaded his wife to set up a tryst with the youth, who was a bit in love with her, and to promise to make the boy's wildest dreams come true.

The lady agreed to the scheme quite voluntarily for in truth she had a taste for no finer venison than this. After a while, the date was set, the hour arrived. The young man and the lady were enjoying their pleasant games, when suddenly, the hidden husband rushed in for the ambush. Nabbing them in the very act, he put a dagger to the boy's throat, and threatened to kill him, as was his right under Italian law, which is somewhat stricter than French law. So the young man was compelled to grant the wishes of the husband who eagerly changed places with his wife. Thus was the husband [*willingly*] cuckolded in an extremely vile way.

—SEIGNEUR DE BRANTÔME

Henri III Is Seduced by a Smell, 1572

On August 18, 1572, the marriages of the King of Navarre to Marguerite de Valois and of Prince de Condé to Marie de Clèves were celebrated at the Louvre. Graceful, charming, sixteen-year-old Marie de Clèves, after dancing a long time and finding herself uncomfortable from the heat of the ballroom, went to a dressing room, where one of the serving women of the queen mother noticed her blouse was completely soaked and gave her another one to wear.

A moment after she left the dressing room, the Duke d'Anjou (the future Henri III), who also had danced a lot, entered the room to fix his wig, and he wiped his face with the first cloth he could find: it happened to be the blouse Marie had just left.

When he returned to the ballroom, he cast his eyes on her and stared at her, it's said, with astonishment, as though he were looking at her for the first time. The feelings, the pain, the passion, and all the eagerness that he started to show were all the more surprising since for the previous six days she had been at the court and he had appeared completely indifferent to these same charms. In that one moment she cast such a vivid impression upon his soul that it would last for a very long time.

—POULLAIN DE SAINT-FOIX

Henri III wrote letters to Marie in blood and promised he would make her the queen of France, but she died mysteriously just as he inherited the throne in 1574. Henri III went into deep mourning, wearing skulls all over his clothes for months afterwards. Some scholars contend he became France's most blatantly homosexual monarch.

Crude Behavior at St. Bartholomew's Day Massacre, 1572

One of the most vicious double-crosses in all history was the St. Bartholomew's Day massacre (August 23–24, 1572), when the Catholic French king, Charles IX, lured all the leading Huguenots (French Calvinists) to Paris for the above-mentioned wedding between his sister and the Huguenot king of Navarre; then he slaughtered them. Mark Twain pegged the death toll at seventy thousand and said that the French showed true genius for massacre: "The Frenchman is nothing if not pious," wrote Twain in The French and the Commanches. *"He is not content to be pious all by himself, he requires his neighbor to be pious also—otherwise he will kill him and make him so."*

And he will also celebrate the aftermath:

After King Charles perpetrated St. Bartholomew's Day, he shouted, laughing and swearing to God: "Teh! what a wonderful c-nt my fat sister Margot has! By God's blood, I don't think there's another like it in the world. It's drawn all the Huguenot rebels like a bird call."

—PIERRE DE L'ESTOILE

The mother of Charles IX was the notorious Catherine de Medici, accused by many of masterminding the massacre. She routinely used her dozens of beautiful ladies-in-waiting as a "flying squadron" of call girls to influence powerful men, and she was certainly as crude as her son.

The night of St. Bartholomew's Day [*massacre*], the queen mother, to get a little fresh air and have a little fun, left the Louvre with her ladies and handmaidens to view the dead bodies of the slain Huguenots. Among them all, she especially wanted to see the nude body of Soubise, to check out his "equipment," since this handsome and powerful gentleman was said to be impotent with the ladies.

—PIERRE DE L'ESTOILE

Soubise (Baron Charles de Quellenec) was in the midst of a nationally known trial for impotency, the gossip scandal of the moment. His mother-in-law had lobbied Catherine de Medici, then sued in court to have her sixteen-year-old-daughter freed from the marriage on the grounds of the husband's impotency. The baron in 1572 actually had to produce an erection before court-appointed experts, and he failed. Before he could demand another trial, he was killed.

Public Impotency Trials, 1611–1627

Very few factors besides death could legally dissolve a Catholic marriage, but impotency—the inability to follow God's commandment to procreate—was one of them. That raises the question of proof.

As astounding as it may sound, church officials from the mid-1500s to the 1700s, with the help of doctors and midwives, actually conducted physical tests for impotency: husbands underwent erection tests; wives, virginity checks; and, ultimately, there were even "trials by congress"— basically, marital intercourse for a select audience.

(This is all carefully reported in Pierre Darmon's superb book, Damning the Innocent, Viking, 1986.*)*

Trial by Congress, 1611

Each of the participants is inspected naked from the crown of their head to the soles of their feet in all parts of the body— even in their anus—to discover whether they're hiding anything that could help or hinder the sexual trial.

To prevent the wife from using astringents to tighten herself up and make it more difficult for the man to enter, she's put in a half bath for a little while.

Next, the condition of the privy parts is then examined, and by this means, they seek to judge the difference in her opening and her dilation before and after the sexual trial and to determine whether or not intromission [*i.e., penetration*] has taken place.

That done, the man and the woman lie down in broad daylight on a bed, the attending experts either remain or retire . . . leaving the door ajar and matrons stationed by the bed.

The [bed] curtains are drawn, it falls to the man to go about proving his potency. Often squabbling and silly fights break out: the husband complaining that his spouse doesn't want to let him do it and is blocking insertion while she denies it and claims that he wants to put his finger in there and dilate her and open her up by this means. . . .

A man would have to be amazingly determined and even brutish if he didn't lose his erection—that is, if he ever had one. And if notwithstanding these indignities and obstacles, if he survives long enough to insert himself, he would not be able to unless someone held the hands and feet of his partner.

Finally, after the couple has spent maybe an hour or two in bed, the experts are summoned, or else they come on their own because they're bored; they approach and open the curtains to inspect what's happened and examine the woman to see whether she's more open than before she got in bed, and to see if any intromission has occurred (also whether there's any ejaculation: where? how? and what sort?). This is all done without candle or eyeglasses, used by old people, though not without extremely perverse and shameful questions and arguments. They draw up their reports which they deliver to the judge in another room off to one side. The prosecutors and elite of the Ecclesiastical Court await the final results of this drama, whose verdict always goes against the man, unless he achieved intromission.

—JURIST VINCENT TAGEREAU

Christmas Eve Pardon, 1613

The inability to procreate could take another form. The Ecclesiastical Court granted Magdeleine de Charbonnier a separation from her husband, Jean Fauré, on December 24, 1613:

. . . because her said husband's virile organ was too huge and beyond the capacity of any virgin to accommodate it.

—COURT RECORDS

Virginity Test: Examining the Wife

One way to prove that a husband has never succeeded in having intercourse with his wife is to show that the woman's virginity is still absolutely intact. But, cautioned one Dr. Nicolas Venette, "In all of medicine there is nothing more difficult to determine than virginity." And Dr. Venette compared the difficulty of following the path of a penis inside a vagina to "tracking the course of a ship on the sea, an eagle in the air or a snake on a rock."

Here's how jurist Louis Servin described the test:

Do you want this spectacle to be represented in words? Chaste ears, forgive me, if my words wallow in a shameful thing, I don't know anything less chaste and shameful. The girl is caused to lie on a bed, stretched out on her back, her thighs splayed apart, one here, the other over there. One clearly sees her privy parts, those that Nature wanted to hide for pleasure and the satisfaction of men. The matrons—midwives and old women—and the doctors carefully examine those parts, handling them and opening them. The judge, who is present, tries to keep a straight face and stop himself from laughing. The matrons recall their long past flames, which have long since frozen over. The doctors, depending to their age, muse to themselves about their bygone prowess. The others, busying themselves, absorb this vain and useless spectacle. The surgeon, who is holding either an instrument made just for this purpose, a "mirror of the womb," or is holding a virile organ made of wax or some other substance, plumbs the depth of the entrance of her lair of Venus; he makes an opening, dilates it, stretches it and enlarges its bounds. The girl sprawled on the bed feels her privy parts tingle so much that even if she came to the exam a virgin, she will never leave one, but rather corrupted and spoiled. It's shameful to say anymore.

—LOUIS SERVIN

Sir Walter Raleigh Wasn't Always a Gentleman, 1570s

Sir Walter Raleigh (1554–1618) was painted as the ultimate gentleman for casting his coat into a puddle so Queen Elizabeth could keep her feet dry. A respected biographer noted another side of Raleigh:

He loved a wench well; and one time getting one of his maids of honor up against a tree in a wood (twas his first lady) who seemed at first boarding to be something fearful of her honor, and modest, she cried, "Sweet Sir Walter, what do you me ask? Will you undo me? Nay, sweet Sir Walter! Sweet Sir Walter! Sir Walter!" At last as the danger and the pleasure at the same time grew higher, she cried in ecstasy, "Swisser

Swatter Swisser Swatter." She proved with child and I doubt not but this hero took care of both as also that the product was more than an ordinary mortal.

—JOHN AUBREY, *BRIEF LIVES*

Chastity Shoes in Venice, 1589

Try to picture these outfits, observed in Venice by a French traveler:

Married Venetian women wear gowns padded in front and behind. They wear their hair dyed blond, prettily braided, and raised up in front to form two horns almost half a foot high. They keep these up not by iron mold or other means but simply by delicate braiding. They wear nothing on their heads other than a veil of black crepe that reaches below their shoulders. However, they make sure it doesn't prevent anyone from admiring the beauty of their hair, shoulders, and breasts, which they expose almost to their belly.

They seem a foot taller than their husbands because they wear wooden shoes covered in leather that are at least a foot high. They need to have one servant help them walk and another to carry the train of their dress. There they walk along, with an air of dignity, while completely exposing their breasts, the old ones as much the young.

—SEIGNEUR DE VILLAMONT

A British traveler visited Venice about fifty years later, and he found shoes a foot and a half tall:

When I complained about the shoes, I was told there's more

to the custom than meets the eye. It's a subtle way to keep the wives at home, or at least prevent them from going far, or going alone, or secretly.

—RICHARD LASSELS

The Turkish Harem, 1599–1640

The Turkish harem was not the figment of some overheated Victorian pornographer's imagination. It really existed for almost five hundred years, from 1453 forward. The basic setup: One Ottoman sultan with three hundred or more beautiful half-naked virgins at his beck and call. Within the harem, though, there were elaborate rules of conduct.

(See also "An Englishwoman at the Turkish Baths, 1717.")

An Englishman Peeps into the Turkish Harem, 1599

Thomas Dallam, an English organ maker on loan to the sultan, became in 1599—during a tour by a friendly eunuch— the first European to have a confirmed sighting of the Seraglio, according to Harem, *by N. Penzer.*

When he had showed me many other things which I wondered at, then crossing through a little square court paved with marble, he pointed me to go to a grate in a wall, but made me a sign that he might not go thither himself. When I came to the grate, the wall was very thick, and grated on both sides with iron very strongly; but through that grate, I did see thirty of the grand seignor's concubines that were playing with a ball in another court.

At the first sight of them, I thought they had been young men, but when I saw the hair of their heads hang down on their backs, plaited together with a tassel of small pearls hanging in the lower end of it, and by other plain tokens, I did know them to be women, and very pretty ones indeed.

They wore upon their heads nothing but a little cap of cloth of gold, which did but cover the crown of her head; no bands about their necks, nor anything but fair chains of pearl and a jewel hanging on their breast, and jewels in their ears; their coats were like a soldier's mandilion [*cloak*], some of red satin, some of blue, and some of other colors and girded like a lace of contrary color; they wore britches of scamatie, a fine cloth made of cotton wool, as white as snow and as fine as lawn; for I could discern the skin of their thighs through it. These britches came down to their mid-leg; some of them did wear fine cordevan buskins, and some had their legs naked, with a gold ring on the small of her leg; on her foot a velvet pantoble [*slipper*] four or five inches high. I stood so long looking upon them that he which had showed me such kindness began to be very angry with me. He made a wry mouth, and stamped with his foot to make me give over looking; which I was very loath to do, for that sight did please me wondrous well.

—THOMAS DALLAM

The Selection Process

Paul Rycaut, British ambassador to Turkey, described the workings of the harem in his 1668 book, The State of the Ottoman Empire:

When the Grand Seignor resolves to choose himself a bedfellow, he retires into the lodgings of his women, where (according to the story in every place reported, when the Turkish seraglio falls into discourse) the damsels being ranged in order by the "Mother of the Maids," he throws his handkerchief to her, where his eye and fancy best direct, it being a token of her election to his bed. The surprised virgin snatches at this prize and good fortune with [such] eagerness that she is ravished with the joy before she is deflowered by the sultan, and kneeling down first kisses the handkerchief, and then puts it in her bosom, when immediately she is congratulated by all the ladies of the court, for the great honor and favor she has received.

And after she has been first washed, bathed, and perfumed, she is adorned with jewels and what other attire can make her appear glorious and beautiful; she is conducted at night, with music and songs of her companions chanting before her to the bed chamber of the sultan, at the door of which attends some favorite eunuch, who upon her approaching gives some advice to the Grand Seignor, and permission being given her to enter in, she comes running and kneels before him, and sometimes enters in at the foot of the bed, according to the ancient ceremony, or otherwise as he chances to like her, is taken in a nearer way with the embraces of the Grand Seignor.

—PAUL RYCAUT

The Fetishes of Sultan Ibrahim, 1645

Demetrius Cantemir, in his History of the Growth and Decay of the Ottoman Empire *(1734), describes the preferences of Ibrahim (reigned 1640–1648), one of the more crude and unbalanced sultans. Before he became sultan, Ibrahim—as a potential rival of his older brother for the throne—was locked up until age twenty-four in an isolated prison called the Cage, served by deaf-mutes and barren women; this was considered more humane than the earlier "Law of Fratricide," which called for killing all the sultan's brothers.*

Every Friday, which is the Turkish sabbath, he dedicated to Venus, and commanded a beautiful virgin richly habited to be brought to him by his mother, prime vizier, or some other great man. He covered the walls of his chamber with looking glass, that his love battles might seem to be acted in several places at once. He ordered his pillows to be stuffed with rich furs, that the bed destined for the imperial pleasure might be the more precious. Nay, he put whole sable skins under him, in a notion that his lust would be inflamed, if his love toil were rendered more difficult by the glowing of his knees. In the palace garden called "Chas," he frequently assembled all the virgins, made them strip themselves, and himself naked, neighing like a stallion, ran among them, and as it were ravished one or other kicking and struggling by his order. Happening once to see by chance the privy parts of a wild heifer, he sent the shape of them in gold all over the empire, with orders to make enquiry whether a woman made just in the manner could be found for his lust.

—DEMETRIUS CANTEMIR

Rycaut, in The History of the Turkish Empire *(1680), describes the discovery:*

At length they happily procured a huge tall Armenian woman, well proportioned according to her height, and a giantess for her stature; which being found, she was presently washed and perfumed in the bath, and as richly clothed and adorned as the shortness of time would permit. There was no difficulty to persuade her to become Turk, having so high preferment in her prospect. So that being introduced to the Grand Seignor's presence, he became immediately enamored, and was so pleased with her society that he preferred her before all the other women of his court. . . . He could not deny her in any request she could make. . . .

[*But*] the queen mother becoming jealous, one day inviting her to dinner, caused her to be strangled, and persuaded Ibrahim that she had died suddenly of a violent sickness, at which the poor man was greatly afflicted.

—PAUL RYCAUT

Ibrahim himself was by no means harmless. Once, in a rage, he had his entire harem of three hundred women cast into the Straits of Bosporus, tied up in weighted sacks.

5

The Seventeenth Century

King James (of Bible Fame) Falls in Love with a Poor Young Scotsman, 1615

King James I (1566–1625)—best known for commissioning a fresh translation of the Bible—hardly concealed his strong affection for several young men. Did his love for them ever get physical? It appears very likely.

When Robert Carr, a handsome seventeen-year-old penniless Scot, fell off a horse at a royal joust and broke his leg in 1607, the forty-one-year-old king helped nurse him back to health, tried to teach him some Latin, and fell in love. "The prince leaneth on his arm, pinches his cheeks, smooths his ruffled garment, and when he looketh at Carr, directeth discourse to others," *wrote Thomas Howard, Earl of Suffolk, in a letter in 1611.*

Over the years, King James showered Carr with gifts. But by 1615, the relationship between the king and Carr, now the wealthy (and married) earl of Somerset, had soured.

This letter, written by James in early 1615, runs through a long list of complaints, and then adds:

> I leave out of this reckoning your long creeping back and withdrawing yourself from lying in my chamber, notwithstanding my many hundred times earnest soliciting you to the contrary, accounting that but as a point of unkindness. Now whether all your great parts and merits be not accompanied with a sour and distasteful sauce, yourself shall be the judge.
>
> . . . Consider that I am a freeman, if I were not a king. Remember that all your being, except your breathing and soul, is from me. I told you twice or thrice that ye might lead me by the heart and not by the nose. I cannot deal honestly if I cannot deal plainly with you. If ever I find that ye think to retain me by one sparkle of fear, all the violence of my love will in that instant be changed in[to] as violent a hatred. God is my judge my love hath been infinite towards you.

In 1616, Carr and his wife were convicted of poisoning a prisoner in the Tower and sentenced to die. King James commuted the sentence to imprisonment and they wound up spending six years themselves in the Tower before eventually gaining a pardon. Carr lived out his days at his fine country estate.

A Genital Medical Emergency, 1621

Victorian sex researcher Havelock Ellis cited the following as the oldest recorded instance of a woman suffering a masturbation accident and needing surgical help. He found it in the book On the Procreative Organs *(1621), by Dr. Francesco Plazzoni.*

Once, a respectable virgin, troubled by a tingling in her womanly penis [*clitoris*], began masturbating with a bone needle in order to soothe this itch, and because the orifice of the bladder is nearby, she slipped the needle into her bladder. She suffered horrendous pains, which required the hand of a doctor. [*Famed physician*] Aquapendente performed the cure while I stood by. We noticed that her clitoris jutted out about half a finger's length.

(One theory popular then was that large clitorises caused masturbation and lesbianism. Apparently, Dr. Plazzoni was a bit of a connoisseur of that part of the female anatomy.)

For in the clitoris, the greatest pleasure is believed to reside, to such a degree that even a finger drawn across it makes semen pour forth; hence, it's called "gadfly of Venus," the "goad of lust," the "bon-bon of love."

—Dr. Francesco Plazzoni

The Beastly Loves of Some Forgotten Puritans, 1629–1641

All the Puritans escaping England and coming over to the New World weren't the black-hatted, buckle-shoed, missionary-position Puritans we know. In fact, according to court records and governors' memoirs, a number of the first settlers in America experimented with bestiality, homosexuality, and lesbianism. But when they were caught, the real (central casting) Puritans made very sure the others paid the price.

A Sheep Lineup: Ewe, Ewe, Ewe, and Ewe

The Puritans, following strictly after Leviticus, regarded bestiality as a capital offense for both the man and the animal. This could lead to some unusual problems, as recorded in History of Plymouth Plantation, *by Governor William Bradford:*

September 8, 1642

There was a youth whose name was Thomas Granger. He was servant to an honest man of Duxbury, being about sixteen or seventeen years of age. (His father and mother lived at the same time at Sityate.) He was this year detected of buggery, and indicted for the same, with a mare, a cow, two goats, five sheep, two calves, and a turkey. Horrible it is to mention but the truth of the history requires it. He was first discovered by one that accidentally saw his lewd practice towards the mare. (I forebear particulars.) Being upon it, examined and committed, in the end he not only confessed the fact with that beast at that time, but sundry times before and at several times with all the rest of the forenamed in his indictment. And this his free confession was not only in private to the magistrates (though at first he strived to deny it) but to sundry, both ministers and others; and afterwards upon his indictment, to the whole court and jury, and confirmed it at his execution.

And whereas some of the sheep could not so well be known by his description of them, others with them were brought before him and he declared which they were and which were not.

And accordingly he was cast by the jury and condemned, and after executed about the 8th of September, 1642. A very sad spectacle it was; for first the mare and then the cow and the rest of the lesser cattle were killed before his face, according to the law, Leviticus 20:15, and then he himself was executed. The cattle were all cast into a great and large pit that was digged of purpose for them and no use made of any part of them.

—WILLIAM BRADFORD

A Man and a Pig, 1646

Governor Theophilus Eaton of New Haven colony (not yet merged into Connecticut) visited a barn to witness the trial-by-masturbation between a man and a pig. The man's name, improbably enough, was Thomas Hogg. And he stood accused of fathering a piglet that resembled him: it too was wall-eyed on the right side.

The governor and deputy, intending to examine him, caused him to be [*led*] down to Mrs. [*Lamberton's*] yard, where the swine were, then bid him scratt [*fondle*] the sow that had the monsters and immediately there appeared a working of lust in the sow, insomuch she poured out seed before them and then they asked what he thought of it, he said he saw a hand of God in it. Afterwards he was bid to scratt another sow as he did the former but it was not moved at all, which Thomas Hogg acknowledged to be true but said he never had to do with the other sow.

—RECORDS OF NEW HAVEN COLONY

Hogg was convicted of the lesser charges of filthiness, lying, and pilfering, and was sentenced to a severe whipping and prison "with a mean diet and hard labor that his lusts may not be fed."

Deadly Serious

The crime of bestiality might seem almost comical from the distance of three centuries, but it only takes the following item to remind us that teenage boys were actually killed for it. An eighteen-year-old servant, William Hackett, was caught buggering a cow on a Sunday in 1641 by a woman who was too sick to go to church:

When the day of execution came, after he had been at the lecture [*sermon*], he went to the place of execution sadly and silently, and being up the ladder, he said nothing; but the cow (with which he had committed that abomination), being brought forth and slain before him, he broke out into a loud and doleful complaint against himself, bewailed his sinful course of life, his disobedience to his parents, his slighting and despising their instructions and the instructions of his dame, and other means of grace God had offered him, etc. Then Mr. Wilson, the pastor of Boston (the rest of the elders and the people there present joining with him), prayed earnestly to the Lord for him a good space. He attended duly thereto, and prayed also himself, crying oft and earnestly for mercy; yet with a trembling body, and amazed with the apprehension of death so near at hand, to which he quietly yielded himself, when he was required. There is no doubt to be made but the Lord received his soul to his mercy.

—Governor John Winthrop, *History of New England*

Accused of Raping His Own Wife, 1631

In England, Lord Audley, second earl of Castlehaven, was accused in court on April 25, 1631, of raping his own wife:

Lady Castlehaven testified:

That shortly after the Earl marry'd her, viz., the first or second night, Amptil [*the stableman*] came unto the Bed's side whilst she and her husband were in bed, and the Lord Audley spake lasciviously to her, and told her that now her body was his, and that if she lov'd him she must love Amptil, and that if she lay with any other man with his consent, it was not her fault but his and that if it is his will to have it, she must obey and do it.

That he attempted to draw her to lie with his servant Skipwith, and that Skipwith made him believe he did it, but did it not.

That he would make Skipwith come naked into his chamber, and delighted in calling up his servants to shew their privities and would make her look on, and commended those that had the largest.

That one night being abed with her at Founthill, he called for his man Broadway, and commanded him to lie at his bed's feet, and about midnight (she being asleep), call'd him to light a pipe of tobacco, Broadway rose in his shirt, and my Lord pull'd him into bed to him and her, and made him lie next to her, and Broadway lay with her, and knew her carnally, whilst she made resistance, and the Lord held both her hands and one of her legs the while, and that as soon as she was free, she would have killed herself with a knife but that Broadway forcibly took the knife away from her and broke it. Before that act of Broadway she had never done it.

Castlehaven was also accused of aiding a similar act against his twelve-year-old daughter-in-law:

The servant Skipwith testified:

That the Earl often sollicited him to lie with the young lady, and persuaded him that his son lov'd her not, and that in the end he usually lay with the young lady, and that there was Love between them both before and after; and that my Lord said, he would rather have a boy of his begetting than any others; and that she was but twelve years of age when he first lay with her, and that he could not enter her body without art and that the Lord Audley fetch'd oil to open her body but she cry'd out and he could not enter, and then the Earl appointed oil the second time, and then Skipwith enter'd her body and knew her carnally.

. . . That he spent 500£ per annum of the Lord's purse and for the most part he lay with the said Earl. . . .

—Court records

Castlehaven complained bitterly about what would happen to England if wives and servants were allowed to testify against their masters. Nonetheless, he was convicted of raping his own wife and of sodomy with two servants, and he was beheaded soon after.

A Sinful Error, 1632

Mr. Baker, an English printer, was called before a London ecclesiastical court in 1632 and punished for the following offense:

For false printing of the Bible in diverse places of it, in the edition of 1631, viz., in the 20 of Exodus, "Thou shalt commit adultery."

The Old Lemon Juice Defense, 1635

Mademoiselle de La Fayette eagerly wanted to become the king's new mistress. She did everything to attract King Louis XIII's attention.

The writer of these memoirs was Pierre de la Porte, then the queen's messenger.

[*Mlle. de La Fayette*] sang, she danced; she played games with the utmost charm; she was solemn when appropriate; she laughed with all her heart upon occasion, and a few times almost like a madwoman. One evening at St. Germain, something struck her as funny and she laughed so hard, she wet herself; in fact, so much so that for a long time, she didn't dare move. The king was willing let her stay there, but the queen wanted her to move. Pretty soon a giant lake appeared.

Her enemies weren't able to control their laughter, especially the queen, who announced in a loud voice that it was La Fayette who had peed. One of La Fayette's supporters, Mademoiselle de Vieux-Pont, contradicted the queen, right to her face, and claimed that it appeared to her to be lemon juice, and that she had a few lemons in her pocket that must have gotten squeezed. That little speech so incited the queen that she ordered me to smell what it was: I did so immediately and told her it did not smell the least bit like lemon; so that now everyone knew the queen had been telling the truth.

The queen, then and there, wanted to examine each of the young ladies to determine who had peed because almost all of them proclaimed that it certainly wasn't Mlle. La Fayette. But

they all ran off to their rooms. This entire incident pissed off
the king, almost as much as the song someone made up about it.

—PIERRE DE LA PORTE

The Restoration in England:
Fast Times at the Court of the Well-Endowed
Monarch, Charles II, 1660–1685

*Once the repressive Puritans of Oliver Cromwell lost
control in 1660 and King Charles II (1630–1685) was restored
to the throne, England—especially the upper classes—plunged
in for a cursing, carousing, lecherous romp. Playing the lewd
court jester and typifying the national mood during the
Restoration was one bawdy boozehound poet: John Wilmot,
Earl of Rochester (1647–1680).*

*First, to get a flavor of life at the court, here's a day in the
life of Rochester:*

The Ribald Routine of a Restoration Poet

I rise at eleven, I dine at two,
I get drunk before seven, and the next thing I do
I send for my whore when, for fear of the clap,
I come in her hand and I spew in her lap.
Then we quarrel and scold till I fall fast asleep,
When the bitch growing bold, to my pocket doth creep.
She slyly then leaves me, and to revenge my affront
At once she bereaves me of money and cunt . . .
I storm and I roar, and I fall in a rage,

And, missing my whore, I bugger my page.
Then crop-sick all morning, I rail at my men,
And in bed I lie yawning 'till eleven again.

Big King Charles II, 1676

Towering over the debauchery and leading by example was King Charles II, whose impressive royal member is described in Rochester's poems and the diary of Samuel Pepys.

Rochester was temporarily banished from court in 1676 for the following satire:

. . . Nor are his high Desires above his strength,
His Sceptre and his Prick are of a length
And she may sway the one, who plays with th'other
And make him little wiser than his Brother.
Restless he rolls about from Whore to Whore
A merry Monarch, scandalous and poor.
Poor Prince thy Prick like thy Buffoons at Court
Will govern thee because it makes thee sport.
'Tis sure the sauciest that e're did swive
The proudest peremptoriest Prick alive.
Though Safety, Law, Religion, Life lay on't,
'Twould break through all to make its way to Cunt. . . .

The Royal Priorities Are Clear

May 15, 1663

The king doth mind nothing but pleasures and hates the very sights or thoughts of business. That [*the king's mistress*] my Lady Castlemayne rules him; who he says hath all the tricks of Aretin [*erotic writer Pietro Aretino*] that are to be practiced to give pleasure—in which he is too able, hav[*ing*] a large—but that which is the unhappiness is that, as the Italian proverb says, "Cazzo dritto non vuolt consiglio [*A stiff prick doesn't want any advice*]."

—DIARY OF SAMUEL PEPYS

To the King's Health

Perfectly in the spirit of the Restoration was this incident, which starred Sir Charles Sedley, one of the king's closest advisers, drunk in front of a crowd:

July 1, 1663

Sir Charles Sedley . . . coming in open day into the balcony and showed his nakedness—acting all the postures of lust and buggery that could be imagined, and abusing of scripture and, as it were, from thence preaching a Mountebanke sermon from that pulpit, saying that he hath to sell such a powder as should make all the cunts in town to run after him—a thousand people standing underneath to see and hear him.

And that being done, he took a glass of wine and washed his prick in it and then drank it off; and then took another and drank to the king's health.

—DIARY OF SAMUEL PEPYS

The King: Disguised, Penniless in a Whorehouse

It fell to Rochester, an extremely unlikely reformer, to try to break Charles II of a dangerous habit:

[*Rochester*] agreed to go out one night with him to visit a celebrated house of intrigue, where he told his Majesty the finest women in England were to be found. The King [*didn't hesitate*] to assume his usual disguise and accompany him, and while he was engaged with one of the ladies of pleasure, being before instructed by Rochester how to behave, she pick'd his pocket of all his money and watch, which the king did not immediately miss. Neither she nor the people of the house were made acquainted with the quality of their visitor, nor had the least suspicion who he was.

When the intrigue was ended, the King enquired for Rochester but was told he had quitted the house, without taking leave. But into what embarrassment was he thrown when upon searching his pockets, in order to discharge the reckoning, he found his money gone; he was then reduced to ask the favour of the jezebel to give him credit till tomorrow, as the gentleman who came with him had not returned, who was to have pay'd for both. The consequence of this request was, he was abused, and laughed at; and the old woman told him, that she had often been served such dirty tricks, and would not permit him to stir till the reckoning was paid, and then called one of her bullies to take care of him.

In this ridiculous distress stood the British monarch, the prisoner of a bawd, and the life upon whom the nation's hopes were fixed, put in the power of a ruffian. After many altercations the King at last proposed that she should accept a ring which he took off his finger, in pledge for her money, which she likewise refused, and told him, that as she was no judge of the value of the ring, she did not choose to accept such a pledge. The King then desired that a jeweler might be called to give his opinion on the value of it but he was answered that the expedient was impracticable as no jeweler could then be supposed to be out of bed. After much entreaty, his Majesty at last prevailed upon the fellow to knock up a jeweler and show him the ring, which as soon as he had inspected, he stood amazed and enquired, with eyes fixed upon the fellow: who he had got in his house? To which [*the man*] answered "A black-looking ugly son of a wh-re who had no money in his pocket and was obliged to pawn his ring."

"The ring," says the jeweler, "is so immensely rich that but one man in the nation could afford to wear it; and that one is the King."

The jeweler being astonished at this incident, went out with the bully, in order to be fully satisfied of so extraordinary an affair; and as soon as he entered the room, he fell on his knees, and with the utmost respect presented the ring to his Majesty. The old jezebel and the bully finding the extraordinary quality of their guest were now confounded and asked pardon most submissively on their knees. The King in his best natured manner forgave them, and laughing asked them whether the ring would bear another bottle.

Thus ended this adventure, in which the King learned how dangerous it was to risk his person in night frolics.

—THEOPHILUS CIBBER

Eyewitness Account of Sex with the Devil, 1662

Isabel Gowdie, a married woman, confessed four times in elaborate detail to witchcraft before a tribunal of clergymen and elders in Aulderne, Scotland (spelling and some wording modernized from seventeenth-century Scottish):

First as I was going between the towns of Druwdewin and The Headis, the Devil met with me and there I covenanted with him and promised to meet him in the night time, in the Kirk of Aulderne, which I did. He stood at the reader's desk, and a black book in his hand, where I came before him and renounced Jesus Christ and my baptism; and all between the sole of my foot and the crown of my head. I got up freely and went over to the Devil. Margaret Brodie, in Aulderne, held me up to the Devil, until he re-baptized me, and marked me in the shoulder, and with his mouth sucked out my blood at that place, and spouted it in his hand, and sprinkling it upon my head and face, he said, "I baptize ye, Janet, to my self, in my own name!" Within a while, we all left.

And within a few days, he came to me, in the New Ward's of Inshoch, and there had carnal copulation with me. He was a very huge, black, rough man, very cold; and I found his nature [*semen*] within me all cold as spring well water. He will lie all heavy upon us, when he has carnal dealing with us, like a sack of barley malt. His member is exceedingly great and long; no man's member is so long and big as his. He would be among us like a stud horse among mares. He would lie with us in the presence of the multitude; neither of us had any kind of shame; but especially he has no shame at all. He would lie and have carnal dealing with all, at every time, as he pleased. He would have carnal dealing with us in the shape of a deer or any other shape that he would be in. We would never refuse him. He would come to my house-top in the shape of a crow, or like a deer, or in any other shape now and then. I would recognize his voice, at the first hearing of it, and would go forth to him and have carnal copulation with him. The youngest and lustiest women will have very great pleasure in their carnal copulation with him, yea much more than with their own husbands; and they will have an exceedingly great desire for it with him, as much as he can give them and more, and never think shame of it. He is abler for us that way than any man can be (Alas! that I should compare him to any man!) only he is heavy like a sack of barley malt; a huge nature [*outpouring of semen*], very cold as ice.

—Isabel Gowdie

A French Love Manual, 1687

Frenchman Dr. Nicolas Venette (1622–1698), a royal professor of surgery, wrote an enthusiastic sex manual for married couples aimed at promoting enjoyable procreational sex. This popular bedside book, Tableau de l'Amour Conjugale *(1687), went into numerous editions and was translated into English, Dutch, and German. Venette blends the whacky misconceptions of his predecessors with a surprising commonsense approach to problems such as impotence, post-deflowering soreness, and penises that are too long.*

Right Size for Men

Nature, which does nothing without a plan, established laws for all the body parts: those which serve amorous functions generally have a certain dimension among men and women. The member of the man, according to these laws, should not usually be more than six or eight inches in length, and three or four inches in circumference.* That's just the right size which Nature has maintained in forming this organ in the majority of men. If the penis is bigger and thicker, then it takes too much artifice to make it move. For that reason the inhabitants of Midi [in southern France] are less suited for procreation than we are.

*In the British edition (1740) of Venette's work, the average length of a penis is translated as "six or seven inches." The British translator left the circumference unchanged.

Too Big

Penises that are too long or too fat are not the best, either for recreation or procreation. They irritate women and signify nothing special. If for no other reason than to make the sex act easier, the man's member should be medium sized and the woman's should be proportioned the same, so that they can join one to the other, and touch each other pleasurably everywhere.

Too Small

Chastity and mortification of the flesh are often the strongest causes for the shrinking of the genitals. A good example of this is St. Martin, who throughout his life punished his body through unheard of austerities and rebelled against the lewdness of his age. So much so, that after his death, if we believe Sulpicius, his penis became so small that it couldn't have been found if one hadn't known the exact spot where to look.

Right Size for Women

Dr. Venette is just as pragmatic about the size of a woman's genitals.

The canal of the woman's private parts is usually six or eight inches long, and the internal circumference doesn't have any fixed measure; because by an admirable structure, this canal can well adapt itself to the man's sexual organ, becoming wider or narrower as needed.

Clitoris

Like Hippocrates and Maimonides cited earlier, he further dispels the modern myth that men didn't discover the clitoris until the twentieth century:

One sees above the inner labia an organ about half-a-finger's-breadth tall, which the anatomy doctors call the "clitoris." I could call it the passion and guide of Love. It's there that Nature has placed the throne of pleasures and sensuous joys. It's there that Nature has endowed excessive sensitivity and has established the zone of wantonness for women. Thus, in the action of Love, the clitoris fills itself with life forces and stiffens like the penis of a man. It lacks neither a gland nor a foreskin and if it had a little hole on the tip, one would say that it was exactly the same as the man's member.

It's this organ that lewd women abuse. Sappho the Lesbian never would have gained her notorious reputation if she had had a smaller clitoris. . . . I once saw an eight-year-old girl who had a clitoris half the length of a little finger; and if this organ grows with age, as it appears it will, then I'm convinced it will soon become as thick and as long as the one Platerus claimed to have seen: which was as thick and as long as the neck of a goose.

Remedy for Too Big: The "Bourlet"

There was a young woman who complained loudly to the [Church] authorities that her husband's penis was too long. His mere approach was cruel torture. And the pain she felt from the impact of his organ was enough to make her pass out.

When her husband tore apart her vaginal lips, when he scraped the remnants of her hymen, when he split open her canal and bore to the depth of her womb; all that caused much bleeding and dysentery and other illnesses.

But perhaps there's a cure for these problems.

If one carefully cuts a hole in the middle of a piece of cork that's, say, one or two inches in thickness, matching the excessive length of the penis. Then one wraps the cork above and below with cotton, then this cotton is in turn wrapped with a soft cloth which should be tightly sewn on, so that this "bourlet," or to put it better, this "shield," is covered from top to bottom. Next, one sews on each side two little ribbons, and when Love's fire flares up again, then the man slips his member through the hole of the shield and ties the two little ribbons onto each thigh to keep it fixed in place, after that one can enjoy fresh pleasures thanks to the device. This way, the young wife won't flee the caresses of her husband and will no longer refuse his amorous embraces. If, by accident, her husband forgets his shield, she should take care to carry another, or in a pinch use her hand so that she can avoid those past agonies and not renew her despair, wondering whether she can ever have children in her marriage.

Thickness

The thickness of a penis is not as annoying to a woman as excessive length. She has only to enlarge her private parts, which since they're fleshy and membranous will easily enlarge as much as one wants.

Venette adds elsewhere a caveat:

I am not at all speaking here, though, of the humongous size of some men's penises. One realizes these men are not destined for marriage, and one would be very wrong to want the man mentioned by Fabrice of Hilden to remarry, because he had an organ as big and fat as a newborn baby.

If the Woman's Too Loose . . .

Dr. Venette realizes the danger of publishing these remedies that could be used for restoring lost virginity. So he wants his motives known:

My aim is not to promote crime but rather to cure illnesses

which plague women, and to maintain a loving relationship among married persons. . . . I shouldn't have to worry about the evil tendencies of some people who abuse the finest things in the world.

Women from warm climates prevent the [*looseness*] problem that we've been discussing by bathing their genitals in distilled myrtle berry juice, that they perfume with a bit of clove or with a few drops of ambergris, or they use astringent mixtures.

Advice on Deflowering

I wouldn't be surprised if it's true that the Phoenicians, as reported by St. Athanasius, legislated that their daughters must be deflowered by servants before marriage. Nor would I be shocked if the Armenians, as states Strabo, "sacrificed" their daughters in the temple of the goddess Anaitis, to be deflowered there to make the genitals more suited to [*marriage*].

Because it's impossible to predict all toil and pain a man will suffer in this first foray. . . . Far from igniting the passion of his wife, one often sparks such pain and anger that this can be quite a common reason for divorce. It's much sweeter to embrace a woman accustomed to the pleasures of love than to caress one who has never known a man.

It's the same as when we call a locksmith to make the springs move in a brand new lock to avoid the annoyance we'd face the first day; thus those ancient races, mentioned above, had valid reasons for establishing those types of laws.

—DR. NICOLAS VENETTE

Englishmen Sell Their Wives by the Pound, 1696

From the time of Queen Elizabeth up to Victoria, wives were actually sold in the public marketplace in England, according to Wives for Sale, *by Samuel Menefee. How pervasive the practice was is unclear, but Thomas Hardy included a scene of it in his* Mayor of Casterbridge, *and newspaper accounts and church records documenting it have survived.*

One printer made up the following song:

Come all you kind husbands who have scolding wives
Who thro' living together are tired of your lives,
If you cannot persuade her, nor good-natur'd make her,
Place a rope round her neck & to market pray take her.

So How Much Do Wives Cost?

The Church court records from Thame, Oxfordshire, 1696, give a clue:

[*Thomas Heath testifies*] that he did buy the wife of George Fuller at two pence [*per*] pound and brought her behind him to a publick house in Thame where she stayed two days and two nights and that he did not see her above one hour in a day while she stayed there . . . and after that he carried her to the White Hart in Benson and that he did sit on the bedside with her both here and at Benson but denies that he had carnal knowledge of her body.

. . . John Pricket of Thame maketh oath that he was not at the bargain making but came time enough to see [*the wife of George Fuller*] weighed and the money paid which amounted to 29 shilling. *(At 12 pence in a shilling, that means she weighed 174 pounds.)*

Heath was found guilty and did public penance.

Newspaper Ad, 1796

To be sold for <u>five shillings</u>, my wife, Jane Hebland. She is stout built, stands firm on her posterns and is sound wind and limb. She can sow and reap, hold a plough, and drive a team, and would answer any stout able men, that can hold a <u>tight rein</u>, for she is damned <u>hard mouthed</u> and headstrong; but if properly managed would either lead or drive as tame as a rabbit. She now and then, if not watched, will make a <u>false step</u>. Her husband parts with her because she is too much for him. —Enquire of the printer.

N.B. All her body clothes will be given with her.

Sale of a Wife at Thomas Street Market, 1823

May 29, 1823

This day another of those disgraceful scenes which of late have so frequently annoyed the public markets in this country took place at St. Thomas' market, in this city; a man (if he deserves the name) of the name of John Nash, a drover, residing in Rosemary Street, appeared there leading his wife in a halter, followed by a great concourse of spectators; when arrived opposite the Bell-yard, he publicly announced his intention of disposing of his better half by public auction, and stated that the biddings were then open; it was a long while before anyone ventured to speak, at length a young man who thought it a pity to let her remain in the hands of her present owner, generously bid six d. [*pennies*]! In vain did the anxious seller look for another bidding, no one could be found to advance one penny, and after extolling her qualities, and warranting her sound, and free from vice, he was obliged, rather than keep her, to let her go at that price. The lady appeared quite satisfied, but not so the purchaser, he soon repented of his bargain, and again offered her to sale, when being bid nine-pence, he readily accepted it and handed the lady to her new purchaser, who, not liking the transfer, made off with her mother, but soon was taken by her purchaser, and claimed as his property, to this she would not consent but by order of a magistrate, who dismissed the case. Nash, the husband, was obliged to make a precipitate retreat from the enraged populace.

—BRISTOL NEWSPAPER

Sacred Order of Glorious Pederasts, *circa* 1680

A *quartet of the highest-ranking French noblemen—Manicamp, Grammont, Tilladet, Biran—formed a secret pederasty society, according to Comte de Bussi-Rabutin in his* Amorous History of the French *(1695).*

Bussi-Rabutin records the club's nine by-laws:

1) That no one will be admitted to the club who hasn't been physically inspected by the grand-masters, to make sure all body parts are healthy, so that they can support the austerities.
2) That they swear vows of obedience and chastity [*from women*], and if anyone breaks them, they will be banned from the club, and not be allowed to return no matter what excuse.
3) That anyone may be admitted to the club, without distinction to rank, so long as nothing prevents them from submitting to the rigours of the noviciate, which last until the beard comes to the chin.
4) If any of the brothers marry, he must declare that it was for practical reasons, or because his parents forced him to, or because he'd lose an inheritance. That he must promise at the same time never to love his wife, to sleep with her only until there's a boy from it, and that meanwhile he will ask permission for doing so, which shall not be granted more than once a week.

Sometimes the whole thing sounds like a pyramid scheme for the founding members.

5) That the brothers will be divided into four classes, so that each grand-master will have as many as another; and as for those who apply for membership, the grand-masters will have them each in turn, so that jealousy cannot taint their union.
6) That everyone will tell everyone else in detail everything that occurred, so that whenever an accusation surfaces, it

will survive only on merit, which will be well known by this means.

7) As for outsiders, it is absolutely forbidden to reveal the mysteries to them, and whoever does it, will be denied all privileges for eight days, and even longer, if his grand-master deems it appropriate.

8) Nonetheless, one can open up to those whom they might hope to attract to join; but it's necessary that this be done with much discretion, and that one is certain of success before undertaking this tactic.

9) That whoever brings new members to the club would enjoy the same privileges for two days as the grand-masters enjoy. But it's well understood nonetheless that they must allow the grand-masters to go first, and that they must content themselves to have the leftovers from their table.

—BUSSI-RABUTIN

Members were also expected to wear a cross, showing a man trampling a woman underfoot. King Louis XIV had the club disbanded when he discovered a close relative and several other very top-tier noblemen about to join.

6

The Eighteenth Century

The Governor of New York in a Ball Gown, 1702

Like so many of the early British governors in the colonies, Lord Cornbury, of New York and New Jersey (in office 1702–1708), was notorious for his greed and incompetence. But Cornbury had an added claim to fame:

[*Lord Cornbury's*] great insanity was dressing himself as a woman. Lord Orford says that when Governor in America [*Cornbury*] opened the Assembly dressed in that fashion. When some of those about him remonstrated, his reply was, "You are very stupid not to see the propriety of it. In this place and particularly on this occasion, I represent a woman (Queen Anne) and ought in all respects to represent her as faithfully as I can."

Mr. Williams says his father has told him that he has done business with him in woman's clothes. He used to sit at the open window so dressed, to the great amusement of the neighbours. He employed always the most fashionable milliner, shoemaker, staymaker, etc. Mr. Williams has seen a picture of him at Sir Herbert Packington's in Worcestershire, in a gown, stays, tucker, long ruffles, cap, etc.

—The Diaries of Sylvester Douglas, Lord Glenbervie

This first cousin to Queen Anne even had his portrait painted in ball gown and five o'clock shadow, and it now hangs in the New York Historical Society.

His Wife

Cornbury contemporary Gertrude van Cortlandt gave this account to her granddaughter, Janet Livingston Montgomery:

My Lord Cornbury and my Lady was a theme never done. That they were extraordinary people is true and worth perhaps recording from their oddity. He, in consequence of a vow, obliged himself for a month in every year to wear every day women's clothes. He was a large man, wore a hoop and a headdress, and with a fan in his hand was seen frequently at night upon the ramparts. . . .

The Lady of this very just nobleman was equally a character. He had fallen in love with her because she had a beautiful ear; otherwise she was extremely plain. The ear soon ceased to please, and he treated her with neglect. Her pin money was withheld, and she had no other resource but begging and stealing.

—JANET LIVINGSTON MONTGOMERY

Turkish Empire: Tourist Tales

Travelers to the vast Turkish (Ottoman) Empire rarely failed to come home with exotic stories, and what's more, many of the following appear to be true.

The Tricks of Christian Surgeons in Constantinople, 1716

The Koran requires Moslems to be "clean" or "pure" for prayer; hence, after urinating, Moslem men were expected to wipe the head of the penis with one to three bits of stone, clay, or sand, according to Sir Richard Burton.

In the early 1700s in Constantinople, some unscrupulous Christian doctors took advantage of this practice to drum up a little extra business for themselves:

When [*Moslem men*] make water, they squat down like women, for fear some drops of urine should fall into their breeches. To prevent this evil, they squeeze the part very carefully and rub the head of it against the wall; and one may see the stones, worn in several places by this custom. To make themselves sport, the Christians smeer the stones sometimes with Indian pepper, the root called Calf's foot, or some other hot plants, which frequently causes an inflammation in such as happen to use the stone. As the pain is very smart, the poor Turks commonly run for a cure to those very same Christian surgeons, who were the authors of all the mischief; they never fail to tell them it is a very dangerous case, and they should be obliged perhaps to make an amputation; the Turks, on the contrary, protest and swear they have had no communication with any sort of woman that could be suspected. In short, they wrap up the suffering part in a linen dipped in Oxicrat, tinctured with Bole-Armenic; and this they sell them as a great specifick for this kind of mischief.

—M. Tournefort, *A Voyage into the Levant*

An Englishwoman at the Turkish Baths, 1717

The baths became the social hub of most women's lives, the one semipublic place where Moslem women could mingle for hours with friends without arousing suspicion. Gradually, more and more amenities were added: restaurants, shops, music, plays. Even bridal showers took place there.

Lady Mary Montagu, wife of the British ambassador, was an eye-witness to the baths in 1717:

The first sofas were covered with cushions and rich carpets, on which sat the ladies; and on the second, their slaves behind them, but without any distinction of rank by their dress, all being in the state of nature, that is, in plain English, stark naked, without any beauty or defect concealed. . . .

I was here convinced of the truth of a reflection I have often made, that if it was the fashion to go naked, the face would be hardly observed. I perceived that the ladies of the most delicate skins and finest shapes had the greatest share of my admiration, though their faces were sometimes less beautiful than those of their companions. To tell you the truth, I had wickedness enough to wish secretly that Mr. Jervis [*an Irish painter*] could have been there invisible. I fancy it would have very much improved his art, to see so many fine women naked, in different postures, some in conversation, some working, others drinking coffee or sherbet, and many negligently lying on cushions, while their slaves (generally pretty girls of seventeen or eighteen) were employed in braiding their hair in several pretty fancies. In short, it is the women's coffee-house where all the news of the world is told. . . .

The Nude Bridal Shower

One thing to note for picturing the following scene: the married women were completely smooth and depilated, while the virgins—as perhaps yet another means of ensuring chastity until marriage—were tufted, according to nature.

Those that were or had been married placed themselves round the room on the marble sofas; but the virgins very hastily threw off their clothes and appeared without any other ornament or covering than their own long hair braided with pearl or ribbon. Two of them met the bride at the door, conducted by her mother and another grave relation. She was a beautiful maid of about seventeen, very richly dressed, shining with jewels, but was presently reduced by them to the state of nature. Two others filled silver gilt pots with perfume, and began the procession, the rest following in pairs to the number of thirty. The leaders sung an epithalamium, answered by the others in chorus, and the two last led the fair bride, her eyes fixed on the ground, with a charming affectation of modesty. In this order, they marched round the three largest rooms of the bagnio. It is not easy to represent to you the beauty of this sight, most of them being well proportioned and white skinned: all of them perfectly smooth and polished by the frequent use of bathing. After having made their tour, the bride was again led to every matron round the rooms, who saluted her with a compliment and a present, some of jewels, others pieces of stuff, handkerchiefs, or little gallantries of that nature, which she thanked them for by kissing their hands.

—LADY MARY MONTAGU

Lady Mary either didn't witness or omits one key part of the ceremony. From the diary of one John Richards:

The Bride Gets Fleeced, 1699

Upon solemn occasions, when a virgin does prepare herself for her husband's bed, they make a feast in the baths to which they invite their friends, at which she takes off the hair of her body which she never does before, and is always practiced afterwards in these hot countries. With how much modesty this is done, I cannot tell, but I am told that it is very expensive.

—JOHN RICHARDS

Egypt: Adultery and Poison, 1717

C. S. Sonnini, a French engineer, visited Egypt (then part of the Turkish Empire) and discovered that the wives in the South didn't allow any unfaithfulness by their husbands, even if, as the Frenchman tolerantly notes, it was merely an "animal passion while the heart is totally unaffected."

These women . . . are not willing to inflict a quick and sudden death [*on their cheating husbands*]; with this, their remorseless jealousy would not be gratified but they bring on a gradual decay more intolerable than death itself. In themselves they find the poison. . . . The periodic menstrual discharge, which Nature employs to preserve their existence and health, becomes, in their hands, a means of destroying others. Mixed with some food, a portion of their discharge is a poison which immediately throws him who swallows it into languor and a consumption and leads him to the grave. . . . The symptoms are nearly the same as the scurvy. The body dries up; all the limbs become excessively feeble; the gums rot; the teeth are loosened; the beard and hair fall off. . . . No remedy is known.

Good Luck Crocodiles

Sonnini took a boat trip to the Upper Nile and noted the following:

In the neighborhood of Thebes, the small boat in which I sailed upriver was often surrounded by crocodiles, on a level with the surface; they saw us pass by with indifference. . . . The noise occasioned by musket shot was alone able to disturb them in their state of tranquil apathy. . . .

It is upon the muddy coast of the Nile that they deposit their eggs; it there also that they copulate. The female, which in the act of copulation is laid on her back, has much difficulty in rising again; it is even said that she can neither change her position nor turn without the assistance of the male. Will it be believed, that in Upper Egypt there are men to be found, who, hurried on by the excess of an unexampled depravity and bestiality take advantage of this forced situation of the female crocodile, hunt away the male, and replace him in a commerce that shocks humanity? Horrible embraces, frightful enjoyments, the knowledge of which should never have stained the disgusting pages of the history of human perversity!

—C. S. SONNINI

Infamous traveler Sir Richard Burton observes in his notes on the "Arabian Nights" that Sonnini left out an important detail: There was a strong superstitious belief that intercourse with a crocodile would act as the ultimate good luck "charm for rising to rank and riches."

The Painful Loves of Jean-Jacques Rousseau, 1720

While most memoirists paint flattering self-portraits, novelist/philosopher Jean-Jacques Rousseau (1712–1778) does just the opposite, by spotlighting his most humiliating and comic sexual escapades.

First Thrill

Jean-Jacques, an eight-year-old orphan, received his first spanking from thirty-year-old Mlle. Lambercier, who was taking care of him and his cousin Bernard:

I found in the pain and even in the shame a blend of sensuality that left me craving rather than fearing to feel it again from the same hand.

By the second spanking, Mlle. Lambercier realized that little Jean enjoyed it far too much:

Mademoiselle Lambercier undoubtedly perceived by some sign this penalty wasn't achieving its goal, and she declared she was giving it up because it was too strenuous. We had until then slept in her bedroom, and a few times during the winter even in her bed. Two days later, we were told to sleep in another room; I had from then on the honor, which I would certainly have forsaken, of being treated by her as a big boy.

Who would have thought this childhood punishment, received at the age of eight from the hand of a woman of thirty, would determine my tastes, my desires, my passions, my very being for the rest of my life, and set it in a direction precisely contrary to what it should have naturally followed?

Rousseau Exposes Himself to Ridicule, 1728

He's sixteen, a virgin, and very restless:

My aroused blood filled my brain with an incessant parade of girls and women; but since I wasn't familiar with the correct use for them, I kept them occupied acting out my bizarre fantasies [*i.e., spanking him*]—I didn't know anything else to do with them. . . .

My agitation grew to the point that, not being able to satisfy my desires, I instead stirred them up by perpetrating the most eccentric stunts. I used to go seek out dark alleys, hidden little nooks where I could expose myself from afar to women: in the position I would have wanted to be in if in reality I was ever near them. What they saw was not obscene, I would not have dreamed of that; what they saw was ridiculous. The foolish pleasure which I felt in exposing it [*i.e., Rousseau's derriere*] before their eyes cannot be described. It was only a short step from there for me to receive the desired treatment and I have no doubt that some hardy woman passing by would have eventually granted me the favor, if I had had the boldness to wait. But my folly created a catastrophe that was almost equally comic, though perhaps less amusing for me.

One day I went to station myself at the end of a courtyard with a well where servant girls frequently used to come for water. In the back there, a short stairwell led down to some cellars via several passageways. In the gloomy half-light, I investigated these underground passageways and finding them long and dark, I guessed that they ran on forever and that if I were seen and surprised, I could find a guaranteed safe haven. Backed by this confidence, I presented to the girls coming to the well a spectacle that was more laughable than seductive. The smarter ones pretended to see nothing; others began to laugh while yet others felt themselves insulted and started shouting. I ran off to my secret refuge; I was followed. I heard the voice of a man, which I hadn't expected, and which alarmed me. I raced deeper into underground passages, ever in danger of getting lost: the noise, the voices, the voice of a man, kept pursuing me always. I had counted on the darkness, I saw light. I trembled; I plunged deeper. A wall stopped me. I could go no further; I was forced to await my fate. In a moment I was caught and grabbed by a big man, with a big mustache and a big hat, a big sword, accompanied by four or five old women each armed with a broomstick. Among them, I noticed the little scamp who had betrayed me; she no doubt wanted to see my face.

The man with the sword grabbed me by the arm and harshly asked me what I was doing there. I had no pat answer ready; still, I recovered. Rallying myself at this critical moment, I spun a romantic excuse that saved me. I asked him, in a pleading voice, to take pity because of my age and my condition. I said that I was a stranger of noble birth whose brain was deranged, that I had escaped from my father's home because they wanted to lock me up, and that I would be ruined if he revealed me, but that if he would be kind enough to let me go, that someday perhaps I could repay his good deed. As unlikely as it may seem, my little speech and my demeanor convinced him; the terrifying man was touched. And after a short enough scolding, he gently let me go, without interrogating me further. But judging by the way the girl and the old women glowered at me as I left, I realized that the man whom I had so feared had actually been very useful to me, and that with just the women, I would not have gotten off so easily. I heard them muttering unintelligible things that I hardly cared about; because, thanks to the sword and the man they didn't meddle and I was quite certain, agile and vigorous as I was, that I could have saved myself from them and their broomsticks.

A Romantic, 1731

Rousseau, still a virgin at nineteen, was madly in love with the plump vivacious Mme. de Warens, who was ten years older than he.

I would never finish if I tried to recount in detail all the follies which thoughts of my sweet Madame caused me to commit when I wasn't in her presence. How many times have I kissed my bed day-dreaming about how she had slept there, kissed my curtains, my furniture, since they were hers and her beautiful hand had touched them, even the floor on which I prostrated myself musing that she had walked upon it! Several times even in her presence, I committed the most extravagant acts that only the most violent love could seem able to inspire.

One day, at the dinner table, just as she had put a piece in her mouth, I cried out that I had seen a hair in it; she spit out the morsel on her plate; I grabbed it eagerly and swallowed it. In a word, between me and the most passionate lover, there was only one single difference, but it was an essential one, and it rendered my condition almost inconceivable to a rational mind.

Rousseau called her "Mama"; she called him "little one." He was twenty-four; she was about thirty-five when she finally convinced him he was ready to lose his virginity:

I saw myself for the first time in the arms of a woman, and of a woman I adored. Was I happy? No, I tasted the pleasure. I don't know what unconquerable sadness poisoned its charm. I felt as though I was committing incest. Two or three times, in holding her with rapture in my arms, I flooded her breast with my tears. As for her, she was neither sad nor bubbly; she was caressing and calm. Since she wasn't very sensual and hadn't explored voluptuous pleasures, she felt neither joys nor did she have any regrets.

—JEAN-JACQUES ROUSSEAU

First Awakening of Love, 1738

Another French writer, Restif de la Bretonne (1734–1806), who wrote a book on utopian prostitution, had a fetish of a different sort. He reveals in his Calender *of lovers that it all started at age four:*

AGATHE TILDEN: Beautiful peasant of Sacy, dark, clean and who always had a blue ribbon to attach to her shoes. It was she who gave me, from the age of four, my first concept of a pretty foot. I used to love to see hers and I would touch and kiss her shoes, socks, stockings with pleasure—at the same time I had the greatest disgust for those of men and old women.

—RESTIF DE LA BRETONNE

Kidnapping Virgin Heiresses, 1727

Daniel Defoe (1660–1731), author of Robinson Crusoe, *also wrote* Conjugal Lewdness *(1727), in which he hyped the subject of heiresses duped or forced into marrying:*

The arts and tricks made use of to "trapan," and as it were, kidnap young women away into the hands of Brutes and Sharpers, were very scandalous, and it became almost dangerous for anyone to leave a fortune to the disposal of the person that was to enjoy it, and where it was so left, the young lady went always in danger of her life, she was watched, laid in wait for, and, as it were, besieged by a continual gang of Rogues, cheats, gamesters and such like starving crew, so that she was obliged to confine herself like a prisoner to her chamber, be locked and barred and bolted in, and have her eyes every moment upon the door, as if she was afraid of bailiffs and officers to arrest her; or else she was snatched up, seized upon, hurried up into a coach and six, a fellow dressed up in a clergyman's habit to perform the ceremony, and a pistol clapt to her breast to make her consent to be married: And thus the work was done. She was then carried to the private lodging, put to bed under the same awe of swords and pistols, a fellow that she never saw in her life and knows nothing of, comes to bed to her, deflowers her or, as may be well said, ravishes her, and the next day she is called a wife, and the fortune seized upon in the name of the husband, and perhaps, in a few days more, played all away at the box and dice, and the lady sent home again naked, and a beggar.

—DANIEL DEFOE

Casanova Loses His Virginity, 1741

Giacomo Casanova (1725–1798) was a man of extraordinary talents, many of them practiced outside the bedroom. Born in Venice, he was made an abbot at fifteen, earned his Doctor of Laws at sixteen, then renounced the Church and went on to become ambassador, poet, businessman, violinist, duel fighter, historian, and magician, to name a few professions. He conducted a national lottery for Louis XV of France, advised the Polish king on a business deal, left Spain under threat of death, and departed England under mountains of debt.

He certainly wooed his share of beautiful and powerful women, but he wasn't the ranking Lothario of his day. He was, however, the Lothario who wrote the best memoirs.

His twelve-volume autobiography paints perhaps the fullest picture of eighteenth-century Europe, and it reads like a thriller; his rooftop escape from the "Leads" prison in Venice tops any Indiana Jones adventure. However, here we focus on escape of a different sort: from virginity.

Casanova was sixteen in 1741 and was longing for one coquettish Angela, who agreed to meet him late one night. Her two young orphan cousins, aged fifteen and sixteen, acted as go-betweens, and much more:

Three quarters of an hour later, I heard the street door shut, and soon I saw Nanette and Marton appear before me.

"So where's Angela?" I said to Nanette.

"She must not have been able to come, or to let us know; nonetheless she has to know you are here."

"She thinks she has tricked me; and really I didn't expect it. But at least, you now know her true colors. She's just toying with me; she wins. She used you to trap me and she succeeded. But if she had come, I would have been the one who had toyed with her."

"Oh, please. Permit me to doubt that."

"I permit you to doubt nothing, pretty Nanette. You will be won over by the delightful night we are going to spend without her."

"That's to say, that being a clever fellow, you'll make do with the dregs; but you will sleep here, and we will sleep on the couch in the other room."

"I'm not stopping you, but that really would be a dirty trick; in any case, I don't plan on sleeping."

"What! You have the strength to pass seven hours alone with us? I am sure that when you run out of things to say, you will fall asleep."

"We'll see. But until then, here's some supplies. Would you be so cruel as to make me eat alone? Do you have any bread?"

"Yes. And we won't be cruel; we will eat a second dinner."

"It's you I should be in love with. Tell me, pretty Nanette, if I had a crush on you, as I had on Angela, would you have made me as unhappy as she did?"

"How could you even think of asking such a question? She's a ninny. All I can say to you, is that I know nothing about it."

They quickly set three places at the table, brought over

some bread, Parmesan cheese, and water, giggling at
everything, and soon we were eating. The Cyprian wine, which
they weren't accustomed to, went to their head, and their
gaiety became delicious. I was amazed, watching them, that I
had never recognized their qualities before.

After our little supper, which was delicious, seated between
the two of them, I lifted their hands to my lips and asked if
they were my true friends and if they approved of the
humiliating way Angela had treated me. They answered
together that they had spilled tears on my behalf.

"Then let me," I replied, "love you both like a brother, and
share my love as though you were my sisters. Let's give each
other pledges in the innocence of our hearts and let's swear
eternal fidelity."

The first kiss I gave them sprang neither from love nor the
desire to seduce. And on their part, they assured me a few
days later that they gave me a kiss only to convince me they
shared my honest feelings of brotherly affection.

But those innocent kisses didn't take long to flare up and
ignite in us a roaring fire which must have stunned us all
because we stopped a few seconds later and looked at each
other, completely amazed and very serious. They stood up
simply and I found myself alone with my thoughts.

It wasn't surprising that the fire that those kisses had
alighted in my soul and which raced through my veins had
caused me to fall madly in love with these lovable creatures.
They each were prettier than Angela, and Nanette with her
wit and Marton with her gentleness and naïveté were infinitely
superior to her.

I was surprised that I hadn't recognized their merits sooner,
but since these mademoiselles were noble and honest, the

fluke of fate that had tossed them in my hands must not be fatal for them. I wasn't silly enough to think they loved me, but I believed my kisses had had the same effect on them as theirs had on me. With this logic, I could clearly see that by using tricks and twists unknown to them, it would not be difficult during the course of the long night together, to make them consent to certain pleasures whose end results could prove very decisive for them.

That thought sickened me and I imposed on myself the strictest law to treat them with respect, never doubting that I would have the force needed to observe it.

The moment they re-appeared, I saw on their faces signs of trust and contentment, and I quickly gave myself the same outward polish, quite determined not to expose myself again to the ardour of their kisses.

We spent an hour talking of Angela and I told them I felt determined not to see her again, convinced as I was that she didn't love me.

"She loves you," naive Marton told me, "and I'm sure of it; but if you're not thinking of marrying her, you would do well to break it off completely with her, because she has decided not to give you even one single kiss so long as you're not her fiancé. You must choose: either drop her or count on her never granting you anything."

"You reason like an angel, but how can you be sure she loves me?"

"I'm very sure of it, and in the fraternal friendship we've sworn, I can tell you how. When Angela sleeps with us, she kisses me tenderly and calls me her 'darling Abbot.'" [*Casanova had been recently ordained.*]

At these words, Nanette burst out laughing, then covered

her mouth with her hand, but Marton's naïveté charmed me so I had trouble controlling myself.

Marton said to Nanette that since I was such a man of the world, it was impossible that I didn't know what happens when young girls sleep together.

"Of course," I rushed to say, "no one's in the dark about that silliness, and I can't believe, my dear Nanette, you find this friendly secret sharing of your sister's overly indiscreet."

"What's done is done, but this is the sort of thing you just don't tell. If Angela ever knew!"

"She would be crushed. But Marton showed such a sign of friendship that I will be grateful to her until death. Besides, it's over: I detest Angela, and I will never mention her again. She is a phoney. She plotted only my ruin."

"But if she loved you, she wasn't wrong to want you for a husband."

"Agreed. But she thinks only of herself. If she loved me, and knew how I am suffering, how could she act this way? Meanwhile, to calm her own desires, she simply used her imagination with the charming Marton who quite willingly acted as her husband."

At these words, Nanette's bursts of laughter redoubled, but I remained quite serious and continued to speak to her sister in the same tone, pronouncing an ode to her sincerity. I said to her finally that without a doubt the laws of returning favors must have required Angela to play her husband as well, but she said Angela was only Nanette's husband and Nanette had to agree.

"But who does Nanette in her moments of passion call her husband?"

"Nobody knows anything about him."

"You do love someone then, Nanette?"

"Yes, but no one will find out my secret."

This deep secrecy suggested to me that I might be part of that secret and that Nanette was the rival of Angela. So seductive a conversation made me little by little lose the urge to spend a passion-free night with these two charming girls made for love.

"I am very happy," I told them, "to feel for you only the feelings of friendship, because without that I would find it very hard to spend the night with you, without being tempted to give you proofs of my affection and to receive some in return. Both of you are gorgeous and made to turn the heads of every man you meet."

And continuing to speak that way, I pretended to want to go to sleep. Nanette, noticing it first, said to me:

"Don't try to hide it; go to bed: we will go to the other room and sleep on the couch."

"I would consider myself," I told them, "the rudest of men if I allowed that. Let's chat some more. The urge to sleep will pass; I'm only worried about you. You go to sleep, and I, my charming friends, will go into the other room. If you're afraid of me, lock yourselves in, but you would be mistaken because I love you only with brotherly affection."

"We would never do that," Nanette told me. "But you let yourself be persuaded; sleep here."

"I can't sleep in my clothes."

"Take your clothes off. We won't look at you."

"I wasn't worried about that, but I could never fall asleep knowing you had to stay up because of me."

"We will go to sleep too," Marton told me, "but without getting undressed."

"That's an insult to my honor. Tell me, Nanette. Do you think I'm an honorable man?"

"Yes, certainly."

"Well then, you must convince me, and to do that, sleep on either side of me, completely undressed, and count on my word of honor that I will not touch you. What's more, you are two against one: what do you have to fear? Will you not be able to leave the bed if I stop being wise? In short, if you do not consent to give me this mark of confidence, at least once you see that I'm asleep, otherwise I will not go to sleep at all."

Then, I stopped talking and pretended to drift off. They whispered to each other. Marton told me to go to sleep and that once they saw me asleep, they would come to bed. Nanette confirmed this promise, then I turned my back to them, undressed, and after wishing them "Goodnight," I went to bed. As soon as I was in bed, I pretended to fall asleep, but soon real sleep overcame me, and I didn't wake up until they had just climbed into bed. I rolled over as though to go back to sleep, I remained motionless until I was certain they had fallen asleep, and if they weren't, it was their choice to pretend.

They both had turned their backs toward me, and the light was extinguished. I acted purely by chance and offered my first homages to the one on my right, not knowing whether it was Nanette or Marton. I found her all tucked in a ball, and covered in the single garment she had kept on. Without badgering her and carefully protecting her modesty, I gradually put her in a position where she had to admit defeat, with her best option left to continue pretending to be asleep and let me do what I wanted. Soon, the animal Nature within set her to move in rhythm with me, and I attained my goal and my efforts crowned with obvious success left me no doubt that

I had obtained those first fruits to which the prejudice forces us to attach such importance. Thrilled to have savoured a pleasure that I had just experienced completely for the first time, I gently left my lovely one to deliver to the other a new tribute of my ardor. I found her motionless, sleeping on her back, in a deep and tranquil sleep. Managing the approach as though I was afraid of waking her, I started by caressing her senses, assuring myself that she was as much a novice as her sister; and as soon as a natural movement made me feel that love invited the offering, I set myself to consummate the sacrifice. Then she, yielding suddenly to the passionate feelings stirring within her and as though tired of the play-acting she had adopted, she held me tightly in her arms at the moment of the crisis, covered me in kisses and matched me transport for transport and love flooded our souls with an equal rapture.

By these signs, I knew it had to be Nanette; I told her so.

"Yes, it's me," she said. "And I consider myself as happy as my sister if you remain honorable and faithful."

"Until death, my angels. And since everything we have done is the handiwork of love, let there no longer be any question of Angela among us."

I begged them to get up and light the candles; but Marton, so agreeable, got up immediately and left us alone. When I saw Nanette in my arms animated by the fire of love, and Marton near to us, a candle in her hand, looking at us as though accusing us of being ingrates for not saying anything to her since she had been the first one to surrender herself to my caresses, I felt completely happy.

"Let us all get up, my friends," I told them, "and let's swear a vow of eternal friendship."

As soon as we were up, we started washing ourselves, which set all of us laughing, and which revived our passion; then in the costume of the Golden Age, we finished the leftovers from our supper. Afterwards, we said a hundred things in the drunkenness of our senses that only love can interpret, then we climbed back into bed and the most delicious of nights was spent in reciprocal proofs of our ardor. It was Nanette who received the last proof of my affection. Since Madame Orio had left for mass, I was obliged to rush away, swearing that they had extinguished in my heart all feelings for Angela. Once I reached home, I went straight to bed and slept the most peaceful sleep until dinnertime.

—GIACOMO CASANOVA

Benjamin Franklin Recommends Older Women, 1745

Benjamin Franklin (1706–1790), son of a poor candlemaker, became a world-class inventor and a Founding Father. Here is a letter of advice he once wrote to a young acquaintance:

June 25, 1745, Philadelphia

My dear Friend:

I know of no medicine fit to diminish the violent natural inclinations you mention, and if I did, I think I should not communicate it to you. Marriage is the proper remedy. It is the most natural state of man, and therefore the state in which you are most likely to find solid happiness. Your reasons against entering into it at present appear to me

not well founded. The circumstantial advantages you
have in view by postponing it are not only uncertain, but
they are small in comparison with that of the thing itself,
the being married and settled. It is the man and woman
united that make the complete human being. Separate,
she wants his force of body and strength of reason; he,
her softness, sensibility, and acute discernment.
Together they are more likely to succeed in the world. A
single man has not nearly the value he would have in the
state of union. He is an incomplete animal. He
resembles the odd half of a pair of scissors. If you get a
prudent healthy wife, your industry in your profession,
with her good economy, will be a fortune sufficient.

But if you will <u>not</u> take this counsel and persist in
thinking a commerce with the sex inevitable, then I
repeat my former advice, that in all your amours you
should prefer older women to young ones.

You call this a paradox and demand my reasons. They
are these:

1) Because they have more knowledge of the world
and their minds are better stored with observations,
their conversation is more improving and more lastingly
agreeable.

2) Because when women cease to be handsome they
study to be good. To maintain their influence over men,
they supply the diminution of beauty by an
augmentation of utility. They learn to do a thousand
services small and great, and are the most tender and
useful of friends when you are sick. Thus they continue
amiable. And there is hardly such a thing to be found as
an old woman who is not a good woman.

3) Because there is no hazard of children, which irregularly produced may be attended with much inconvenience.

4) Because through more experience they are more prudent and discreet in conducting an intrigue to prevent suspicion. The commerce with them is therefore safer with regard to your reputation. And with regard to theirs, if the affair should happen to be known, considerate people might be rather inclined to excuse an old woman, who would kindly take care of a young man, form his manners by good counsels, and prevent his ruining his health and fortune among mercenary prostitutes.

5) Because in every animal that walks upright the deficiency of the fluids that fills the muscles appears first in the highest part. The face first grows lank and wrinkled; then the neck; then the breast and arms; the lower parts continuing to the last as plump as ever: so that covering all above with a basket, and regarding only what is below the girdle, it is impossible of two women to tell an old one from a young one. And as in the dark all cats are gray, the pleasure of corporal enjoyment with an old woman is at least equal, and frequently superior; every knack being, by practice, capable of improvement.

6) Because the sin is less. The debauching a virgin may be her ruin, and make her unhappy for life.

7) Because the compunction is less. The having made a young girl miserable may give you frequent bitter reflection; none of which can attend making an old woman happy.

8th and lastly. They are so grateful!

Thus much for my paradox. But still I advise you to
marry directly; being sincerely
Your affectionate friend,
Benjamin Franklin

A Terrifying Case of Priapism, 1758

*Medical books written around this time were sometimes a
collection of case histories, such as the following:*

A doctor named Chauvel had been called in 1758 to
Caderousse, a little town near his home, to see a man struck by
priapism. At the doorway of the house, he found the wife of the
sick man, who complained bitterly about her husband's demonic
lust. She said that he had mounted her forty times in a single
night, and that he always has an erection. The woman then
showed the doctor her husband's erection so that he might be
able to prescribe some cure to bring down the swelling.

Her husband's problems stemmed from a cantharide
potion, given to him by a woman who runs a clinic for curing
tierce fever which afflicted him. But he fell into such a frenzy
from it that they had to tie him up as though he were
possessed by the devil. The local vicar came to exorcize him,
even while Dr. Chauvel was there. The patient begged them
both to let him die in pleasure. The women folded him in a
sheet moistened with water and vinegar and left him until the
next day.

When they came back to check on him, they found his
furious lust had finally abated and disappeared. That's because
he was dead, stiff as a corpse. And in his gaping mouth, they
saw his teeth and his gangrenous penis.

—PABROL, *OBSERVATIONS ANATOMIQUES*

Buggery on the High Seas, 1762

Winston Churchill once reportedly groused to an admiral in the Royal Navy: "Don't talk to me about naval tradition; it's nothing but rum, sodomy, and the lash." During the following court martial, the main witness, seaman Joshua James, testified to observing this behavior:

They were behind a chest, Martin Billin with his face to the chest & James Bryan's belly to Martin Billin's back. I then threw myself down on the chest and run my hand, down between the forepart of Bryan & the hinder part of Billin; Billin's breeches were about half down his thigh, & Bryan's trousers were down on his knees. I laid hold of Bryan's yard & pulled it out of Billin's fundament. . . .

More questions during the court martial:

Q: When you had Bryan's yard in your hand, did you observe whether there had been any emission from it?

A: I cannot tell whether there was any emission but my hand was moist after handling it.

Q: By what means are you sure Bryan's yard had penetrated the body of Billin?

A: Because as I laid hold of part of his yard, the other part came out with a spring, as if a cork had been drawn out of a bottle.

—ADMIRALTY COURT RECORDS QUOTED IN *BUGGERY AND THE BRITISH NAVY*, BY ARTHUR GILBERT

The court chose not to impose the death penalty. Bryan and Billin were each sentenced to receive one thousand lashes.

Thomas Jefferson

As a kind of footnote to the above item, here's what Jefferson came up with as a punishment for sodomy when he was working on a revision of the Virginia law code. His suggestion was considered liberal compared to the death penalty.

June 18, 1779

Whosoever shall be guilty of Rape, Polygamy, or Sodomy with man or woman shall be punished; if a man, by castration, if a woman, by cutting through the cartilage of her nose a hole of one half inch in diameter at the least.

However, the statute was never passed into law.

James Boswell: Young Lust and Rousseau's Mistress, *circa* 1763

James Boswell (1740–1795) is probably the best known biographer in the English language ("Every Johnson needs his Boswell"). However, before he chose Samuel Johnson for his subject, he considered doing Rousseau instead. And Boswell might have chronicled the famed Frenchman, if not for an encounter with Rousseau's mistress over a five-day trip from Paris to London in 1766.

First, here's a glimpse of the amorous side of young Boswell:

Safe Sex

March 31, 1763, Boswell's journal

At night I strolled into the park and took the first whore I met, whom I, without many words, copulated with free from danger, being safely sheathed. She was ugly and lean and her breath smelt of spirits. I never asked her name. When it was done, she slunk off. I had a low opinion of this gross practice and resolved to do it no more.

London Pickup

May 19, 1763, Boswell's journal

I then sallied forth to the Piazzas in rich flow of animal spirits and burning with fierce desire. I met two very pretty little girls who asked me to take them with me.

"My dear girls," said I, "I am a poor fellow. I can give you no money. But if you choose to have a glass of wine and my company and let us be gay and obliging to each other without money, I am your man." They agreed with great good humour. So back to the Shakespeare I went.

"Waiter," said I, "I have got here a couple of human beings; I don't know how they'll do."

"I'll look, your honor," cried he, and with inimitable effrontery stared them in the face and then cried, "They'll do very well."

"What," said I, "are they good fellow-creatures? Bring them up, then."

We were shown into a good room and had a bottle of sherry before us in a minute. I surveyed my seraglio and found them both good subjects for amorous play. I toyed with them and drank about and sung "Youth's the Season" [*from "The Beggar's Opera"*] and thought myself Captain Macheath; and then I solaced my existence with them, one after the other, according to their seniority. I was quite "raised," as the phrase is: thought I was in a London tavern, the Shakespeare's Head, enjoying high debauchery after my sober winter. I parted with my ladies politely and came home in a glow of spirits.

Rousseau and His Longtime Companion, Thérèse

The twenty-four-year-old Boswell made a pilgrimage to visit the fifty-two-year-old Rousseau.

December 4, 1764, Boswell's diary

Mademoiselle [*Thérèse Le Vasseur, forty-four years old*] always accompanies me to the door. She said, "I have been twenty-two years with Monsieur Rousseau; I would not give up my place to be Queen of France. I try to profit by the good advice he gives me. If he should die, I shall have to go into a convent." She is a very good girl, and deserves to be esteemed for her constancy to a man so valuable. His simplicity is beautiful. He consulted Mademoiselle and her mother on the merits of his [*novels*] "Héloïse" and his "Émile."

Boswell's letter to Rousseau, January 4, 1766:

I am told you are going to England. What a wonderful prospect for me! I am sure there is no man on earth more keenly disposed to contribute to your happiness than I, and you will be sure of it too.

When Rousseau reached England, Boswell happened to be in Paris, and so was Rousseau's own Thérèse Le Vasseur. They agreed to travel together, but before they left, Boswell found out his mother had died.

January 31, 1766

Yesterday morning after having been up all night and written sixteen or seventeen letters, and felt spirits bound in veins, kept post-horses waiting from six till nine, then was still in confusion. Cried, "Is it possible that my mother is dead?" Set out and at Hotel de Luxembourg took up Mademoiselle. Was serious and composed. . . . Now and then thought mother was alive and gave starts. Night was manly, but hurt by Mademoiselle's mean kindness to servants, &c. Talked much of Rousseau always.

Seduction and Censorship

Sir William Forbes, a prudish executor of Boswell's estate, tore out the next twelve pages and inserted a slip of paper, marked "Reprehensible Passage." Fortunately, the buyer, Col. Ralph Isham, had read them, and his recollection of the eroto-comic episode formed the basis for the following account by editors Frank Brady and Frederick Pottle.

February 1–11, 1766

It does not appear that before leaving Paris Boswell had formed any scheme of seducing Thérèse, and the day of his departure found him tense and harassed by difficulties in getting started, and deeply unhappy over his mother's death.

But the intimacy of travel and the proximity in which the pair found themselves at inns at night precipitated an intrigue almost immediately. On the second night out they shared the same bed; Boswell's first attempt, as often with him, was a fiasco. He was deeply humiliated, the grief he was trying to repress came back upon him, and he wept. Thérèse, with a Frenchwoman's tenderness and sympathy, put her arm around him to console him and laid his hand on her shoulder. His grief and embarrassment waned; as he recorded on another occasion, his powers were excited and he felt himself vigorous. Next day, he was very proud of himself, and in the coach, he congratulated Thérèse (who was almost twenty years his senior) on her good fortune in having at last experienced the ardours of a Scotch lover. Thérèse stunned him by denying that she had great cause for gratitude: "I allow," she said, "that you are a hardy and vigorous lover, but you have no art." Then, with quick perception seeing him cast down, she went on, "I did not mean to hurt you. You are young, you can learn. I myself will give you your first lesson in the art of love."

Since Boswell's success as a lover depended on his maintaining a feeling of superiority, this announcement filled him with terror. The apartment in which they were lodged that night was in the shape of an L: a private dining room with a bed in an alcove at one end. As bedtime approached, he grew more frightened. In the earlier period of his life, as the journal printed in the present volume shows, he drank little, but on this occasion he secured from the servant a full bottle of wine and concealed it in the dining room. Thérèse retired; Boswell remained reading. Thérèse called him; he went in clutching the wine, but instead of joining her, he paced up and down asking questions about Rousseau. At last, when no further diversion would avail, he drained the bottle and reluctantly slipped into bed.

He gave some details of her instruction. He must be gentle though ardent; he must not hurry. She asked him, as a man who had traveled much, if he had not noticed how many things were achieved by men's hands. He made good technical progress, though he was not wholly persuaded of her right to set up for a teacher; he said she rode him "agitated, like a bad rider galloping downhill." After a while her lectures bored him, and he brought up the subject of Rousseau, hoping at least to gather a few "dicta philosophi" [*words of the philosopher*] for his journal. Thérèse in her turn found that dull. It was a mistake, he finally reflected, to get involved with an old man's mistress.

A Baker's Dozen

The journal resumes.

February 12, 1766, Dover

Yesterday morning had gone to bed very early, and had done it once: thirteen in all. Was really affectionate to her. . . . Mademoiselle was much fatigued. Came to London about six. . . . Carried her to David Hume.

A Big Hug With . . .

(Boswell addresses himself in the second person here.)

February 13, 1766

Then went to Mlle. Le Vasseur, with whom was Hume. You breakfasted, and then carried her out to Chiswick. . . . You gave her word of honour you would not mention "affaire" till after her death or that of the philosopher. Went to Rousseau; delivered her over. "Quanta oscula" [*such kissing*] &c.! He seemed so oldish and weak you had no longer your enthusiasm for him. Told him all about Corsica and he cried, "Pardi! I am sorry not to have gone there." He was incited by what he heard. He was to go to Wales. You asked if Scotland had not a claim to him. He said, "I shall act like the kings; I shall put my body in one place, and my heart in another."

Back to London. Immediately to Johnson; received you with open arms. You kneeled, and asked blessing. Miss Williams glad of your return. When she went out, he hugged you to him like a sack, and grumbled, "I hope we shall pass many years of regard."

—JAMES BOSWELL

Turned out to be a bit of an understatement.

British Sailors Barter for Sex in Tahiti, 1767

Capt. Samuel Wallis landed the first European ship at Tahiti. After a few armed skirmishes, the British settled into friendly trading relations with the islanders. The sailors were quite pleased to discover that the Tahitian women preferred iron nails to gold and silver.

The women are all handsome, and some of them are extremely beautiful. Chastity does not seem to be considered as a virtue among them, for they not only readily and openly trafficked with our people for personal favors, but were brought down by their fathers and brothers for that purpose;

they were, however, conscious of the value of beauty, and the size of the nail that was demanded for the enjoyment of the lady, was always in proportion to her charms. The men who came down to the side of the river, at the same time that they presented the girl, shewed a stick the size of the nail that was to be her price, and if our people agreed she was sent over to them, for the men were not permitted to cross the river. The commerce was carried on a considerable time before our officers discovered it; for while some straggled a little way to receive the lady, the others kept a look-out. . . . I no longer wondered that the ship was in danger of being pulled to pieces for the nails and iron that held her together.

—JOURNAL OF CAPT. SAMUEL WALLIS

We pick up the story in the journal of the ship's master, George Robertson:

Shore Leave Canceled

July 21, 1767

The carpenter came and told me every cleat in the ship was drawn, and the nails carried off. At the same time, the boatswain informed me that most of the hammock nails was drawn and two-thirds of the men obliged to lie on the deck for want of nails to hang their hammocks, I immediately stopped the liberty men and called all hands, and let them know that no man in the ship should have liberty to go ashore until they informed me who drew the nails and cleats.

—GEORGE ROBERTSON

The officers were angry for another reason as well: the stolen nails had caused inflation in the marketplace. The Brits used to be able to buy a twenty-pound pig for one three-inch nail; now the price had tripled. And the crew was angry because some of the sailors had been overpaying (with giant spikes), spoiling it for the guys with only two-inchers to offer.

Kangaroo Court

Ship's master Robertson sneaked below deck.

July 21, 1767, nighttime

I observed a great murmuring amongst the people. I therefore stepped forward to see if I could find who had drawn the nails and cleats. At this time, the galley was full addressing their suppers and some blamed one, some another. It being dark none of them observed me. Therefore with their mind plain, at last I found out that most of them was [*involved*], and several said they had rather receive a dozen lashes than have their liberty stopped. At last there was a trial among them, and six were condemned for spoiling the old trade by giving large spike nails, when others had only a hammock nail, which three declared was refused, they being much smaller [*than*] the spikes.

But two [*sailors*] cleared themselves by proving that they got double value for the spikes. After that a battle ensued, about the one interfering with the other in the way of trade. That obliged me to call out, "What was the matter?" and all was quiet immediately.

The sailors offered up a scapegoat as three witnesses accused a "poor" convicted thief named Francis Pinckney of stealing a cleat. He had to run the gauntlet three times around the ship, being flogged with nettles by the sailors.

I acquainted the whole [*crew*] that if any such complaint [*of stolen nails*] came again, they might rely on a much severer punishment and none of them would ever be allowed to go on liberty anymore. Then they all declared to a man that they should take great care that no such thing should ever be done again.

—George Robertson

The Real-Life Crimes of the Marquis de Sade, 1768

The name Marquis de Sade (1740–1814) has come to stand for cruelty, vicious rough sex, for deriving pleasure from inflicting pain. One gets the image of this fiend wielding the whip and red-hot poker from morning till night in some castle, the screams echoing up the stone staircases while he laughs and downs glass after glass of vintage brandy. Actually, de Sade's criminal reputation rests mainly upon three incidents (the Rose Keller whipping, the Spanish Fly poisoning, and the kidnapped virgins). He dreamed up the rest of the foul deeds during his twenty-seven years in prisons and put them into his novels. De Sade once indignantly wrote to his wife: "Madam, I may be a libertine but I am neither a criminal nor a murderer."

Rose Keller: "Doctor" de Sade

This first contemporary account of de Sade's crime was contained in a letter from French arts patron Mme. du

*Deffand to English author Horace Walpole, written nine days
after the incident:*

Paris, April 12, 1768

. . . Here is a tragic and very unusual story:

A certain Count de Sade, nephew of the abbot and
"Petrarch" author, encountered on Tuesday of Easter
Week a tall well-proportioned woman, thirty years old,
who begged for some charity from him; he asked her
many questions, displayed much interest, proposed to
pluck her from her misery, and to make her
housekeeper of a little country home he had outside
Paris. That woman accepted; he told her to meet him
there the following morning; she did. He first conducted
her throughout all the rooms in the house, in all the
nooks and crannies, and then he led her to the attic.
Once there, he locked himself in with her, ordered her
to strip naked; she resisted this request, threw herself at
his feet, said to him that she was an honest woman; he
showed her a pistol which he drew from his pocket, and
told her to obey, which she did immediately. Then, he
tied her up and cruelly whipped her; when she was
bleeding everywhere, he drew a bottle of ointment from
his pocket, dressed her wounds and left her. I do not
know whether he fed her or gave anything to drink, but
he did not see her again till the following morning; he
examined her wounds, and saw that the ointment had
delivered the expected results. Then, he took out a
penknife and slashed her entire body. He then took
more of the same ointment and covered all her wounds,

and went away. That despairing woman figured out a way to break her bonds and jumped out of a window overlooking the street. It's unclear whether she hurt herself falling; a crowd gathered around her; the police lieutenant was informed; Monsieur de Sade was arrested; he is, it's said, at the castle in Saumur; no one knows what's going to happen with this incident, and whether the punishment will be limited to this [*imprisonment*]—which is quite possible since he comes from a powerful and respectable family; it's said the motive for the horrible crime was to test out his ointment.

April 13, 11 A.M.

. . . Since yesterday I heard the rest about Monsieur de Sade. The village where his country house is located, is Arcueil. He whipped and slashed the unfortunate woman the same day, and immediately he put some salve on her wounds and flayed skin; he untied her hands, wrapped her in lots of linen and laid her down on a good bed. As soon as she was alone, she made use of her arms and bedsheets to save herself via the window; the judge at Arcueil told her to take her complaints to the Procurer-General and police lieutenant. The latter went looking for de Sade, who far from disavowing and blushing at his crime, claimed to have done a noble deed, and to have rendered a great service to humanity by discovering a salve which heals wounds on the spot; it is true that it did achieve that result on that woman. She dropped her complaints, apparently in exchange for some money. Thus there's every reason to believe he will be freed from prison.

De Sade spent seven months in prison.

The Spanish Fly Bon Bons

In 1772, de Sade eloped with his wife's sister, ensuring the eternal enmity of his powerful mother-in-law. This contemporary account was in M. de Bachaumont's Secret Memoirs:

July 25, 1772

Someone writes from Marseille that Count de Sade—who was so notorious in 1768 for the mad horrors to which he subjected a girl, under the pretext of testing ointments—has just provided that city with a spectacle, which at first was very pleasant but wound up terrifying in its final outcome. He gave a ball, where he had invited lots of people, and for dessert he served them chocolate pastilles, so delicious that many people devoured several. The candies were everywhere and no one could miss them; but he had mixed in powdered "Spanish fly." The attributes of this drug are well known. Anyone who had eaten some started to burn with a shameless ardor and unleashed themselves to commit the most excessive acts of brutal lust. The ball degenerated into one of those lewd orgies notorious among the Romans: even the most modest women couldn't resist the uterine fire that raged through them. It's thus that M. de Sade sported with his sister-in-law, with whom he fled to save himself from his just punishment. Several people died from the excesses which they indulged in during their fearful priapism, and others are still suffering from the after-effects.

De Sade was sentenced to death in absentia by the Parliament at Aix on September 11, 1772, charged with sodomy and poisoning. (Most de Sade scholars claim that there was no grand ball, but rather a small orgy of prostitutes and that no one died.) Thanks to several escapes and a shrewd lawyer, he stayed mostly out of prison until 1777, when his outraged mother-in-law pulled strings to have him locked up for good. He wrote a long letter to his wife, defending himself regarding those two incidents and a third, which took place at the castle at La Coste in 1775.

De Sade's Self-defense

February 20, 1781, Vincennes Prison

To Madame de Sade

. . . Seeing myself reduced to passing time alone in a very remote castle, almost always without your company and suffering from the trifling weakness (I must confess) of being a little too fond of women, I applied to a very well-known procuress in Lyon and said, "I want to take three or four servant girls home with me; I want them young and pretty; supply me with them." The said procuress, Nanon, for Nanon was the recognized procuress in Lyon—I will prove it when proof is required—promises me the girls and sends them. I go off with them; I use them. Six months later, some parents come to demand their return, assuring me that they are their children. I give them back; and suddenly a charge of abduction and rape is brought against me. It is a monstrous injustice. The law on this point is. . . . It is expressly forbidden in France for any procuress to supply virgin maidens, and if the girl supplied is a virgin and lodges a complaint, it is not the man who is charged, but the procuress who is punished severely on the spot. But even if the male offender has requested a virgin, he is not liable to punishment: he is merely doing what all men do. It is, I repeat, the procuress who provided him with the girl and who is perfectly aware that she is expressly forbidden to do so, who is guilty.

Therefore, this first charge against me in Lyon of abduction and rape, was entirely illegal. I have committed no offense. It is the procuress to whom I applied who is liable to punishment—not I. But they cannot get anything out of the procuress and the girls' parents hope to extract some money from me. Let's pass on.

Originally, I had an adventure at Arcueil, in which a woman [*i.e., Rose Keller*], who proved both a liar and a cheat, had, with the purpose of gaining money (which was foolishly paid), spread the rumor all over Paris that I was carrying out experiments and that my garden was a graveyard in which I buried the corpses which I had used for my purposes.

The rumor was only too useful: it served my enemies' fury too well for them not to resist the temptation to dish it up in every shape in any matters that might concern me.

As a result, in the Marseilles affair it was, of course,

another of my "experiments" . . . and also an experiment
carried out on girls who were destined to disappear. But
if they have not all reappeared in Lyon, they have not
failed to turn up in other parts of the world.

*De Sade traces the whereabouts of each girl, and then goes
on to defend himself from more charges, such as the abortion
formula found in his wallet ("never used it"), and the bones
with which he decorated a room ("just a prank"). Near the end
of this long letter, he sums up his philosophy.*

I am guilty of nothing more than simple libertinage;
such as it is practiced by all men, more or less according
to their natural temperaments or tendencies. Every man
has his weaknesses; comparisons are odious: my gaolers
themselves would perhaps not gain by a parallel.

Yes, I admit that I am a libertine; I have devised
everything that can be done in that line, but I have not
practised all that I have devised and I never intend to
do so.

I may be a libertine, but I am neither a criminal nor a
murderer. . . .

*De Sade desperately hoped his wife could free him from
prison. He closed with a flourish:*

You will reread [*this letter*] and you will see that the one
who will love you to the grave wished to sign it with his
blood.

De Sade

*A year later, when writing to a female friend, Marie-
Dorothée de Rousset, de Sade puts a bit of a different spin on
his memories. He's describing a former servant:*

April 17, 1782

Despite all her faults, Gothon was attached to me. She gave pleasant, prompt, nimble service; she was a good mare and loved her master's stud. This poor wench . . . would have provided a complete household. In truth, I miss her.

Furthermore, I should add, yes, now that we have been discussing virtues, we can consider physical qualities: Gothon had, it is claimed, the loveliest "c——." Devil take me, how am I to explain? The dictionary lacks a synonym for this word, and decency forbids me to write it in full even though it is only a four-letter word. Oh, well, yes, truly, mademoiselle, it was the most fetching "c——" that ever escaped from the mountains of Switzerland for more than a century. . . .

But I perceive [*by mentioning all this*] that I am in danger of forgetting a famous proverb: "You should never mention rope in the house of a hanged man." And that I should not therefore be occupying my mind with these immodest objects since it's claimed that my attachment to them has been responsible for all my misfortunes.

De Sade was jailed in the Bastille but missed being freed during the dramatic storming there on July 14, 1789, during the French Revolution. He had recently been transferred to a mental hospital because on July 2 he had used a voice trumpet to inform passers-by about the sexual habits of the governor of the prison.

He died at Charenton mental hospital in 1814.

Voltaire: Curmudgeon Views on Sex, 1769

Voltaire (1694–1778) had such a great talent for satire that he spent much of his life forced to live outside of France. He's probably best known in America for Candide, *his spoof of blind optimism. In his* Dictionaire Philosophique *(1769), he takes a contrarian view to some conventional wisdom:*

On Semen

What do you want to do with a precious liquid formed by Nature for the propagation of the human species? If you just squander it recklessly, it can kill you; if you keep it all bottled up, that too can kill you.

On Masturbation

It's been observed that men and monkeys are the only animals that masturbate.

On Birching

It's shameful and horrible that such a punishment is inflicted upon the buttocks of young girls and boys. It used to be the punishment of slaves. I have seen in colleges some barbarians strip the children almost naked and then a ghoul, often drunk, whips them with long rods, causing bleeding and horrible swelling. Then again, others spank them with a certain gentleness, which leads to an inconvenience of a different sort. The two nerves traveling from the sphincter to the pubis become irritated and bring on orgasms; this often happens with young girls.

Right of the First Night

Voltaire examines the notorious custom that allowed powerful men the right to take virgin brides to bed before their husbands:

. . . It is astonishing that in Christian Europe a kind of feudal law for a long time existed, or at least was deemed a customary usage, to regard the virginity of the female vassal as the property of the Lord. The first night of the nuptials of the daughter of this "vilain" [*tenant farmer*] belonged to him without dispute.

This right was established in the same manner as that of walking with a falcon on his fist, or of being saluted with incense at mass. The lords, indeed, did not enact that the wives of their "vilains" belonged to them; they confined themselves to the daughters; the reason of which is obvious. Girls are bashful and sometimes might exhibit reluctance. This however yielded at once to the majesty of laws, when the condescending baron deemed them worthy of personally enforcing the custom.

It is undoubted that some abbots and bishops enjoyed this privilege in their capacity as temporal lords; and it is not very long since that these prelates compounded their prerogative for acknowledgments in money, to which they have just as much right as to the virginity of the girls.

But let it be well remarked that this excess of tyranny was never sanctioned by any public law. If a lord or a prelate had cited before a tribunal a girl affianced to one of his vassals, in claim of her quit-rent, he would doubtless have lost his cause with court costs.

Let us seize this occasion to rest assured, that no partially civilized people ever established formal laws against morals. I do not believe a single instance can be furnished. Abuses creep in and are borne: they pass as customs and travelers mistake them for fundamental laws. It is said that in Asia greasy Mahomettan saints march in procession entirely naked and that devout females crowd round them to kiss that part which is not worthy to be named; but I defy any one to discover a passage in the Koran which justifies this brutality.

The phallum, which the Egyptians carry in procession, may be quoted, in order to confound me, as well as the idol Jaggernaut, of the Indians. I reply that these ceremonies war no more against morals than circumcision at the age of eight days. In some of our towns, the holy foreskin has been borne in procession; and it is preserved yet in certain sacristies, without this piece of drollery causing the least disturbance in families. Still, I am convinced that no council or act of parliament ever ordained this homage to the holy foreskin.

I call a public law which deprives me of my property, which takes away my wife and gives her to another, a law against morals. And I am certain that such a law is impossible.

Some travelers maintain that in Lapland, husbands, out of politeness, make an offer of their wives. Out of still greater politeness, I believe them; but I nevertheless assert that they never found this rule of good manners in the legal code of Lapland, any more than in the constitutions of Germany, in the ordinances of the kings of France, or in the "statutes at large" of England, any positive law adjudging the right of "cuissage" [*first night*] to the barons.

Absurd and barbarous laws may be found everywhere; formal laws against morals nowhere.

—VOLTAIRE

Catherine the Great and Her Young Lovers, 1770s

No, she did not die when the harness broke, while having sex with some stallion in a barn.

Catherine the Great (1727–1796) didn't love horses, she loved officers in the Imperial Horse Guard, handsome young ones. Over time, this passionate woman developed a system whereby her close confidante (either Countess Bruce or Mlle. Protassov) would act as "eprouveuse," or "court tester," and sample the love-making skills of the chosen young man; then British Dr. Rogerson would examine him. If he passed both tests, he was installed as the favorite and would usually last a year or two and earn tens of thousands of rubles, and property and serfs.

Did Catherine deserve her reputation as possibly the lustiest female monarch of all time? Hardly. She had only twelve lovers over a forty-four-year period. What might have shocked some was that her last, Plato Zubof, was twenty-one, when Catherine was in her sixties.

Potemkin

The love of Catherine's life was Gregory Potemkin, who graduated to be her chief minister and, in later years, her chief procurer of young men.

Letters of Catherine to Potemkin, 1774

Sweetheart, what funny stories you told me yesterday. I haven't stopped laughing thinking about them. What happy moments I spend with you! We stay together four

hours without a shadow of boredom and I always leave
you against my will. My dear little pigeon, I love you
very much; you are handsome, intelligent, amusing. I
forget the entire world when I'm with you. I have never
been as happy as right now. I try often to hide my
feelings, but my heart betrays my passion. Evidently, it's
too obvious, it overflows. I didn't write to you earlier
because I woke up late and I know you're on duty today.
Adieu, my friend, conduct yourself well before everyone
so that no one suspects what's happening between us. It
amuses me much to dupe the world.

✳

Sweetheart, I'm going to go to bed and the door will be
locked. If, against all expectations, you come and are not
able to enter to my bedroom, I will cry warm tears
tomorrow. So I beg you to stay home and to be sure that
no one could love you more than I love you, my little soul.

They could be quite frank with each other:

My beloved soul, precious and unique, I can find no
words to express my love for you. Do not be upset
because of your diarrhea—it will clean up your bowels
well. But do be careful, my beloved, my adored one.

✳

If you really must see me, send someone to tell me;
since six o'clock in the morning I have the most
atrocious diarrhea; I am afraid that, passing through the
nonheated corridor, and especially with this bad
weather, would only make my pains worse, which are

bad enough as it is. I am sorry you are so ill. Try to be quiet, my friend, that is the best remedy.

—CATHERINE THE GREAT

Social Adviser

Within a few years, Potemkin was introducing Catherine to handsome young men. French ambassador Chevalier de Corberon kept a diary:

June 9, 1777, Monday

On Saturday on the day of our dinner in the country, the Empress dined on the Islands of [*Newski*], under a tent, overseen by Potemkin, who had built in this place a Cossack pavilion. This favorite—who is better than ever and who plays the role played by Mme. Pompadour at the end of her life with Louis XV—introduced to her a man named Zoritz, major of the hussars who's been promoted to lieutenant-colonel and inspector of all the light troops. This new favorite dined with her. It's said that he received 1,800 serfs for his first attempt. After dinner, Potemkin toasted the health of the Empress and kneeled down to her. Upon leaving the table, which was made of porcelain, she was in the gayest mood, and the freest; since it's said that the good woman was tipsy.

Not a Bad Career Choice

June 19, 1777

I have learned that Zavadovski, a previous favorite of the Empress, has received from Her Majesty 50,000 roubles, a

5,000-rouble pension, and four thousand serfs in the Ukraine, where they are worth a lot. Admit it, my friend, that this isn't a bad career choice.

—CHEVALIER DE CORBERON

Just a Theory, 1770s

A former British envoy, George McCartney, thought he had figured out why German-born Catherine always chose Russian-born lovers:

It is evident from the lists of the Empress' favourites that she has always of late preferred a Russian to one of any other nation. This may be partly owing to a fear of exciting any jealousy in the nation but by some is attributed to an idea that the Russians excel even the Irish in a certain Manly accomplishment, or rather feature of their persons. The Russian nurses it is said make a constant practice of pulling it, when the child is young, which has a great effect of lengthening the "virile instrument." It is very certain that pulling and stroking the nose lengthens and raises it much and a similar plan may have some effect on other parts of the body.

—GEORGE MCCARTNEY

A Little Joke, 1792

English scholar John Parkinson heard the following anecdote during his tour of Catherine's ambitious building projects in St. Petersburg:

A party was considering which of the Canals had cost the most money when one of them archly observed there was not a doubt about the matter; Catherine's Canal (this is the name of one of them) had unquestionably been the most expensive.

—JOHN PARKINSON

Final Lover, 1789

Frenchman Charles Masson wrote the following in Memoirs of the Court of St. Petersburg, *which was published anonymously in 1801:*

Plato Zubof was a young lieutenant in the horse-guards. . . . He spoke French fluently, he had some education, was of a polite and pliant disposition, could converse a little on literary subjects and had learned music. He was of middle size, but supple, muscular and well made. He had a high and intelligent forehead, and fine eyes, and his own countenance had not that air of coldness and severity, mixed with vanity, which it afterwards assumed. When the Empress went to Tzarsko-selo in the spring of 1789, he solicited from his patron the favor of being appointed to command the detachment that attended her, and having obtained it, dined with Catherine.

The Court had scarcely arrived when the rupture with [*current favorite*] Mamonof took place. This favorite was married and dismissed. Zubof was the only young officer in sight; and it appears that he was indebted rather to this fortunate circumstance than to the deliberate choice of Catherine, for the preference he obtained. Potemkin being absent, Nicholas Soltikof, at that time in high credit, introduced and served up the young Zubof with so much more zeal, hoping to find in him a protector against the haughty Potemkin, whom he heartily disliked. After some secret conferences, Zubof was approved and sent for more ample information to Miss Protasof and the Empress' physician. The account they gave must have been favorable for he was named aide-de-camp to the Empress, received a present of a hundred thousand roubles to furnish himself with linen, and was installed in the apartment of the favorites, with all the customary advantages. The next day, this young man was seen familiarly offering his arm to his Sovereign, equipped in his new uniform, with a large hat and feather on his head, attended by his patron and the great men of the Empire, who walked behind him with their hats off, though the day before, he had danced in attendance in their antechambers.

In the evening, after her card party was over, Catherine was seen to dismiss her Court, and retire, accompanied only by her favorite.

Next day, the antechambers of the new idol were filled with aged generals and ministers of long service, all of whom bent the knee before him. He was a genius discerned by the piercing eye of Catherine; the treasures of the Empire were lavished on him.

—CHARLES MASSON

Catherine died in 1796 of natural causes; she suffered a stroke on her way to the water closet.

Mozart's Scatological Love Letters, 1777

Wolfgang (1756–1791), the musical genius, was giving recitals at three, composing minuets at five; but as for emotional maturity, well . . . In his early twenties, Mozart scribbled some very unusual love letters to his pretty cousin, Maria Anna Thekle Mozart:

November 5, 1777, Mannheim

Dearest Coz Fuzz!

. . . Well, I wish you good night but first shit into your bed and make it burst. Sleep soundly, my love, into your mouth your arse you'll shove. Now I'm off to fool about and then I'll sleep a bit, no doubt. Tomorrow we'll talk sensibly for a bit vomit. I'll tell a things of lot to have you, you imagine can't simply how have I much say to; but hear all tomorrow it will you. Meanwhile, good-bye. Oh, my arse is burning like fire!—Perhaps some muck wants to come out? Why yes, muck, I know, see and smell you . . . and . . . what is that?—Is it possible . . . Ye gods!—can I believe those ears of mine? Yes indeed, it is so—what a long melancholy note! . . .

November 13, 1777, Mannheim

Ma très chere Nièce! Cousine! Fille! Mère, Soeur, et Épouse!
[*My very dear Niece! Cousin! Daughter! Mother, Sister, and Wife!*]

. . . Such a parcel to get, but no portrait as yet! I was all eagerness—in fact, I was quite sure—for you yourself had written the other day that I was to have it soon, very, very soon. Perhaps you doubt that I shall keep my word? Surely you do not doubt me? Well, anyhow, I implore you to send me yours—the sooner, the better. And I

trust that you will have it done, as I urged you, in
French costume.

How do I like Mohmheim? As well as I could like any
place without my little cousin. Forgive my wretched
writing, but the pen is already worn to a shred, and I've
been shitting, so 'tis said, nigh twenty-two years through
the same old hole, which is not yet frayed one whit,
though I've used it daily to shit, and each time the muck
with my teeth I've bit.

On the other hand, I hope that, however that may be,
you have received all my letters. . . . Now I must close,
however that may be, for I am not yet dressed and we
are lunching this very moment, so that after we may shit
again, however that may be. Do go on loving me as I
love you, then we shall never cease loving one another,
though the lion hovers round the walls, though doubt's
hard victory has not been weighed and the tyrant's
frenzy has crept to decay; yet Codrus, the wise
philosopher, often eats soot instead of porridge, and the
Romans, the props of my arse, have always been and
ever will be—half-castes. Adieu. J'espere que . . . [*rest
of letter is in French*] I hope you have already taken
some French lessons and I have no doubt that you will
soon know French better than I; since it's certainly two
years since I have written a word in that language.
Good-bye, for now. I kiss your hands, your face, your
knees and your—in a word, wherever you permit me to
kiss. I am with all my heart

your very affectionate Nephew and Cousin

WOLFG: AMADÉ MOZART

Mozart Wants to Marry

First cousin Maria sent Mozart her portrait, a pencil drawing, in February 1778, but the relationship didn't exactly have much of a chance. In three years, the twenty-five-year-old Mozart, still a virgin, decided it was time to marry. He wrote a letter to his domineering father, explaining his plans:

December 15, 1781, Vienna

Mon très cher Père!

. . . You are horrified at the idea? But I entreat you, dearest, most beloved father, to listen to me. I have been obliged to reveal my intentions to you. You must, therefore, allow me to disclose to you my reasons, which, moreover, are very well founded. The voice of Nature speaks as loud in me as in others, louder, perhaps, than in many a big strong lout of a fellow. I simply cannot live as most young men do in these days. In the first place, I have too much religion; in the second place, I have too great a love of my neighbor and too high a feeling of honor to seduce an innocent girl; and, in the third place, I have too much horror and disgust, too much dread and fear of diseases and too much care for my health to fool about with whores. So I can swear that I have never had relations of that sort with any woman. Besides, if such a thing had occurred, I should not have concealed it from you; for, after all, to err is natural enough in a man, and to err *once* would be mere weakness—although I should not undertake to promise that if I had erred once in this way, I should stop short at one slip. However, I stake my life on the truth of what I have told you. I am well aware that this reason (powerful as it is) is not urgent enough. But owing to my disposition, which is more inclined to a peaceful and domesticated existence than to revelry, I who from my youth up have never been accustomed to look after my own belongings, linen, clothes and so forth, cannot think of anything more necessary to me than a wife.

I assure you that I am often obliged to spend unnecessarily, simply because I do not pay attention to things. I am absolutely convinced that I should manage better with a wife (on the same income which I have now) than I do by myself. And how many useless expenses would be avoided! True, other expenses would have to be met, but—one knows what they are and can be prepared for them—in short, one leads a well-ordered existence. A bachelor, in my opinion, is only half alive. Such are my views and I cannot help it.

I have thought the matter over and reflected sufficiently, and I shall not change my mind. But who is the object of my love? Do not be horrified again, I entreat you. Surely, not one of the Webers? Yes, one of the Webers—but not Josefa, nor Sophie, but Constanze, the middle one. In no other family have I ever come across such differences of character. The eldest is a lazy, gross perfidious woman, and cunning as a fox. Mme. Lange [*who had scorned Mozart*] is a false malicious person and a coquette. The youngest—is still too young to be anything in particular—she is just a good-natured but feather-headed creature! May God protect her from seduction! But the middle one, my good, dear Constanze, is the martyr of the family and, probably for that very reason, is the kindest, the cleverest and, in short, the best of them all. She makes herself responsible for the whole household and yet in their opinion she does nothing right. Oh, my most beloved father, I could fill whole sheets with descriptions of all the scenes that I have witnessed in that house. If you want to read them, I shall do so in my next letter. But before I cease to plague you with my chatter, I must make you better acquainted with the character of my dear Constanze. She is not ugly, but at the same time far from beautiful. Her whole beauty consists in two little black eyes and a pretty figure. She has no wit, but she has enough common sense to enable her to fulfill her duties as a wife and a mother. It is a downright lie that she is inclined to be extravagant. On the contrary, she is accustomed to be shabbily dressed, for the little that her mother has been able to do for her children, she had done for the two others, but never for Constanze. True, she would like to be neatly and cleanly dressed, but not smartly, and most things that a woman needs she is able to make for herself; and she dresses her own hair every day. Moreover she understands housekeeping and has the kindest heart in the world. I love her and she loves me with all her heart. Tell me whether I could wish myself a better wife?

W: A: MOZART

Constanze and Wolfgang were married August 4, 1782. Their marriage appears to have been a happy one, although neither had a clue about career planning or money management. Mozart died in 1791, so penniless that he was buried in a pauper's grave.

Inside Paris' Most Notorious Bordello, 1779

In the Paris of Casanova and de Sade, Madame Gourdan ran the most notorious brothel—complete with fake virgins, peepholes, hidden entrances, mail-order dildoes, and sound-proof torture rooms. An explicit description has survived in a curious publication called The English Spy; or Secret Correspondence between Milord the Eye and Milord the Ear. *It was published anonymously in London in 1779 and represents the pre-Revolutionary grumblings of one Pidanzat de Mairobert. Is this a spoof? Is this reportage? Maybe a little of both.*

We pick up the author midway through his private tour conducted by a local official, the president of Tournelle, just after the authorities shut down the brothel:

Piscine, or Bathroom

I move on to the "piscine." It's a bathroom where are introduced the girls, recruited incessantly for Madame Gourdan from the provinces, the countryside and from Paris. One would shrink back in horror if one saw them leaving their village but here they're scrubbed, their skin softened, whitened, perfumed. In a word, Cinderella is pampered as though she were a superb horse. Someone next opened an armoire where there were several different essences, liqueurs and perfumes for use by the young women. There was

"Essence of Virgin"; it's a very strong astringent, with which Madame Gourdan treats the most tattered beauties and restores what can be lost only once.

Ballroom

The ballroom was next and although it doesn't function for dancing, it's not badly named because it's where everyone plays masquerade, where the peasant is metamorphosed into bourgeoisie and the noble lady sometimes into a chambermaid. Only in Paris are these subtle amenities for vice provided. There was an armoire, inside of which we were amazed to discover a door [*which led to an identical armoire in the back of the neighbor's curio shop*]. This was how prelates, judges and noble ladies could enter. By arriving via this secret way, they could change careers back here. The churchman could go secular, the judge go military, and free themselves from the fear of being discovered. Wives—hiding their rank and their titles, under the guise of a cook, could receive the vigorous assaults of a crude rustic selected [*by Gourdan*] to assuage their burning lust.

Infirmary: Sexual Healing

Next we enter the Infirmary. Milord, you'll be shocked to know that the main concern here is not venereal diseases but rather aging voluptuaries whose jaded senses need to revived by all the resources of the sensual arts.

The room received light only from above; the walls on all sides were covered with erotic paintings and prints, full of lascivious scenes and positions, invented to set fire to the imagination and to resurrect desires; these were repeated in sculptures and also further to titillate the clientele, the most obscene selections from poets were framed.

In glancing everywhere, my eyes alighted on little bundles of perfumed furze [*prickly evergreen*]. I asked ingenuously what these were used for. The president [*i.e., a local government official*] laughed in my face and said, "Your ignorance is to your credit; I congratulate you on never having need of this remedy. But since that might someday happen, I should teach you the usage of these switches. These are real ones and are destined to be used in a flagellation, often a violent one. Unfortunate dotards hope that these wielded by the arm of one or two courtesans will stir up their blood, and enable libertines to rediscover a vigor they thought they had lost.

"Still others resort to remedies," he added, "which appear less repugnant, but are actually more deadly." While speaking, he took from a small armoire a little box, in which were pastilles in the form of bon bons of every color. "You need to eat only one," he continued, "and you'll soon feel like a new man." They were labeled: "Pastilles a la Richelieu." I asked him why. He said that this Seigneur regularly used them not for himself but to persuade those women he lusted after but found reluctant.

"In addition," continued the president, "say that you don't have access to this stimulant and a woman falls into your hands, especially some she-wolf too difficult to satisfy, then here's what would soothe her and set her straight."

He showed me a little ball made out of stone, called "apple of love" [*i.e., "ben-wa ball"*]. He assured me that this item is so effective that if a woman inserts it into her pleasure center, it will start titillating her so and giving her so much enjoyment that she will have to remove it before it kills her. He couldn't tell me if chemists had analyzed the stone (probably an alloy), which is much in use among the Chinese.

I picked up one of those ingenious instruments, invented in girls' convents to provide the functions of manhood [*i.e.*, *a dildo*], and observed that no doubt female connoisseurs would ignore these in favor of the "apple of love."

"Yes they would," replied the president, "but since the apples of love can't be gathered in this country and at most are owned by a few curious people, it's necessary to stick with the tried and true commodity. You would not believe the number of letters found in Madame Gourdan's pile of correspondence, from abbesses and nuns writing to her requesting to be furnished with a 'consolateur.'

I saw next a quantity of little black rings, that were much too big to be finger rings. I asked what they were for. "Another aid," the judge told me, "for lechers who find a courtesan cold—since the women often become jaded, irritated, exhausted from too much exercise of Venus—and the men desire to spur her on; that's why they call these rings 'helpers.' They are put, you can guess where; they are furnished, according to the thickness of the cavalier. They are very supple, but at the same time, they are studded with little bumps, which excite such a titillation in the female that she is forced to follow the thrusts of her partner and to match his pace.

To finish the inventory of these curiosities of the cabinet of Madame Gourdan, one mustn't omit the "redingotes" of England. You know the many types of shields, which block poisonous diseases and which dull the pleasures. (*The French called condoms "redingotes," a corruption of "riding coats," because they thought they resembled long overcoats, then fashionable.)*

Chambre de la Question

We just glanced into the "chambre de la question." It's a closet where through secret peepholes the mistress and her confidants can see and hear whatever is said and done there.

Salon de Vulcain

We finished up at a room which the concierge called Vulcan's room. I found nothing unusual there except an armchair, whose singular design caught my eye. "Sit down," the president told me. "You will find out its purpose." Just as soon as I threw myself there, the movement of my body tripped a counterweight. The back flipped backwards and so did I. I found myself spread-eagled, legs bound apart and arms as well, in a sort of a cross. "My faith!" I shouted. "The trap of the god of Lemnos wouldn't work better." The judge told me that these are called the "trap of Fronsac" because it was dreamed up by this Seigneur, to overcome a virgin who, although she was of a much lesser rank, had resisted all his seduction attempts, all his gold and his threats. Mad to possess her, he committed three crimes to soothe his lust. He made himself guilty of arson, kidnapping and rape.

One fine night, he had the young girl's house set on fire, by his orders. An old lady, taking advantage of the chaos caused by this accident, steered the young girl away under the pretext of giving her shelter, and beneath the eyes of her mother, conducted her to her hovel. The duke of Fronsac was there; she was rushed into this infernal chair and there ignoring her tears, her screams, her struggles, he indulged in all the infamies suggested to him by his guilty lust. The place was so situated that the noise of her complaints, her sobs, even her screams could not be heard outside. It wasn't until several days later that thanks to a police investigation, the shrewish old accomplice of the duke was forced to release her prey.

I shuddered at the horror of this recital, didn't they draw and quarter this scoundrel who was guilty of such horrible crimes? "No," said the president, "the late king, when informed of the facts, exiled him from court. An investigation was begun and money did the rest. When the public brouhaha had died down, he reappeared; he continued the functions of 'gentleman of the chamber,' which he had inherited and he still has the job today for the reigning king."

—PIDANZAT DE MAIROBERT, *THE ENGLISH SPY; OR CORRESPONDENCE BETWEEN MILORD THE EYE AND MILORD THE EAR*

This chair also turns up in the writings of journalist/ pornographer Restif de la Bretonne; only he one-ups "the English Spy" by having his version of the chair not only spread-eagle the girl but open her mouth.

Catholic Theologians Debate Sexual Sins

Catholic theologians—who have analyzed and quoted Scripture to delve into the Trinity and the Eucharist—have also applied the same exhaustive techniques to answer elaborate questions on sexual behavior, such as:

Does a man commit a mortal sin by beginning the act of copulation in the hinder vessel [*i.e., the ass*], that he may afterwards finish it in the proper vessel [*i.e., the vagina*]?

—ALFONSO MARIE DE LIGUORI, 1696–1787

If a woman, after entering holy matrimony, is found to be too tight, should she undergo an incision?

—PIERRE DENS, 1690–1775

Are touches and lecherous looks between a husband and wife a mortal sin, if they are done for pleasure alone and not leading to the act of copulation?

—LIGUORI

The answers are so learned and complicated that one brief excerpt will suffice:

Is Oral Sex a Mortal Sin?

That [*it's a mortal sin*] is denied by Sanchez and others, provided there is no danger of pollution. But it is more truly affirmed [*as a mortal sin*] by Spor. de Matrim & others, for two reasons: because in this case, owing to the heat of the mouth, there is proximate danger of pollution, and because this appears of itself a new type of sensual sin against nature (called by some "Irrumation"). . . .

However Spor. & others make an exception [*for oral sex*] if it be done casually; and in truth, Sanchez seems to agree: he excuses that act from [*being a*] mortal sin, should all danger of pollution cease.

Pal. also makes an exception, "if the husband does this to excite himself for natural copulation." But from what has been said before, I think neither ought to be admitted.

Just as Sanchez condemns a man of mortal sin who in the act of copulation introduces his finger into the hinder vessel of his wife, because (he says) in this act, there is a disposition to sodomy. . . . I say husbands practicing a foul act of this nature ought always to be severely rebuked.

—LIGUORI

A French Revolutionary Collects Sexual Anecdotes, 1783

Mirabeau (1749–1791), an aristocrat by birth and sympathetic to the king, nonetheless became one of the leaders of the French Revolution, thanks mostly to his impassioned speeches. The count brought the same passion to his carousing, several times winding up in prison.

About a decade before the French Revolution, Mirabeau wrote a curious book, Erotika Biblion *(1783), a kind of wise-ass collection of sexual anecdotes from history, blending solid research with erotic fantasy.*

The Invention of Lipstick

The Phoenician men [*notorious in antiquity for their bisexuality*] . . . were the first to redden their lips in order to imitate perfectly the entrance of the true sanctuary of love [*i.e., the vagina*].

Invention of Oral Sex

Lesbians [*the original Greeks from the island of Lesbos*] are credited with the innovation of making the mouth the most frequent organ of pleasure. . . .

Etymological Roots of Lesbian Love

From ancient days comes the word "clitoriazein" [*Greek*] which means "the contraction of two clitorises"; it's an act, which [*dictionary compilers*] Hesychius and Suidas took the trouble to explain, informing us that it's accomplished like the rubbing of carp against each other: one partner moves when the other stops and vice versa.

Bestiality

Bestiality was so widespread among the Jews that it was decreed to burn the offspring along with the participants (Exod. 22:19; Lev. 7:21, 18:23). Here's what I find bizarre: I can understand how a country bumpkin or a lout, driven by aching need or bizarre fantasies, could try a goat, a mare or even a cow; but nothing can prepare me for the idea of a woman who wants to be impaled by a donkey.

Airborne Oriental Lesbians

Monsieur Poivre informs us during his voyages that the most notorious lesbians in the universe are the Chinese. And since in that country, noblewomen walk very little, they "tribad" [*make lesbian love*] across suspended hammocks.

These hammocks are made of plaited silk, woven with two-inch squares; they gently stretch their bodies down, then they balance themselves and titillate each other or themselves without the annoyance of having to move around. It's a great luxury for the Mandarin lords to have beneath their eyes in one room, rich with aroma, twenty airborne women diddling each other.

Tailed Man of Manilla

Mirabeau is here needling the Catholic theologians, the type cited on page 271. You might need to draw a diagram, but try to picture the anatomical geography.

Marco Polo, described in his "Travels" printed in 1566, men with tails in the kingdom of Lambri. Struys had mentioned those of the island of Formosa and Gemelli Carreri those of the island of Mindors, near Manilla. Such a wealth of authorities were more than sufficient to prompt Jesuit missionaries to try to make converts in that region. They brought back word of these tailed men, who by an extension of the coccyx bear actual tails of seven, eight and ten inches, which are sensitive and as far as mobility, able to do all the movements demonstrated by the trunk of an elephant.

Now, if one of these tailed men slept between two women—one of whom has a large-sized clitoris—and positioned himself head to foot to her, and then placed her clitoris pederastically into himself while this islander's tail furnished seven inches to her legitimate vessel [*i.e.*, *vagina*]; the islander who was easy-going let this be done, and to occupy all his faculties, he approached the other woman and enjoyed her as Nature invites him to [*i.e., vaginally*]. . . . This is assuredly something that would exercise the prince of casuists [*Father Tomas Sanchez*].

Sanchez interprets it thus: For the first act, he says, double sodomy although ultimately incomplete, because neither the tail nor the clitoris can spill any libation; they are doing nothing contrary to the paths of God and the purpose of Nature; as for the second act, simple fornication.

Homosexual Prostitution in Paris

Famed traveler Sir Richard Burton quoted Mirabeau as an authority on the topic of homosexual prostitution, and perhaps a few facts do lie hidden in this spoof of the French obsession for bureaucracy:

The taste for homosexuality makes considerable inroads here—although it is less in vogue now than it was during the reign of Henri III when men groped each other under the very porticoes of the Louvre.

Since Paris is a masterpiece of police control, public places have been designated for this purpose.

Young men destined for the profession are carefully classified, for the bureaucratic system extends this far. They are examined, and those who can play both an active and a passive role, who are handsome, rosy-cheeked, well-made with nice plump figures, are reserved for the high-ranking noblemen; or they will be amply rewarded by bishops or financiers.

Those who are deprived of their testicles, or to use a euphemism (since our language is more chaste than our habits) those who do not have their "weaver's weights," but who give and receive, form the second class; they are even more expensive because women can use them while they are serving men.

Those jaded ones who can't get an erection although they still have their genitals, are registered as "pure passives" and compose the third class; but whoever officiates over these pleasures, must verify their impotence. To do this, they are placed completely nude on a bed with the bottom half of the covers pulled up; two girls caress them with all their skill, while a third gently whips with fresh nettles the seat of their venereal desires. After a quarter hour of this test, a long red pepper is inserted in their anus which causes considerable irritation; then a fine mustard of Caudebec is smeared on the welts caused by the nettles; and camphor is rubbed on the head of the penis. Whoever is immune to all these attempts, and shows absolutely no sign of an erection will serve as a passive partner at one-third pay only.

—MIRABEAU

Poet Robert Burns Gets a Bonny Lass Pregnant, 1786

This lusty Scottish poet, who loved to hoist a glass, wrote some great bawdy poetry, but in America, Burns (1759–1796) is sometimes remembered for just one line: "The best laid plans of mice and men gang aft aglay." And that was certainly true in the following case. The church court records of his sinning with Jean Armour have survived:

Penance in Church

Mauchline, Ayrshire, Scotland, 1786

The Session [*i.e., church court*] being informed that Jean Armour, an unmarried woman, is said to be with child, and that she has gone off from the place of late, to reside elsewhere, the Session think it their duty to enquire.

. . . James Carrie reports that he spoke to Mary Smit, mother to Jean Armour, who told him that she did not suspect her daughter to be with child, that she was gone to Paisley to see her friends, and would return soon.

. . . Jean Armour sent a letter directed to the minister, the tenor whereof follows: "I am heartily sorry that I have given and must give your Session trouble on my account. I acknowledge that I am with child, and Robert Burns in Mossgiel is the father. I am, with great respect, your humble servant, Jean Armour."

. . . Compeared [*appeared*] Robert Burns and acknowledged himself the father of Jean Armour's child. . . . Robert Burns, John Smith, Mary Lindsay, Jean Armour, and Agnes Auld appeared before the congregation professing their repentance for the sin of fornication, and they having each appeared two several Sabbaths formerly were this day rebuked and absolved from the scandal.

It wasn't the first time for Burns, who had written a poem about an earlier church penance:

The Fornicator, 1785

Before the congregation wide,
I pass the muster fairly,

My handsome Betsey by my side,
We got our ditty rarely;
But my downcast eye by chance did spy
What made my lips to water,
Those limbs so clean where I between
Commenced a Fornicator.

—ROBERT BURNS

John Paul Jones Accused of Rape in Russia, 1789

John Paul Jones (1747–1792), the most celebrated American sailor in the Revolutionary War, the man who said, "I have not yet begun to fight," was accused of raping a young girl, Katerina Goltzwart, on March 30, 1789, in St. Petersburg. Jones had ventured to Russia as a soldier of fortune hired to serve Catherine the Great.

We have two very different versions of the incident, both by Jones himself. Watch the story change over time:

Note to the Police Chief

Written in French, three days after the incident:

April 2, 1789
The accusation against me is an imposture invented by the mother of a depraved girl, who came several times to my house and with whom I have often sported [*Fr. badiné*], always giving her money, but whose virginity I

have absolutely NOT taken. . . . I thought her to be several years older than Your Excellency says she is, and each time that she came to my house she lent herself very amiably to do all that a man would want of her. The last time passed off like the rest, and she went out appearing content and relaxed, and having in no way been abused. If one has checked on her having been deflowered, I declare that I am not the author of it, and I shall as easily prove the falseness of this assertion as of several other points included in the deposition which you have sent to me.

I have the honor to be, etc.

John Paul Jones

Tells the Sympathetic French Ambassador

A few days later, French ambassador Comte de Ségur visited Jones, a hero for the French because he had so roughed up the British Navy during the Revolutionary War. Ségur reveals in his memoirs what Jones told him during that visit:

A few days ago, in the morning, a young girl came to my house to ask whether I had any linen or lace for her to mend. She then made me some rather sudden and indecent propositions. I was astonished at such boldness in one so young, and I felt sorry for her. I advised her not to enter upon so vile a career; I gave her some money and told her to leave, but she was determined to stay.

I was annoyed by her insistence, so I took her by the hand and led her to the door; but at the instant when the door opened, the little scamp tore her sleeve, her kerchief, started screaming loudly, charging that I had molested her, and threw herself in the arms of an old woman, who called herself her mother and who certainly wasn't stationed there by accident. The mother and the daughter fill the house with their cries, then depart and go off to denounce me. Now you know all.

So How Old Was the Girl?

Jones was desperate to prove that the girl was not ten years old, as his accusers claimed. He succeeded in tracking down the girl's father and got a deposition, which he sent to Prince Potemkin:

> SIGNED AFFADAVIT
> Saratowka, April 7th 1789
> "I certify that my daughter is twelve years old."
> —Signed Stephen Koltzwarthen.

Jones also sent the prince a passionate letter:

> April 13, 1789, St. Petersburg
>
> . . . The charge against me is an unworthy imposture. I love woman, I confess, and the pleasures that one only obtains from that sex; but to get such things by force is horrible to me. I cannot even contemplate gratifying my passions without their consent, and I give you my word as a soldier and an honest man that, if the girl in

question has not passed through hands other than mine, she is still a virgin.

—JOHN PAUL JONES

We will probably never know all—perhaps it was a plot by rival British soldiers of fortune—but, in any case, Catherine the Great never forgave him. In August 1789, Kontradmiral Pavel Ivanovich Jones started the long carriage ride to Warsaw, leaving Russia in disgrace, never to return.

Marie-Antoinette's Last Love Note, 1793

Years before the French Revolution, Marie-Antoinette (1755–1793) liked to eat cake with a Swedish soldier-diplomat named Axel Fersen:

April 10, 1780

I must confide in your majesty that the young count de Fersen has so charmed the Queen that people have started whispering. I swear that I'm unable NOT to believe that she has a crush on him; I've seen too many signs to doubt it.

The young count has acted admirably by his discretion and above all by his decision to go off to America.

—LETTER OF COMTE DE CREUTZ TO KING GUSTAVE III OF SWEDEN

Count Fersen joined a French expeditionary force and fought valiantly in the Revolutionary War. Marie-Antoinette was sentenced to death in 1793; Fersen wound up sounding like a Dickens character:

August 24, 1793

If I could still do something, could try to free her, I would suffer less. Not being able to do anything, that's what's so horrid. . . . My greatest happiness would be to die for her, but that happiness is denied me. . . .

—COUNT FERSEN, LETTER TO HIS SISTER

Marie-Antoinette had a brief note smuggled to Fersen from her prison cell:

Adieu. My heart is completely yours.

The note arrived after she had lost her head at the guillotine, October 16, 1793.

Napoleon, Josephine, and Josephine's Dog, 1796

Napoleon marched pell-mell over most of Europe, but he met strong resistance in Josephine's bed on their wedding night.

After a small civil ceremony in which the twenty-six-year-old Napoleon married the thirty-two-year-old widow Josephine Beauharnais, the couple returned to her apartment. They started to get amorous, but Josephine's pampered dog, Fortune, an ugly little pug with a corkscrew tail, was parked right in the middle of the bed.

I wanted to boot him off it: a hopeless wish. I was told I must resolve to sleep somewhere else or agree to share. That annoyed me quite a bit, but it was "take it or leave it." So I resigned myself. The favorite, however, was less accommodating than I.

—NAPOLEON, TO PLAYWRIGHT A. V. ARNAULT, *SOUVENIRS*

Napoleon and Josephine resumed their love-making, and things were going well, when suddenly the future emperor cried out. Josephine thought it a cry of passion. It wasn't. Fortune had sunk his teeth in Napoleon's leg.

All night the disappointed Josephine had to put compresses on her invalid's wound. He huddled in the bed and loudly moaned that he was dying of rabies.

—M. DE RAVINE, *MEMOIRS*, QUOTED IN GUY BRETON'S *NAPOLEON AND HIS LADIES*

Napoleon's Wildly Passionate Love Letters

Just a few days after his wedding, Napoleon rushed off to conquer Italy. He was madly in love, and his letters burn with passion. He tells Josephine that he has sped up battle plans so he can see her again sooner. He closes his letters with phrases such as "A thousand kisses to your neck, your breasts and lower down, much lower, that little black forest I love so well."

10 Germinal [*of the French Revolutionary calender*]

March 30, 1796, Nice [*France*]

I have not passed a day without loving you; I have not passed a night without holding you in my arms; I have not drunk a cup of tea without cursing the glory and the ambition which keeps me so far from the soul of my life. In the middle of battle, at the head of the troops, in touring the camps, my adorable Josephine is alone in my heart, occupies my spirit, absorbs my thoughts.

If I rush away from you with the speed of a torrent of the Rhone river, it's only so that I can see you again sooner. If, in the middle of the night, I wake myself in order to work some more, it's so that I can advance by a few days the arrival of my sweet friend, and meanwhile in your letter [*March 13–16*], you address me formally with "Vous." You of all people! Ah! Miserable! How could you write such a letter? How cold it is! And between the [*13th and 16th*] are four days; what did you do, since you did not write to your husband? Ah! my lover, that "Vous" and these four days make me miss my former indifference. Woe to him who is the cause! May he, for pain and suffering, undergo what I would feel if I had proof and evidence about him. Hell has no torture, nor the Furies any serpent! You! you! Ah! what will happen in fifteen days? My soul is sad; my heart is a slave and my imagination frightens me. . . . I demand neither eternal love nor fidelity, but only truth, honesty without limits.

Bonaparte

Addresse: A la citoyenne Bonaparte, chez la citoyenne Beauharnais, rue Chantereine, n. 6, a Paris.

(Napoleon repeatedly risked the lives of couriers to sneak these letters through battle lines.)

April 24, 1796, Carru

A kiss to your breasts, then another lower down, much
lower down.

*By this time, Josephine had taken a handsome young lover,
named Hippolyte Charles, and she kept making excuses to
avoid leaving Paris, including saying she was pregnant. The
soldiers soon started calling Napoleon "Commander Cuckold."*

June 15, Tortone

You realize well that I could not see you with a lover,
much less offer you one. To rip out his heart and to see
him would for me be the same thing. And afterward, if I
could, raise my hand toward your sacred person. . . . No,
I would never dare that; but I would exit a life in which
the most virtuous person had deceived me. But I am
steadfast and confident in your love. These misfortunes
are the tests which reveal to us the power of passion. A
baby adorable as its mother will someday see the light of
day and could pass several years in your arms. Wretch! I
must content myself with a day. A thousand kisses on
your eyes, on your tongue, on your c–. Adorable wife,
what is your influence? I am certainly sick of your
sickness. I have a burning fever. . . . Don't keep the
courier Le Simple more than six hours, and let him
return to me immediately carrying a beloved letter from
my queen.

*They spent a few brief days together in July in Italy, which
only kindled Napoleon's lust for more:*

November 21, 1796, Verona

I am going to sleep, my little Josephine, my heart full of
your adorable image, and sick of spending so long apart
from you. But I hope that in a few days, I will be
happier, and that I can give you a leisurely proof of the
ardent love which you have inspired in me.

You no longer write to me. You no longer think of
your good friend, cruel woman! Don't you realize that
without you, without your heart, without your love, your
husband has neither happiness nor life. Good God! How
happy I would be if I could watch you get dressed, your
little shoulders, your little white breasts, elastique, so
firm; above that, a little face . . . to devour. You know, of
course, that I haven't forgotten my little visits to the
little black forest. I give it a thousand kisses, and I wait
with impatience the moment of being there. Everything
to you; life, happiness, pleasure they're all only what you
make them.

To live in a Josephine is to live in Paradise. A kiss to
your mouth, your eyes, your shoulder, your breasts,
everywhere, everywhere!

*Napoleon raced to meet Josephine in Milan on November
26, but when he arrived, she had already left town with
Hippolyte Charles.*

*Napoleon eventually got the message. He took numerous
lovers himself and he did get some manner of revenge on
Josephine: He divorced her, and, perhaps more satisfyingly, he
got to witness the cruel death of her beloved pug dog:*

[*Fortune*] had an extreme arrogance, as to be expected; he

attacked, he bit everybody, even other dogs. Less polite than humans, the dogs didn't always forgive him.

One evening, he met in the gardens of Montebello a big mongrel which although he belonged to a servant of the house, didn't think himself inferior to the dog of the master; it was the cook's dog. Fortune pounced on him and bit him on the derriere, the mongrel bit him back on the head and with one chomp of his teeth, killed him on the spot. I will leave you to consider what was the sadness of his mistress. The conqueror of Italy could not help but sympathize; he was sincerely grieved by an accident that rendered him sole owner of the conjugal bed. But that widowhood didn't last long. To console herself at the loss of her dog, Josephine did just what many a woman has done at the loss of a lover, she took another, another pug dog. This breed wasn't yet dethroned.

Inheritor of the same rights and flaws as his predecessor, "Carlin" was reigning for several weeks, when the general noticed the cook taking a walk in a thicket far from the house. Upon seeing the general, this man rushed into the deepest woods.

"Why do you hide from me?" Bonaparte called to him.

"General, after what my dog did . . . "

"Well, so?"

"I was afraid my presence might annoy you."

"Your dog! You don't have it anymore?"

"Forgive me, general, but he never sets foot in your garden anymore, especially since Madame now has another dog. . . ."

"Let him run free anywhere; maybe he will rid me of this other one too."

I love to tell this anecdote because it's characteristic and gives an idea of the power exerted by the most gentle and indolent of Creoles over the most willful and despotic of men. His resolution—before which everyone bowed—was not able to resist the tears of a woman; the man who dictated the laws to Europe, in his home wasn't able to kick out a dog.

—A. V. ARNAULT, *SOUVENIRS D'UN SEXAGINAIRE*

Stendhal: Tips on Incest and Seduction, 1789–1801

Stendhal (1783–1842) was one of France's most popular writers (The Red and the Black). *In his autobiography,* Vie de Henry Brulard, *he confesses an incestuous passion for his mother:*

I wanted to cover my mother in kisses even when she had no clothes on. She loved me passionately and hugged me often. I returned her kisses with such a fire that she often was obliged to run away. I hated my father when he used to come and interrupt our kisses. I always wanted to kiss her on the breasts, but you must remember I lost her in childbirth when I was barely seven years old. She had a plumpness, a perfect freshness; she was very beautiful. . . .

She could not be offended that I'm taking the liberty to reveal that I loved her; if I ever find her again, I will tell it to her again. In any case, she did not participate at all in this love. As for me, I was as criminal as possible. I passionately loved her charms.

One night when by chance I was put to bed on the floor in her bedroom, on a mattress, this woman spry and light-footed like a deer leaped over my mattress to reach her own bed more quickly.

(*In the manuscript, Stendhal started to tell more of this incident, then heavily crossed out the added material.*)

Seduction Tips

At age eighteen, Stendhal recorded in his diary some curious advice:

August 1, 1801

I am just like many others who find it embarrassing when it comes to scr-wing a respectable woman for the first time. Here's a very simple method. Once you've get her in bed, you smother her in kisses, you d-ddle her, etc.; she starts to get a taste for it. However propriety calls for her always to defend herself. Thus it's necessary, without her noticing, for you to put your left fore-arm on her neck, under her chin, as though to choke her; her first reaction is to bring her hand there. At that moment, you must take your p-nis between your pointer and middle fingers—both of them extended—and calmly put "it" into her machine. For those few who can do it with sang-froid, it never fails. It's necessary to camouflage the decisive movement of the left fore-arm beneath a few whimpers. Percheron gave me this method and he's an expert.

7

The
Nineteenth Century

An Indian Transvestite Chases John Tanner, 1800

Many American Indian tribes have a long, proud transvestite tradition which features men passing their entire adult lives as women—cooking, cleaning, getting married to other men. (Remember Little Big Man *with Dustin Hoffman?) In 1789, nine-year-old John Tanner (1780–1846) was captured by Indians; in 1800, he was propositioned by a male cross-dressing Chippewa (Ojibbeway):*

Some time in the course of this winter, there came to our lodge, one of the sons of the celebrated Ojibbeway chief, called Wesh-ko-bug (the sweet), who lived at Leech Lake. This man was one of those who make themselves women, and are called women by the Indians. There are several of this sort among most, if not all Indian tribes. They are commonly called A-go-kwa. This creature called Ozaw-wen-dib (the yellow head) was now near fifty years old, and had lived with many husbands. I do not know whether she had seen me or only heard of me, but she soon let me know she had come a long distance to see me, and with the hope of living with me. She offered herself [*sexually*] to me, but not being discouraged with one refusal, she repeated her disgusting advances until I was almost driven from the lodge.

Old Net-no-kwa was perfectly well acquainted with her character and only laughed at the embarrassment and shame which I evinced whenever she addressed me. She seemed rather to countenance and encourage the Yellow Head in remaining at our lodge. The latter was very expert in the various employments of the women, to which all her time was given.

At length despairing of success in her addresses to me, or being too much pinched by hunger, which was commonly felt in our lodge, she disappeared and was absent three or four days. I began to hope I should be no more troubled by her. When she came back loaded with dry meat, she stated she had found the band of Wa-ge-to-tah-gun and that the chief had sent by her an invitation for us to join him. He had heard of the niggardly condition of Waw-zhe-kwaw-maisk-koon towards us and had sent the A-go-kwa to say to me, "My nephew, I do not wish you to stay there to look at the meat another kills but is too mean to give you. Come to me and neither you nor my sister shall want anything that it is in my power to give you." I was glad enough of his invitation and started immediately. At first encampment, as I was doing something by the fire, I heard the A-go-kwa at no great distance in the woods, whistling to call me. Approaching the place, I found she had her eyes on game of some kind, and presently I discovered a moose. I shot him twice in succession and twice he fell at the report of the gun but it is probable I shot too high, for at last he escaped. The old woman reproved me severely for this, telling me she feared I should never become a good hunter. But before night the next day, we arrived at Wa-ge-to-te's lodge where we ate as much as we wished.

Here also, I found myself relieved from the persecutions of the A-go-kwa, which had become intolerable. Wa-ge-to-te, who had two wives, married her. This introduction of a new intimate into the family of Wa-ge-to-te occasioned some laughter and produced some ludicrous incidents, but was attended with less uneasiness and quarrelling than would have been the bringing in of a new wife of the female sex.

—A NARRATIVE OF THE CAPTIVITY AND ADVENTURES OF JOHN TANNER, 1830

Tanner married an Indian woman soon afterward. In 1817, he brought his wife and children to live among whites in Kentucky, but he found the transition almost impossible. He spent the last thirty years of his life caught between the two races.

Jefferson and His Slave Girl Sally? 1802

Journalist James T. Callender was the man principally responsible for spreading the charges that Thomas Jefferson (1743–1826) had a long affair with his slave girl, Sally Hemings, and fathered several children by her. What makes the charges suspect is that Callender was an angry alcoholic who had been recently turned down by Jefferson for a cushy post office appointment. Here are excerpts from the original articles written by Callender:

The President and His African Venus

September 1, 1802, Richmond *[Virginia]* Recorder

It is well known that the man, whom it delighteth the

people to honor, keeps, and for many years past, has kept, as his concubine, one of his own slaves. Her name is Sally. The name of her eldest son is Tom. His features are said to be a striking although sable resemblance to those of the president himself. The boy is ten or twelve years of age. His mother went to France in the same vessel with Mr. Jefferson and his two daughters. The delicacy of his arrangement must strike every person of common sensibility. What a sublime pattern for an American ambassador to place before the eyes of two young ladies!

If the reader does not feel himself disposed to pause, we beg leave to proceed. Some years ago, this story had once or twice been hinted at in "Rind's Federalist." At that time, we believed the surmise to be an absolute calumny. One reason for thinking so was this. A vast body of people wished to debar Mr. Jefferson from the presidency. The establishment of this single fact would have rendered his election impossible. . . .

But Callender has now become convinced:

By this wench Sally, our president has had several children. There is not an individual in the neighborhood of Charlottesville who does not believe the story, and not a few who know it. . . .

The AFRICAN VENUS is said to officiate as housekeeper at Monticello. When Mr. Jefferson has read this article, he will find leisure to estimate how much has been lost or gained by so many unprovoked attacks upon . . . J.T. CALLENDER.

Musical Charges

November 17, 1802

The following song was "supposed to have been written by the Sage of Monticello," i.e., Jefferson. Among other claims, it accuses the president of preferring the sexual smell of slaves.

Tune: Yankee Doodle Dandy

Of all the damsels on the green
On mountain or in valley,
A lass so luscious ne'er was seen
As the Monticellian Sally.

Yankee doodle, who's the noodle?
What wife were half so handy?
To breed a flock of slaves for stock,
A blackamoor's the dandy.

Search every town and city through,
Search market, street and alley;
No dame at dusk shall meet your view,
So yielding as my Sally.

Yankee doodle, &c.

When press'd by loads of state affairs,
I seek to sport and dally,
The sweetest solace of my cares
Is in the lap of Sally.

Yankee doodle, &c.

Let Yankee parsons preach their worst—
Let tory wittling's rally!
You men of morals! and be curst,
You would snap like sharks for Sally.

Yankee doodle, &c.

She's black, you tell me—grant she be—
Must colour always tally?
Black is love's proper hue for me—
And white's the hue for Sally.

Yankee doodle, &c.

What though she by the gland secretes;°
Must I stand shilt-I shall-I?
Tuck'd up between a pair of sheets
There's no perfume like Sally.

Yankee doodle, &c.

You call her slave—and pray were slaves
Made only for the galley?
Try for yourselves, ye witless knaves—
Take each to bed your Sally.

Yankee doodle, w.hose the noodle?
Wine's vapid, tope me brandy—

For still I find to breed my kind,
A negro wench the dandy!

✳*In another issue of the newspaper, Callender quotes Jefferson's Notes on Virginia, in which Jefferson explains his theory about the smell of African Americans:*
They have less hair on the face and body—they secrete less by the kidnies, and more by the glands of the skin, which gives them a very strong and disagreeable odour. They are more ardent after their female, but love seems with them to be more an eager desire than a tender delicate mixture of sentiment.

—THOMAS JEFFERSON

In July 1803, Callender was found dead in three feet of water on the edge of the James River. The official verdict: accidental drowning while drunk. Jefferson never responded publicly to the charges of fathering slave children and was reelected president in 1804.

Pauline Bonaparte's Gynecological Report, 1807

Napoleon's sister, widely considered one of the most beautiful women of her day, had an itch. We know this because her gynecologist's report has survived. Pauline (1780–1825) had a reputation for scandal: she posed as a topless Venus for Canova; she was giddy, impetuous, extramaritally minded; and it turns out she had a medical excuse for at least some of her behavior.
In the spring of 1807, Pauline's family doctor requested that Dr. Jean-Noel Hallé, foremost gynecologist of his day, examine her. Hallé wrote a letter to Dr. Peyre, in which he did an

achingly polite dance around what he regarded as the true source of Pauline's problems.

April 21, 1807

My dear colleague,

I have continued to reflect on the condition in which I found Her Highness, and in which we observed her yesterday. That condition is one of hysteria. Her womb continued to be sensitive, though less so than before; her ligaments conserved the signs of that painful irritation for which we put her in the bath last Tuesday. The spasms that I saw in the bath were hysterical spasms; the pain in her head was mysterious. Her general state is one of torpor and exhaustion.

This isn't an ordinary inflammation; the inflamed condition that we have seen was usually only temporary.

[*But*] the habitual and constant inflammation is a state of excitation of the uterine organ, and that condition sustained and continued can become extremely irritating.

That's the problem. I touched on the causes when I spoke in broad hints to the Princess, last Tuesday.

I blamed the internal douches and I gave her an overview of what usually causes irritation in the womb, of what type it is. I thought myself understood, but I fear that I wasn't <u>enough</u> understood.

I can't be sure—but we must hazard a guess using the means given us to guess; and what I've already said about the nature of the symptoms that you and I have observed (and you much more often than I) provides more than enough evidence to solve the riddle.

One cannot always blame the douche and its tube, one must certainly speculate that in a beautiful young passionate woman who is living alone [*away from her husband*] and who is visibly exhausted there is a substantive cause for that exhaustion. Whatever that cause may be, it's time and long past time to remove it.

I have seen some women fall victim to similar illnesses; they all began in the same way. It is evident that unless she hurries, it will be too late. I cannot say more than I have said, since I know nothing absolutely, but nonetheless we must snatch this young and attractive woman from her demise, and if there is someone who encourages her weaknesses and who is an accomplice in them, that person, whoever it is, would not be blamed while we would be blamed for having observed nothing or for allowing it all to happen. I have no desire to be regarded as an idiot or to be accused of a cowardly and perfidious complacency; but more important than all that, we must save this excellent and unhappy woman, whose fate saddens me. Fortunately, I am not giving up hope.

Hurry, then, my dear colleague because there's no time to lose. Use my letter however you wish; and give me the means to speak frankly and directly. If we cannot speak out as professionals, we should leave the case.

Adieu, my dear colleague, remain assured of my high admiration and sincere attachment,

Hallé

Pauline was suffering from salpingitis—inflammation of a uterine tube, according to Imperial Venus, *by Len Ortzen. In effect, the illness gave her an itch, which, the more she "scratched" with her lovers, the more irritated it became.*

Pauline—who wouldn't listen to Napoleon—didn't exactly take the doctor's veiled prescription of celibacy and rest either. Yes, she went to take the waters at Gréoux in southern France, but she also decorated a beautiful summer pavilion for rendezvous with her lover, Auguste de Forbin. She closed her June 10 letter inviting him there: "I am sending you flowers that have nestled on my breasts, that I have covered with kisses. I alone love you."

London Police Crack Down on a Homosexual Club, 1810

The British police in July 1810 raided the Vere Street Coterie, a secret homosexual club. Seven of the members received one- to three-year sentences and public pillory, which turned out to be especially brutal, with eggs, mud, and dead cats thrown at them. The lawyer for the building's landlord, James Cook, published a pamphlet trying to clear his client. Their main strategy: depict him as a greedy heterosexual, quite different from the homosexual club members. In it, he describes the goings-on:

Four beds were provided in one room:—another was fitted up for a ladies' dressing-room, with a toilet, and every appendage of rouge, &c.&c:—a third room was called the Chapel, where marriages took place, sometimes between a <u>female grenadier</u> six feet high, and a petit maitre not more than half the altitude of his beloved wife. These marriages were solemnized with all the mockery of bride maids and bride men; and the nuptials were frequently consummated by two, three, or four couples, in the same room, and in the sight of each other! . . . The upper part of the house was appropriated to wretches who were constantly in waiting for casual customers; who practised all the allurements that are found in a brothel, by the more natural description of prostitutes. . . . Men of rank, and respectable situations in life, might be seen wallowing either in or on the beds with wretches of the lowest description. . . . It seems many of these wretches are married; and frequently, when they are together, make their wives, who they call "Tommies," topics of ridicule; and boast of having compelled them to act parts too shocking to think of. . . .

It seems the greater part of these reptiles assume feigned names, though not very appropriate to their calling in life; for instance, Kitty Cambric is a coal merchant; Miss Selina, a runner at a police office; Black-Eyed Leonora, a drummer; Pretty Harriet, a butcher; Lady Godiva, a waiter; the Duchess of Gloucester, a gentleman's servant; Duchess of Devonshire, a blacksmith; and Miss Sweet Lips, a country grocer. It is a generally received opinion, and a very natural one, that the prevalency of this passion has for its object effeminate delicate beings only; but this seems to be, by Cook's account, a mistaken notion; and the reverse is so palpable in many instances, that Fanny Murray, Lucy Cooper, and Kitty Fisher are now personified by an athletic bargeman, a herculean coalheaver and a deaf tire smith—the latter of these monsters has two sons.

—LAWYER IDENTIFIED AS HOLLOWAY

Prostitution in India, *circa* 1840

Edward Sellon sailed for India in 1834 at age sixteen, was promoted to captain, and spent a decade there. He wrote the following:

The usual charge for the general run of [*native women*] is two rupees. For five, you may have the handsomest Mohammedan girls, and any of the high-caste women who follow the trade of a courtesan. The "fivers" are a very different set of people from their frail sisterhood in European countries; they do not drink, they are scrupulously cleanly in their persons, they are sumptuously dressed, they wear the most costly jewels in profusion, they are well educated and sing sweetly, accompanying their voices on the viol de gamba, a sort of guitar, they generally decorate their hair with clusters of clematis, or the sweet scented bilwa flowers entwined with pearls or diamonds. They understand in perfection all the arts and wiles of love, are capable of gratifying any tastes, and in face and figure they are unsurpassed by any women in the world.

They have one custom that seems singular to a European, they not only shave the Mons Veneris, but take a clean sweep underneath it, so that until you glance at their hard, enchanting breasts, handsome beyond compare, you fancy you have got hold of some unfledged girl. The Rajpootanee girls pluck out the hairs as they appear with a pair of tweezers, as the ancient Greek women did, and this I think a preferable process to the shaving.

It is impossible to describe the enjoyment I experienced in the arms of these syrens. I have had English, French, German and Polish women of all grades of society since, but never, did they bear a comparison with those salacious, succulent houris of the far East.

—EDWARD SELLON

Siberian Hospitality?

The Tschuktschi offer their women to travellers; but, to prove themselves worthy of the offer, they must undergo a disgusting test. The daughter or wife, who would spend the night with a new guest, hands him a cup full of her own urine; he must rinse his mouth with it. If he's man enough to do it, he's regarded as a sincere friend; otherwise, he's treated as an enemy of the family.

—JACQUES ANTOINE DULAURE

Abraham Lincoln Gets Jilted by a Fat Woman, 1837

Abraham Lincoln (1809–1865), the man who preserved the Union, had trouble with unions of another sort—marital ones. In 1837, the twenty-eight-year-old Lincoln, then a freshly accredited lawyer and two-time Illinois state representative, proposed marriage to one Mary Owens.

Lincoln wrote this letter to a close friend, Mrs. Orville Browning, recounting the incident:

April 1, 1838, Springfield, Illinois.

Dear Madam,

. . . It was, then, in the autumn of 1836, that a married lady of my acquaintance, and who was a great friend of mine, being about to pay a visit to her father and other relatives residing in Kentucky, proposed to me, that on her return she would bring a sister of hers with her, upon condition I would engage to become her brother-in-law with all convenient dispatch. I, of course, accepted the proposal; for you know I could not have done otherwise, had I really been averse to it; but privately between you and me, I was most confoundedly well pleased with the project. I had seen the said sister some three years before, thought her intelligent and agreeable, and saw no good objection to plodding life through hand in hand with her. Time passed on, the lady took her journey and in due time returned, sister in company sure enough. This stomached me a little; for it appeared to me, that her coming so readily showed that she was a trifle too willing; but on reflection it occurred to me, that she might have been prevailed on by her married sister to come, without anything concerning me ever having been mentioned to her; and so I concluded that if no other objection presented itself, I would consent to wave [*sic*] this. All this occurred upon my <u>hearing</u> of her arrival in the neighbourhood; for, be it remembered, I had not yet <u>seen</u> her, except about three years previous, as before mentioned.

In a few days we had an interview, and although I had

seen her before, she did not look as my imagination had pictured her. I knew she was over-size, but she now appeared a fair match for Falstaff; I knew she was called an "old maid," and I felt no doubt of the truth of at least half of the appelation; but now when I beheld her, I could not for my life avoid thinking of my mother; and this not from withered features, for her skin was too full of fat, to permit its contracting into wrinkles; but from her want of teeth, weather-beaten appearance in general and from a kind of notion that ran in my head, that <u>nothing</u> could have commenced at the size of infancy, and reached her present bulk in less than thirty-five or forty years; and, in short, I was not at all pleased with her. But what could I do? I had told her sister that I would take her for better or for worse; and I made a point of honor and conscience in all things, to stick to my word, especially if others had been induced to act on it, which in this case, I doubted not they had, for I was now fairly convinced, that no other man on earth would have her, and hence the conclusion that they were bent on holding me to my bargain. Well, thought I, I have said it, and, be consequences what they may, it shall not be my fault if I fail to do it. At once I determined to consider her my wife; and this done, all my powers of discovery were put to the rack, in search of perfections in her, which might be fairly set off against her defects. I tried to imagine she was handsome, which, but for her unfortunate corpulency, was actually true. Exclusive of this, no woman that I have seen, has a finer face. I also tried to convince myself, that the mind was much more to be valued than the person; and in this, she was not inferior, as I could discover, to any with whom I had been acquainted.

Shortly after this, without attempting to come to any positive understanding with her, I set out for Vandalia, where and when you first saw me. During my stay there, I had letters from her, which did not change my opinion of either her intellect or intention; but on the contrary confirmed it in both.

Although this while, although I was fixed "firm as the surge repelling rock" in my resolution, I found I was continually repenting the rashness, which had led me to make it. Through life, I have been in no bondage, either real or imaginary from the thraldom of which I so much desired to be free.

After my return home, I saw nothing to change my opinion of her in any particular. She was the same and so was I. I now spent my time between planning how I might get along through life after my contemplated change of circumstances should have taken place, and how I might procrastinate the evil day for a time, which I really dreaded as much—perhaps more, than an Irishman does the halter.

After all my suffering upon this deeply interesting subject, here I am, wholly unexpectedly, completely out of the "scrape"; and I now want to know, if you can guess how I got out of it. Out clear in every sense of the term; no violation of word, honor or conscience. I don't believe you can guess, and so I may as well tell you at once. As the lawyers say, it was done in the manner following, towit. After I had delayed the matter as long as I thought I could in honor do, which by the way brought me into the last fall, I concluded I might as well bring it to a consummation without further delay; and so I mustered my resolution, and made the proposal to her direct; but, shocking to relate, she answered, No. At first, I supposed she did it through an affectation of modesty, which I thought but ill-become her, under the peculiar circumstances of her case; but on my renewal of the charge, I found she repeled it with greater firmness than before. I tried it again and again, but with the same success, or rather with the same want of success. I finally was forced to give it up, at which I very unexpectedly found myself mortified beyond endurance. I was mortified, it seemed to me, in a hundred different ways. My vanity was deeply wounded by the reflection, that I had been so long too stupid to discover her intentions, and at the same time never doubting that I understood them perfectly; and also, that she whom I had taught myself to believe no body else would have, had actually rejected me with all my fancied greatness; and to cap the whole, I then, for the first time, began to suspect that I was really a little in love with her. But let it all go. I'll try and out live it. Others have been made fools of by the girls; but this can never be with truth said of me. I most emphatically, in this instance, made a fool of myself. I have now come to the conclusion never again to think of marrying; and for this reason, I can never be satisfied with anyone who would be block-head enough to have me. . . .

    Your sincere friend,

A. Lincoln

On November 4, 1842, Lincoln married Mary Todd, a tart-tongued woman subject to bouts of madness, and suspected of being a Confederate sympathizer.

Lincoln's Sleeping Arrangements, 1837

Lincoln's close friend Joshua Speed wrote a brief memoir, Reminiscences of Abraham Lincoln.

It was in the spring of 1837, and on the very day that he obtained his [*law*] license, that our intimate acquaintance began. He had ridden into town on a borrowed horse, with no earthly property save a pair of saddle bags containing a few clothes. I was a merchant at Springfield, and kept a large country store, embracing dry goods, groceries, hardware, books, medicines, bed-clothes, mattresses, in fact everything that the country needed. Lincoln came into the store with his saddle bags on his arm. He said he wanted to buy the furniture for a single bed. The mattresses, blankets, sheets, coverlid, and pillow, according to figures made by me, would cost seventeen dollars. He said that was perhaps cheap enough; but, small as the sum was, he was unable to pay it. But if I would credit him till Christmas, and his experiment as a lawyer was a success, he would pay then, saying in the saddest tone, "If I fail in this, I do not know that I can ever pay you." As I looked up at him I thought then, and think now, that I never saw a sadder face.

I said to him, "You seem to be so much pained at contracting so small a debt, I think I can suggest a plan by which you can avoid the debt and at the same time attain your end. I have a large room with a double bed up-stairs, which you are very welcome to share with me."

"Where is your room?" said he.

"Up-stairs," said I, pointing to a pair of winding stairs which led from the store to my room.

He took his saddle-bags on his arm, went up stairs, set them down on the floor, and came down with a most changed countenance. Beaming with pleasure he exclaimed, "Well, Speed, I am moved!"

Abraham Lincoln shared this double bed with Speed for several years. This is an attested fact. A handful of writers have used it to speculate that Lincoln was gay, but most Lincoln scholars dismiss the notion, pointing out that bed-sharing among men wasn't so uncommon in frontier Illinois, then considered part of the West.

Edgar Allan Poe Stalks Two Women at Once, 1848

When Edgar Allan Poe's wife, Virginia, died of tuberculosis in 1847, the master of the macabre went a bit love-crazy. Poe (1809–1849) wooed several women at once—not light-heartedly but with a tortured fervor, a kind of desolate, dark, maniacal Ulalume obsessiveness.

Here Poe is writing to the widow-poetess, Mrs. Sarah Helen Whitman of Providence, to whom he had just proposed:

November 14, 1848, Steamboat to New York

My own dearest Helen, so kind so true so generous—so unmoved by all that would have moved one who had been less than angel:—beloved of my heart of my imagination of my intellect—life of my life—soul of my soul—dear, dearest Helen, how shall I ever thank you as I ought.

I am calm & tranquil & but for a strange shadow of coming evil which haunts me I should be happy. That I am not supremely happy, even when I feel your dear love at my heart, terrifies me. What can this mean?. . . .

But Poe was even more in love with a twenty-eight-year-old married woman, Annie Richmond, who had earlier told him it was for the best that he go to Providence to propose to Mrs. Whitman. (Note the dates of these two letters.)

November 16, 1848, Fordham, N.Y.

Ah, Annie Annie! my Annie! what cruel thoughts about your Eddy must have been torturing your heart during the last terrible fortnight, in which you have heard nothing from me—not even one little word to say I still lived & loved you. But Annie I know that you felt too deeply the nature of my love for you, to doubt that, even for one moment, & this thought has comforted me in my bitter sorrow—I could bear that you should imagine every other evil except that one—that my soul had been untrue to yours. Why am I not with you now darling that I might sit by your side, press your dear hand in mine, & look deep in down into the clear Heaven of your eyes— so that the words which I now can only write, might sink into your heart, and make you comprehend what it is that I would say—And yet Annie, all that I wish to say—all that my soul pines to express at this instant, is included in the one word, love—To be with you now—so that I whisper in your ear the divine emotion, which agitate me—I would willingly—oh joyfully abandon this world with all my hopes of another:—but you believe this,

Annie—you do believe it, & will always believe it—So
long as I think that you know I love you, as no man ever
loved woman—so long as I think you comprehend in
some measure, the fervor with which I adore you, so
long, no worldly trouble can ever render me absolutely
wretched. But oh, my darling, my Annie, my own sweet
sister Annie, my pure beautiful angel—wife of my soul—
to be mine hereafter & forever in the Heavens—how
shall I explain to you the bitter, bitter anguish which has
tortured me since I left you? You saw, you felt the agony
of grief with which I bade you farewell—You remember
my expression of gloom—of a dreadful horrible
foreboding of ill—Indeed—indeed it seemed to me that
death approached me even then, & that I was involved in
the shadow which went before him.—As I clasped you to
my heart, I said to myself—"it is for the last time, until
we meet in Heaven"—I remember nothing, distinctly
from that moment until I found myself in Providence—I
went to bed & wept through a long, long hideous night of
despair—When day broke, I arose & endeavored to quiet
my mind by a rapid walk in the cold, keen air—but all
would not do—the demon tormented me still. Finally I
procured two ounces of laudanum & without returning
to my Hotel, took the cars back to Boston. When I
arrived, I wrote you a letter, in which I opened my whole
heart to you—to you—my Annie, whom I so madly, so
distractedly love—I told you how my struggles were
more than I could bear—how my soul revolted from
saying the words which were to be said—and that not
even for your dear sake, could I bring myself to say them.
I then reminded you of that holy promise, which was the

last I extracted from you in parting—the promise that, under all circumstances, you would come to my bed of death—I implored you to come <u>then</u>—mentioning the place where I should be found in Boston—Having written this letter, I swallowed about half the laudanum & hurried to the Post-Office—intending not to take the rest until I saw you—for, I did not doubt for one moment, that <u>my own</u> Annie would keep her sacred promise—But I had not calculated on the strength of the laudanum, for, before I reached the Post Office my reason was entirely gone, & the letter was never put in. Let me pass over, my darling <u>sister</u>, the awful horrors which succeeded—A friend was at hand, who aided & (if it can be called saving) saved me—but it is only within the last three days that I have been able to remember what occurred in that dreary interval—It appears that, after the laudanum was rejected from the stomach, I became calm, & to a casual observer, sane—so that I was suffered to go back to Providence—Here I saw <u>her</u> and spoke, for <u>your</u> sake, the words which you urged me to speak—Ah Annie Annie! <u>my</u> Annie!—is your heart <u>so</u> strong?—is there <u>no</u> hope!—is there <u>none</u>?—I feel that I <u>must</u> die if I persist, & yet, how can I retract with honor?—Ah <u>beloved</u>, think—think for <u>me</u> & for yourself—do I not <u>love</u> you Annie? do you not <u>love me</u>? Is not this <u>all</u>? Beyond this blissful thought, what other consideration <u>can</u> there be in this dreary world! It is not much that I ask, <u>sweet sister Annie</u>—my mother[-*in-law*] & myself would take a small cottage at Westford—oh <u>so</u> small—so <u>very</u> humble—I should be far away from the tumult of the world—from the ambition which I loathe—

I would labor day & night, and with industry, I would
accomplish so much—Annie! it would be a paradise
beyond my wildest hopes—I could see some of your
beloved family every day, & you often—oh VERY
often—I would hear from you continually—regularly &
our dear mother would be with us & love us both—ah
darling—do not these pictures touch your inmost heart?
Think—oh think for me—before the words—the vows
are spoken, which put yet another terrible bar between
us—before the time goes by, beyond which there must
be no thinking—I call upon you in the name of God—in
the name of the holy love I bear you, to be sincere with
me—Can you, my Annie, bear to think I am another's? It
would give me supreme—infinite bliss to hear you say
that you could not bear it—I am at home now with my
dear muddie who is endeavoring to comfort me—but the
sole words which soothe me, are those in which she
speaks of "my Annie"—she tells me that she has written
you, begging you to come on to Fordham—ah beloved
Annie, IS IT NOT POSSIBLE? I am so ill—so terribly
hopelessly ILL in body and mind, that I feel I CANNOT
live, unless I can feel your sweet, gentle, loving hand
pressed upon my forehead—oh my pure, virtuous,
generous, beautiful, beautiful sister Annie!—is it not
POSSIBLE for you to come—if only for one little
week?—until I subdue this fearful agitation, which if
continued, will either destroy my life or, drive me
hopelessly mad—Farewell—here & hereafter—

   forever your own

Eddy—

Poe was dead by October 7 of the following year. Before that, though, he did propose to another widow, Mrs. Shelton, a childhood sweetheart.

A French Army Officer Commits Necrophilia, 1849

Sergeant Bertrand was a French army officer, slightly built, a loner. He sat for long interviews with court-appointed doctors, including this one with Dr. Ambroise Tardieu, recorded in his Attentats aux Moeurs:

I began to masturbate at a very tender age without knowing what I was doing; I did not conceal myself from anyone. It was not until the age of eight or nine that I began to think of women, but this passion did not become really strong until the age of thirteen or fourteen. Then I no longer knew any bounds, and I masturbated up to seven or eight times a day; the mere sight of a feminine garment excited me. When masturbating I transported myself in imagination into a room where there were women at my disposal; there, after having assuaged my passion on them and after having tormented them in every possible way, I imagined them dead, and I performed all sorts of profanities on their cadavres.

In 1844, Sergeant Bertrand began mutilating animals; in 1847, he dug up his first corpse; in 1848, he fulfilled his ultimate fantasy:

Having arrived at Douai [*in France,*] I felt the need of mutilating dead bodies. One evening toward the 10th of March [*1848*] I went to the cemetery; it was 9 o'clock and after the tattoo, which beat at 8 o'clock, the soldiers no longer left the village; so to execute my design I found it necessary for me to climb the surrounding wall and to get over a ditch about four meters wide by two deep. These difficulties were not capable of stopping me; after having climbed the wall in a place where it was falling into ruins, I recognized the impossibility of leaping the ditch; I crossed it by swimming, after having thrown my clothes across to the other side. The cold was intense, there was even some ice. No sooner had I entered the cemetery than I began to disinter a young girl who might have been from fifteen to seventeen years of age. This body was the first on which I indulged in indecent excesses. I cannot describe what I experienced at that moment; all that is experienced with a living woman is nothing in comparison. I kissed this dead woman in all parts of her body, I pressed her against myself as if to break her in two; in a word I lavished on her all the caresses that a passionate lover could on the object of his love. After having played with this inanimate body for a quarter of an hour, I began to mutilate it and tear out the entrails as on all the other victims of my fury. Afterward I put the body back into the grave, and having covered it with earth again, I returned to the barracks by the same means employed in going to the cemetery. . . .

We returned to Paris (July 17, 1848) and the regiment occupied the camp at Ivry. After some days of rest, the trouble took possession of me more violently than ever. During the night the sentinels were posted very close together and had rigid instructions; but nothing could stop me. I left the camp almost every night to go to the cemetery at Montparnasse, where I indulged in very great excesses.

The first victim of my madness in this cemetery was a young girl of twelve or thirteen years; her body was all decomposed, but that did not prevent me from profaning it by indecent acts. Finally, after having opened the belly and torn out the entrails and having cut up the genital organs, I masturbated again and withdrew. This violation of the sepulchre took place toward the 25th of July, 1848.

On March 15, 1849, having left the Luxembourg at 10 o'clock at night to go to a rendez-vous that I had made, it was my misfortune to pass near the cemetery at Montparnasse; I was impelled to enter as usual, and it was while scaling the enclosure that I was wounded; I believe that if the trap had missed me that time, I should never in my life have returned to a cemetery; however I am not sure of that. . . .

In all my violations of sepulchres, in no case was the act premeditated; when the attack got possession of me, whether at noon or at midnight, I had to go; it was impossible to postpone it.

Bertrand was sentenced to one year in prison.

Graham Crackers and the American Sex Drive, 1848

Religious zealot Sylvester Graham (1794–1851)—who blamed the nation's sinful excesses on too much meat and spicy food—invented the Graham cracker as a nice bland dietary substitute that would reduce the nation's sex drive and save souls. "Health does not absolutely require that there should ever be an emission of semen from puberty to death," *he wrote,* "though the individual live an hundred years."

Marital Frequency

It is impossible to lay down a precise rule, which will be equally adapted to all men, in regard to their frequency of connubial commerce. But as a general rule, it may be said to the healthy and robust, it were better for you not to exceed, in the frequency of your indulgences, the number of months in the year; and you cannot habitually exceed the number of weeks in the year, without to some degree impairing your constitutional powers, shortening your lives, and increasing your liability to disease and suffering.

Prison Masturbation

Graham was staunchly against masturbation. Here he records a "verbatim" conversation between a prison chaplain and an unfortunate inmate:

Not long since, as I was passing the cell of one of the prisoners, just at twilight, he spoke to me with a low and tremulous voice and downcast look. "I shan't live long," said he, "don't you see how poor I am growing? My flesh is almost all gone off my bones." I observed that what he said was true. When I first knew him, he had a full and ruddy cheek; now it was pale and sunken. I suspected the cause, and made inquiries accordingly. He confessed that he had become a slave to that vice [*i.e., masturbation*], and feared it was doing him harm; but did not dare speak to the doctor about it, and did not know that he could avoid it; "for," he said, "I seem to have no power over myself. I awake from my sleep and find myself in the act. Three times a night for weeks in succession, I have yielded to it, and frequently without being voluntary in the thing." He evinced clearly the reciprocal influence between the brain and the genital organs.

"There are several others in prison whom I know to be

given up to a similar excess; and without exception, they all have that cadaverous look, bloodless lips, impaired memory, bodily weakness and pain, and those internal complaints, of which Mr. G[*raham*] speaks in his lecture."

—SYLVESTER GRAHAM

By way of a "cure" for masturbation, Graham advised a bland diet and exercise; he once recommended, for a young man identified as S.W., three months in handcuffs.

Flaubert Chases Belly Dancers in Egypt, 1850

Madame Bovary, with her ice-cold feet and unspeakable frustration, has been enshrined among the greatest characters ever created. Gustave Flaubert (1821–1880), who dazzles with an uncanny eye for detail and personality, used those same gifts when, at twenty-eight, he traveled to Egypt, searching for the exotic Orient of the Arabian nights.

Flaubert, throughout his life, was quite open to paying for sex:

It may be a perverted taste, but I love prostitution, and for itself, quite apart from its carnal aspects. My heart begins to pound every time I see one of those women in low-cut dresses walking under the lamplight in the rain, just as monks in their corded robes have always excited some deep ascetic corner of my soul. The idea of prostitution is a meeting place of so many elements—lust, bitterness, complete absence of human contact, muscular frenzy, the clink of gold—that to peer into it deeply makes one reel. One learns so many things in a brothel, and feels such sadness and dreams so longingly of love!

Flaubert's travel notes and letters from Egypt deliver a

*picture of a man on a mission: to explore sensuality. His travel
companion was a lech of a journalist named Max du Camp,
who once tried to sneak into the Grand Turk's harem in
Constantinople.*

Letter to Louis Bouilhet

Cairo, January 15, 1850

. . . I'll have this marvelous Hasan el-Belbeissi come
again. He'll dance The Bee for me. Done by such a
bardash [*a homosexual*] as he, it can scarcely be a thing
for babes.

Speaking of bardashes, this is what I know about
them. Here it is quite accepted. One admits one's
sodomy, and it is spoken of at table in the hotel.
Sometimes you do a bit of denying, and then everybody
teases you and you end up confessing. Travelling as we
are for educational purposes, and charged with a mission
by the government, we have considered it our duty to
indulge in this form of ejaculation. So far the occasion
has not presented itself. We continue to seek it,
however. It's at the baths that such things take place. You
reserve the bath for yourself (five francs including
masseurs, pipe, coffee, sheet and towel) and you skewer
your lad in one of the rooms. Be informed, furthermore,
that all the bath-boys are bardashes. The final masseurs,
the ones who come to rub you when all the rest is done,
are usually quite nice young boys. We had our eye on
one in an establishment very near our hotel. I reserved
the bath exclusively for myself. I went, and the rascal

was away that day! I was alone in the hot room, watching the daylight fade through the great circles of glass in the dome. Hot water was flowing everywhere; stretched out indolently I thought of a quantity of things as my pores tranquilly dilated. It is very voluptuous and sweetly melancholy to take a bath like that quite alone, lost in those dim rooms where the slightest noise resounds like a cannon shot, while the naked kellaas call out to one another as they massage you, turning you over like embalmers preparing you for the tomb. That day (the day before yesterday, Monday) my kellaa was rubbing me gently, and when he came to the noble parts, he lifted up my boules d'amour to clean them, then continued rubbing my chest with his left hand he began to pull with his right on my prick, and as he drew it up and down he leaned over my shoulder and said, "baksheesh, baksheesh" [*"tip, tip"*]. He was a man in his fifties, ignoble, disgusting—imagine the effect, and the word "baksheesh, baksheesh." I pushed him away a little, saying, "lah, lah" [*"no, no"*]—he thought I was angry and took on a craven look—then I gave him a few pats on the shoulder saying, "lah, lah" again but more gently—he smiled a smile that meant, "You're not fooling me—you like it as much as anybody, but today you've decided against it for some reason." As for me, I laughed aloud like a dirty old man, and the shadowy vault of the bath echoed with the sound.

. . . A week ago I saw a monkey in the street jump on a donkey and try to jack him off—the donkey brayed and kicked, the monkey's owner shouted, the monkey itself squealed—apart from two or three children who laughed and me who found it very funny, no one paid any attention. When I described this to M. Belin, the secretary at the consulate, he told me of having seen an ostrich try to violate a donkey. Max had himself jacked off the other day in a deserted section among some ruins and said it was very good.

Enough lubricities.

Flaubert's Travel Notes

Here Flaubert is making a pilgrimage to visit Kuchuk Hanem, one of the most notorious dancing girls in Egypt:

Wednesday, March 6, 1850

Reached Esna [*Upper Nile*] about nine in the morning. . . . House of Kuchuk Hanem.

Bambeh [*another dancing girl*] precedes us, accompanied by her sheep; she pushes open a door and we enter a house with a small courtyard and a stairway opposite the door. On the stairs, opposite us, surrounded by light and standing against the backdrop of blue sky, a woman in pink trousers. Above, she wore only dark violet gauze.

She had just come from the bath, her firm breasts had a fresh smell like that of sweetened turpentine; she began by perfuming her hands with rose water.

We went up to the first floor. Turning to the left at the top of the stairs, we entered a square whitewashed room: two divans, two windows, one looking on the mountains, the other on the town.

. . . Kuchuk Hanem is a tall, splendid creature, lighter in coloring than an Arab; she comes from Damascus; her skin, particularly on her body, is slightly coffee-colored. When she bends, her flesh ripples into bronze ridges. Her eyes are dark and enormous, her eyebrows black, her nostrils open and wide; heavy shoulders, full apple-shaped breasts. She wore a large tarboosh, ornamented on the top with a convex gold disk, in the middle of which was a small green stone imitating emerald; the blue tassel of her tarboosh spread out fan-wise and fell down over her shoulders; just in front of the lower edge of the tarboosh, fastened to her hair and going from one ear to the other, she had a small spray of white artificial flowers. Her black hair, wavy unruly, pulled straight back on each side from a center parting beginning at the forehead; small braids joined together at the nape of her neck. She has one upper incisor, right, which is beginning to go bad. For a bracelet she has two bands of gold, twisted together and interlaced, around one wrist. Triple necklace of large hollow gold beads. Earrings: gold disks, slightly convex, circumference decorated with gold granules. On her right arm is tattooed a line of blue writing.

She asks us if we would like a little entertainment, but Max says that first he would like to entertain himself alone with her, and they go downstairs. After he finishes, I go down and follow his example. Ground floor room, with a divan and a cafas [*an upturned palm fiber basket*] with a mattress.

DANCE. The musicians arrive: a child and an old man whose left eye is covered with a rag; they both scrape on the rebabah, a kind of small round violin with a metal leg that rests on the ground and two horse-hair strings. The neck of the instrument is very long in proportion to the rest. Nothing could be more discordant or disagreeable. The musicians never stop playing for an instant unless you shout at them to do so.

Kuchuk Hanem and Bambeh begin to dance. Kuchuk's dance is brutal. She squeezes her bare breasts together with her jacket. She puts on a girdle fashioned from a brown shawl with gold stripes with three tassles hanging on ribbons. She rises first on one foot then the other—marvelous movement: when one foot is on the ground, the other moves up and across in front of the shin-bone—the whole thing with a light bound. I have seen this dance on old Greek vases.

Bambeh prefers a dance on a straight line; she moves with a lowering and raising of one hip only, a kind of rhythmic limping of great character. Bambeh has henna on her hands. She seems to be a devoted servant to Kuchuk. (She was a chambermaid in Cairo in an Italian household and understands a few words of Italian; her eyes are slightly diseased.) All in all, their dancing—except Kuchuk's step mentioned above—is far less good than that of Hasan el-Belbeissi, the male dancer in Cairo. Joseph's opinion is that all beautiful women dance badly.

. . . *Ces dames,* and particularly the old musician, imbibe considerable amounts of raki. Kuchuk dances with my tarboosh on her head. Then she accompanies us to the end of her quarter, climbing up on our backs and making faces and jokes like any Christian tart.

At the cafe of *ces dames.* We take a cup of coffee. The place is like all such places—flat roof of sugar cane stalks put together any which way. Kuchuk's amusement at seeing our shaven heads and hearing Max say: "Allah il allah" etc.

Second and more detailed visit to the temple. We wait for the effendi in the cafe, to give him a letter. Dinner.

We return to Kuchuk's house. The room was lighted by three wicks in glasses full of oil, inserted in tin sconces hanging on the wall. The musicians are in their places. Several glasses of raki are quickly drunk; our gift of liquor and the fact that we are wearing swords have their effect.

Arrival of Safiah Zugairah, a small woman with a large nose and eyes that are dark, deep-set, savage, sensual; her necklace of coins clanks like a country cart; she kisses our hands.

The four women seated in a line on the divan singing. The lamps cast quivering lozenge-shaped shadows on the walls, the light is yellow. Bambeh wore a pink robe with large sleeves (all the costumes are light-colored) and her hair was covered with a black kerchief such as the peasants wear. They all sang, the darabukehs throbbed, and the monotonous rebecs furnished a soft but shrill bass; it was like a rather gay song of mourning.

Coup with Safia Zugairah ("Little Sophie")—I stain the divan. She is very raunchy and writhing, extremely voluptuous. But the best was the second copulation with Kuchuk. Effect of her necklace between my teeth. Her cunt felt like rolls of velvet as she made me come. I felt like a tiger.

Kuchuk dances The Bee. First so the door can be closed, the women send away Faghali and another sailor, who up to now have been watching the dances and who, in the background, constituted the grotesque element of the scene. A black veil is tied around the eyes of the child, and a fold of his blue turban is lowered over those of the old man. Kuchuk shed her clothing as she danced. Finally she was naked except for a fichu which she held in her hands and behind which she pretended to hide, and at the end she threw down the fichu. That was The Bee. She danced it very briefly and said she does not like to dance that dance. Joseph, very excited, kept clapping his hands: "La, eu, nia, oh! eu, nia oh!" Finally, after repeating for us the wonderful step she had danced in the afternoon, she sank down breathless on her divan, her body continuing to move slightly in rhythm. One of the women threw her enormous white trousers striped with pink, and she pulled them up to her neck. The two musicians were un-blindfolded.

When she was sitting cross-legged on the divan, the magnificent absolutely sculptural design of her knees.

Another dance: a cup of coffee is placed on the ground; she dances before it, then falls on her knees and continues to move her torso, always clacking the castanets, and describing in the air a gesture with her arms as though she were swimming. That continues, gradually the head is lowered, she reaches the cup, takes the edge of it between her teeth and then leaps up quickly with a single bound.

She was not too enthusiastic about having us spend the night with her, out of fear of thieves who are apt to come when they know strangers are there. Some guards or pimps (on whom she did not spare the cudgel) slept downstairs in a side room, with Joseph and the negress, an Abyssinian slave who carried on each arm the round scar (like a burn) of a plague sore. We went to bed; she insisted on keeping the outside. Lamp: the wick rested in an oval cup with a lip; after some violent play, *coup*. She falls asleep with her hand in mine. She snores. The lamp, shining feebly, casts a triangular gleam, the color of pale metal on her beautiful forehead; the rest of her face was in shadow. Her little dog slept on my silk jacket on the divan. Since she complained of a cough, I put my pelisse over her blanket. I heard Joseph and the guards talking in low voices; I gave myself over to intense reverie, full of reminiscences. Feeling of her stomach against my buttocks. Her mound warmer than her stomach, heated me like a hot iron. Another time I dozed off with my fingers passed through her necklace, as though to hold her should she awake. I thought of Judith and Holofernes sleeping together. At quarter of three, we awake—another *coup,* this time very affectionate. We told each other a great many things by pressure. (As she slept she kept contracting her hands and thighs mechanically, like involuntary shudders.)

I smoke a sheesheh, then she goes down to talk to Joseph, brings back a bucket of burning charcoal, warms herself, comes back to bed. "Basta!"

How flattering it would be to one's pride if at the moment of leaving you were sure that you left a memory behind, that she would think of you more than of the others who have been there, that you would remain in her heart!

. . . We left Esna at a quarter to noon. Some Bedouins sold us a gazelle they had killed that morning on the other side of the Nile.

—GUSTAVE FLAUBERT

Karl Marx Writes a Love Letter to His Wife, 1856

"Workers of the world unite!" Marx's words launched revolutions. But there was another side to the philosopher (1818–1883), which he reveals in a letter to his wife, Jenny—this, after thirteen years of marriage:

June 21, 1856

My heart's beloved,

. . . I have you [*your photograph*] vividly before me, and I carry you on my hands, and I kiss you from head to foot, and I fall on my knees before you, and I groan: "Madam, I love you."

. . . There are actually many females in the world, and some among them are beautiful. But where could I find again a face whose every feature, even every wrinkle, is a reminder of the greatest and sweetest memories of my life? Even my endless pains, my irreplaceable losses, I read in your sweet countenance, and I kiss away the pain when I kiss your sweet face. "Buried in her arms, awakened by her kisses"—namely, in your arms and by your kisses, and I grant the Brahmins and Pythagoras their doctrine of regeneration and Christianity its doctrine of Resurrection.

—KARL MARX

A Pair of Victorian Explorers

They were the odd couple of exploration: proper Victorian John Hanning Speke and unrepentant sexologist Sir Richard Burton. So it was very ironic that Speke's career should sputter a bit over his reporting of an African marital custom:

Fat Queens and the Source of the Nile, 1861

John Hanning Speke (1827–1864) outraced his former colleague Sir Richard Burton to discover the source of the Nile at Lake Victoria, and during his expedition he also explored the royal family at Karague in East Central Africa.

November 26, 1861

In the afternoon, as I had heard from Musa that the wives of the king and princes were fattened to such an extent that they could not stand upright, I paid my respects to Wazezeru, the king's eldest brother—who, having been born before his father ascended his throne, did not come in the line of succession—with the hope of being able to see for myself the truth of the story. There was no mistake about it. On entering the hut I found the old man and his chief wife sitting side by side on a bench of earth strewed over with grass, and partitioned like stalls for sleeping apartments, whilst in front of them were placed numerous wooden pots of milk, and hanging from the poles that supported the bee-hive-shaped hut, a large collection of bows six feet in length, whilst below them were tied an even larger collection of spears, intermixed with a goodly assortment of heavy-headed assages [*slender javelins*]. I was struck with no small surprise at the way he received me, as well as with the extraordinary dimensions yet pleasing beauty, of the immoderately fat fair one his wife. She could not rise; and so large were her arms that, between the joints, the flesh hung down like large loose-stuffed puddings. Then in came their children, all models of the Abyssinian type of beauty, and as polite in their manners as thorough-bred gentlemen. They had heard of my picture-books from the king, and all wished to see them; which they no sooner did, to their infinite delight, especially when they recognized any of the animals, than the subject was turned by my inquiring what they did with so many milk-pots. This was easily explained by Wazezeru himself, who, pointing to his wife, said, "This is all the product of those pots: from early youth upwards we keep those pots to their mouths, as it is the fashion at court to have very fat wives."

December 14, 1861

After a long and amusing conversation with Rumanika in the morning, I called on one of his sisters-in-law, married to an elder brother who was born before Dagara ascended to the throne. She was another of those wonders of obesity, unable to stand excepting on all fours. I was desirous to obtain a good view of her, and actually to measure her, and induced her to give me facilities for doing so, by offering in return to show her a bit of my naked legs and arms. The bait took as I wished it, and after getting her to sidle and wriggle into the middle of the hut, I did as I promised, and took her dimensions as noted below. ° All of these are exact except the height, and I believe I could have obtained this more accurately if I could have had her laid on the floor. Not knowing what difficulties I should have to contend with in such a piece of engineering, I tried to get her height by raising her up. This, after infinite exertions on the part of us both, was accomplished when she sank down again, fainting for her blood had rushed into her head. Meanwhile, the daughter, a lass of sixteen, sat stark-naked before us, sucking at a milk-pot, on which the father kept her at work by holding a rod in his hand, for as fattening is the first duty of fashionable female life, it must be duly enforced by the rod if necessary. I got up a bit of flirtation with missy, and induced her to rise and shake hands with me. Her features were lovely, but her body was round as a ball.

—JOHN HANNING SPEKE

°*Round arm, 1 ft. 11 in.; chest 4 ft. 4 in.; thigh 2 ft. 7 in.; calf 1 ft. 8 in.; height 5 ft. 8 in.*

Sir Richard Burton's Sex Notes
(1842–1885)

While searching for the source of the Nile, while slipping into the Moslem sanctuary of Mecca, and during all his other adventures, Richard Burton (1821–1890) collected facts about local sexual customs: Arab, African, Indian, Mormon, South American.

Racial Dimensions

Debauched women prefer negroes on the account of the size of their parts. I measured one man in Somali-land who, when quiescent, numbered nearly six inches. This is a characteristic of the negro race and of African animals; e.g., the horse; whereas the pure Arab, man and beast, is below the average of Europe; one of the best proofs by the by, that the Egyptian is not an Asiatic, but a negro partially white-washed. Moreover, these imposing parts do not increase proportionately during erection; consequently the deed of kind takes a much longer time and adds greatly to the woman's enjoyment. In my time, no honest Hindi Moslem would take his womenfolk to Zanzibar on account of the huge temptations there and thereby offered to them.

Nutcracker Surcharge

[*There's*] a peculiarity highly prized by the Egyptians; the use of the constrictor vaginae muscles, the sphincter for which Abyssinian women are famous. The "Kabazzah" (holder), as she is called, can sit astraddle upon a man and can provoke venereal orgasm, not by wriggling and moving but by tightening and loosing the male member with the muscles of her privities, milking it as it were. Consequently the "casse-noisette" [*nut-cracker*] costs treble the money of other concubines.

Clues for the Curious

Burton translated this Arab saying:
A maiden's mouth shows what's the make of her chose;
And man's mentule one knows by the length of his nose.
Then he added his own theory for women's pubes:
And the eyebrows disclose
How the lower wig grows.

Chinese Sex Aid

For the use of men, they have the "merkin," a heart-shaped article of thin skin stuffed with cotton and slit with an artificial vagina: two tapes at the top and one below lash it to the back of a chair.

Prolonging the Act

We do not find in The Nights any allusion to this systematic prolongatio veneris [*prolonging of Venus*] which is so much cultivated by Moslems under the name Imsak (retention, withholding i.e., the semen). Yes Eastern books on domestic medicine consist mostly of two parts; the first of general prescriptions and the second of aphrodisiacs especially those qui prolongent le plaisir as did the Gaul by thinking of sa pauvre mere [*his poor mother*]. The Ananga-Ranga by the Reverend Koka Pandit before quoted, gives a host of recipes which are used either externally or internally, to hasten the paroxysm of the woman and delay the orgasm of the man.

Some of these are curious in the extreme. I heard of a Hindi who made a candle of frogs' fat and fibre warranted to retain the seed till it burned out: it failed notably because, relying upon it, he worked too vigorously. The essence of the retaining art is to avoid over-tension of the muscles and to pre-occupy the brain: hence in coition Hindus will drink sherbet, chew betel-nut and even smoke. Europeans ignoring the science and practice, are contemptuously compared with village-cocks [*roosters*] by Hindu women who cannot be satisfied, such is their natural coldness, increased doubtless by vegetable diet and unuse of stimulants, with less than twenty minutes. Hence while thousands of Europeans have cohabited for years with and have had families by "native women" they are never loved by them—at least I never heard of a case.

Pederasty Brothel in India

The "execrabilis familia pathicorum" [*disgusting species of passive partners*] first came before me by a chance of earlier life. In 1845, when Sir Charles Napier had conquered and annexed Sind, despite a faction (mostly venal) which sought favor with the now defunct "Court of Directors to the Honourable East India Company," the veteran began to consider his conquest with a curious eye. It was reported to him that Karachi, a townlet of some two thousand souls and distant not more than a mile from camp, supported no less than three lupanars or bordels, in which not women but boys and eunuchs, the former demanding nearly a double price, lay for hire. (This detail especially excited the veteran's curiosity. The reason proved to be that the scrotum of the unmutilated boy could be used as a kind of bridle for directing the movements of the animal. I find nothing of the kind mentioned in the Sotadical [*homosexual*] literature of Greece and Rome.)

Caught in the Harem

A favourite Persian punishment for strangers caught in the Harem or Gynaeceum is to strip and throw them and expose them to the embraces of the grooms and negro-slaves. I once asked a Shirazi how penetration was possible if the patient [*i.e., passive partner*] resisted with all the force of the sphincter muscle; he smiled and said, "Ah, we Persians know a trick to get over that; we apply a sharpened tent peg to the crupper-bone [*coccyx*] and knock till he opens." A well-known missionary to the East during the last generation was subjected to this gross insult by one of the Persian Prince-governors, whom he had infuriated by his conversion-mania: in his memoirs he alludes to it by mentioning his "dishonoured person"; but English readers cannot comprehend the full significance of the confession.

Man Cannon

About the same time Shaykh Nasr, Governor of Bushire, a man famed for facetious blackguardism, used to invite European youngsters serving in the Bombay Marine and ply them with liquor till they were insensible. Next morning the middies mostly complained that the champagne had caused a curious irritation and soreness in la parte-poste [*i.e., derriere*]. The same Eastern Scrogin would ask his guests if they had ever seen a man-cannon (Adami-top); and, on their replying in the negative, a grey-beard slave was dragged in blaspheming and struggling with all his strength. He was presently placed on all fours and firmly held by the extremities; his bag-

trousers were let down and a dozen peppercorns were inserted
ano suo [*in his anus*]; the target was a sheet of paper held at a
reasonable distance; the match was applied by a pinch of
cayenne in the nostrils; the sneeze started the grapeshot and
the number of hits on the butt decided the bets.

—SIR RICHARD BURTON

*Burton died on October 20, 1890; two weeks later his wife,
Isabel, burned all his unpublished notebooks and letters and
his just completed translation of* The Perfumed Garden.

A Sadistic Englishman in Paris, 1862

*Fred Hankey (1828–1882), an expatriate Brit who collected
expensive pornography in Paris and smuggled it back to clients
in England, was called* "a second de Sade without the
intellect." *He once begged a favor of an executioner at the
hanging of a murderess; he also gave explorer Sir Richard
Burton his most grotesque commission.*

*The extensive journals of critics Edmond and Jules de
Goncourt are crammed with period detail and arch opinions:*

April 7, 1862

Today I met a madman, a monster, one of those men who
linger in the abyss. Through him, as though through a veil torn
away, I glimpsed an abominable depth, a terrifying side of a
bored rich aristocracy, of an English aristocracy bringing
ferocity to Love, a man who enjoys his libertinage only
through the suffering of women.

At a ball at the Opera, Saint Victor had been introduced to a young Englishman, who said simply to him, by way of starting off the conversation, that "there's hardly anything amusing to do in Paris, while London is infinitely superior, that in London, there's quite a fine house, a house of mistress Jenkins, where there were young girls around the age of thirteen, first you set up a school class; then you whipped the little ones, oh! not very hard, but the bigger girls quite hard. You can also stick them with pins, the pins not very long, long only like this," and he showed us the tip of his finger. "Yes, you can see blood! . . . " The young Englishman placidly and sedately added: "As for me, I have cruel tastes, but I draw the line at men or animals. Once with a friend, I rented a window, for a huge amount of money, to witness the hanging of a murderess and we had with us some women so that we could do "certain things" to them—he always used very civil expressions—"at the very moment when she would be hanged. We had even asked the hangman to lift the murderess' skirt a little bit! while hanging her. . . . But unfortunately, the Queen, at the last moment, pardoned her."

Thus, today, Saint Victor took me to meet this unique ghoul. He is a young man of about thirty years old, his temples puffed out like an orange, his eyes of a clear and piercing blue, his skin extremely thin and revealing the sub-cutaneous network of veins, the head—it's strange—the head is of one of those young emaciated and beatific priests, surrounding the bishops in those old paintings. An elegant young man having a bit of stiffness in his arms and body movements; at the same time mechanical and feverish like someone just attacked by spinal marrow disease and with all that an elaborate courtesy, an exquisite politeness, a gentleness of very refined manners.

He opened a large chest-high cabinet, where was kept a

curious collection of erotic books, admirably bound. He handed me a "MEIBOMIUS—The Uses of Flagellation in the Pleasures of Love and Marriage," bound by one of the premier bookbinders of Paris, with engraved bookplates on the inside representing phalluses, skulls, torture instruments, which he designed himself. He tells us: "Ah these engravings . . . , at first the bookbinder did not want to execute them . . . then I loaned him some of my books . . . now he makes his wife very unhappy . . . he runs after little girls . . . but I have my engravings." And showing us another book all ready for the bookbinder: "Yes, for this volume I'm waiting for a skin, a skin of a young girl . . . that one of my friends got for me . . . it will be tanned . . . it takes six months to tan it . . . . If you want to see my skin? . . . But it's not interesting . . . it would have had to have been lifted off a young girl still alive. . . . Luckily I have my friend doctor Bartsh . . . you know, the one who explores Central Africa . . . and so, during one of the massacres . . . he promised me he'd have a skin like that taken for me . . . from a living negress."

And meanwhile, while examining his fingernails held out in front of him, with the look of a maniac, he speaks, he speaks endlessly, and his voice is a bit sing song, halting; then he starts again just as he stops, his cannibalistic words penetrate your ears like a drill.

—EDMOND AND JULES DE GONCOURT

The African explorer mentioned above as "doctor Bartsh" was apparently Sir Richard Burton, and Burton, while in Dahomey wrote a letter about the skin to the notorious Lord Houghton, one of Hankey's clients for pornography:

I have been here three days and am grievously disappointed. Not a man killed, nor a fellow tortured. The canoe floating in blood is a myth of myths. Poor Hankey must still wait for his peau de femme [*skin of a woman*].

Victorian Conversation Verbatim

Lord Houghton recorded this in his commonplace book:

1860

Burton of Hankey: "There is no accounting for tastes in superstition. Hankey would like to have a Bible bound with bits of skin stripped off live from the cunts of a hundred little girls and yet he could not be persuaded to try the sensations of f . . . g a Muscovy duck while its head was cut off.

— LORD HOUGHTON

Flagellation

For many British schoolboys educated at the likes of Eton or Exeter, a flogging represented their first nonsolitary sexual experience. Some never outgrew a taste for it. The practice of sexual whipping was dubbed the "English Vice," and in England during the Victorian era there grew a huge underground appetite for so-called "flagellant pornography." Thousands of books were clandestinely published. The formula was tried and true: A boy or girl misbehaves and the disciplinarian—often a beautiful mistress—must administer the rod. Excruciating pain melts into excruciating pleasure. But this practice was no mere pornographic fantasy.

The Most Popular Flagellation Parlor in London, 1828

In 1820s London, there were at least a dozen houses catering to flagellation. The most popular was that of Mrs. Theresa Berkley, 28 Charlotte Street, Portland Place. When she died, she left her brother more than £10,000 sterling, which—missionary that he was—he refused to accept.

An introduction to Venus Schoolmistress *(1860), attributed to brothel keeper Mary Wilson, focused on Theresa Berkley:*

She possessed the first grand requisite of a courtesan, viz., lewdness; for [*unless*] a woman is positively lecherous she cannot long keep up the affectation of it, and it will soon be perceived that she only moves her hands or her buttocks to the tune of pounds, shillings and pence. She could assume great urbanity and good humour; she would study every lech, whim, caprice and desire of her customer, and had the disposition to gratify them, if her avarice was rewarded in return.

Her instruments of torture were more numerous than those of any other governess. Her supply of birch was extensive, and kept in water so that it was always green and pliant: she had shafts with a dozen whip thongs on each of them; a dozen different sizes of cat-o-nine tails, some with needle points worked into them; various kinds of thin bending canes; leather straps like coach traces; battledoors made of thick sole-leather, with inch nails run through to docket, and currycomb tough hides rendered callous by many years flagellation. Holly brushes, furze brushes; a prickly evergreen, called butchers brush; and during the summer, glass and China vases filled with a constant supply of green nettles, with which she often restored the dead to life. Thus, at her shop, whoever went with plenty of money, could be birched, whipped, fustigated, scourged, needle-pricked, half-hung, holly-brushed, furze-brushed, butcher-brushed, stinging nettled, curry-combed, phlebotomized, and tortured till he had a belly full.

For those whose lech it was to flog a woman, she would herself submit to a certain extent; but if they were gluttons at it, she had women in attendance who would take any number of lashes the flogger pleased, provided he forked out an "ad valorem" duty. Among these were Miss Ring, Hannah Jones, Sally Taylor, One-Eyed Peg, Bauld-cunted Poll and a black girl called Ebony Bet.

The machine represented in the frontispiece to this work was invented for Mrs. Berkley to flog gentlemen upon, in the spring of 1828. [*The "Berkley Horse" resembles two tall ladders hinged at the top so that they form an upside-down V; a few waist-high rungs are removed from one of the ladders.*] It is capable of being opened to a considerable extent, so as to bring the body to any angle that might be desirable. There is a print in Mrs. Berkley's memoirs, representing a man upon it quite naked. A woman is sitting in a chair exactly under it, with her bosom belly and bush exposed: she is "manualizing" his "embolon," whilst Mrs. Berkley is birching his posteriors. The female, acting as "frictrix," was intended for Fisher, a fine tall dark haired girl, all must remember who visited Charlotte Street at that day as well as the good humoured blonde, Willis; the plump, tight, frisky and merry arsed Thurlow; Grenville, with the enormous bubbies; Bentinc, with breadth of hip and splendour of buttock; Olive, the gypsy, whose brown skin, wicked black eye and medicean form, would melt an anchorite; the mild and amiable Palmer, with luxuriant and well-fledged mount, from whose tufted honors many a noble lord has stolen a sprig; and Pryce, the pleasing and complaisant who, when birch was a question, could both give and take.

When the new flogging machine was invented, the designer told her it would bring her into notice, and go by her name after her death; and it did cause her to be talked of, and brought her a great deal of business. She died in Sept. 1836, having funded ten thousand pounds during the eight years she had been a governess. The original horse is among the models of the Society of Arts at the Adelphi, and was presented by Dr. Vance, her executor.

Mrs. Berkley had also in her second floor, a hook and pulley attached to the ceiling, by which she could draw a man up by the hands.

Mary Wilson also tried to explain the appeal of flagellation:
The men who have a propensity for flagellation may be divided into three classes:

1) Those who like to receive a fustigation, more or less severe, from the hand of a fine woman, who is sufficiently robust to wield the rod with vigor and effect.
2) Those who desire themselves to administer birch discipline on the white and plump buttocks of a female.
3) Those who neither wish to be passive recipients nor active administrators of birch discipline but would derive sufficient excitement as mere spectators of the sport.

Many persons not sufficiently acquainted with human nature and the ways of the world, are apt to imagine that the lech for flagellation must be confined either to the aged, or to those who are exhausted through too great a devotion to venery; but such is not the fact, for there are quite as many young men and men in the prime of life who are influenced by this passion. . . .

It is very true that there are innumerable old generals, admirals, colonels, and captains, as well as bishops judges, barristers, lords, commoners and physicians, who periodically go to be whipped, merely because it warms their blood, and keeps up a little agreeable excitement in their systems long after the power of enjoying the opposite sex has failed them; but it is equally true that hundreds of young men through having been educated at institutions where the masters were fond of administering birch discipline, and recollecting certain sensations produced by it, have imbibed a passion for it, and have longed to receive the same chastisement from the hands of a fine woman.

—MARY WILSON, IN *VENUS SCHOOLMISTRESS*

Fond Memories of a Birching and a Maid, 1859

Victorian erotica collector Henry Spencer Ashbee received this letter:

March 13, 1859

In my boyish days it was customary in preparatory schools to have boys and girls together under a woman, and where the rod was used on all occasions with the

utmost severity. We used to be birched in the presence
of each other, the girls across the knee, or held under the
arm, the boys on the back of a maid servant. The latter
used often to come to our rooms, and play the
schoolmistress, so did most of the girls. I have a vivid
recollection of some of the extraordinary scenes in this
line which have often given me the perfect conviction of
numerous women possessing the taste in question. In
the school mentioned above, the female who always
assisted the mistress was evidently most fond of seeing
the operation, though she liked us all, and was herself a
great favorite with the boys, but it was always with a
giggle and a joke that she told several boys almost every
morning that they were not to get up until Missus had
"paid them a visit," or after seeing them in bed telling
them they were to keep awake until Missus should have
had "a little conversation with them," that moreover she
might be expected every moment with a couple of
tremendous rods. This girl put us up to a great deal, and
I fear developed our puberty far too precociously; for
she had a very large breast, and she arranged her dress
so that while being horsed we had our hands completely
slipped into, and feeling her bubbies; and the rocking
and plunging used repeatedly to bring on emission.
Many of the boys used to try to get whipped merely to
experience this sensation. Although 40 years have
elapsed since all this, yet the remembrance is as vivid as
if it had occurred only yesterday.

—NAME WITHHELD

The Joys of a Victorian Schoolmaster, 1860s

This poem, called "The Rodiad," has been attributed to either George Colman or Lord Houghton; it reads like a rhyming diary entry:

But don't think me a sentimental fool;
I'm a schoolmaster of the good old school,—
One to whose ear no sound such music seems
As when a bold big boy for mercy screams—
Mercy, which with my will he will not get
Till his low breeches with his blood be wet,—
One who enjoys far more than any farce
The writhings of a flagellated arse;
When the sharp ends of long fresh-budded rods
Wrap round the thighs and twinge the burning cods;
Or the more spicy play of waxy whips,
Dissects that buttocks and tattoos the hips.
For want of better sport, I hold with glee
Some naughty urchins tight across my knee;
And while his puny pipe for pardon begs,
Stripe the skin between his straddling legs.

. . . Oh, hour that comes too late and goes too soon,
My day's delight,—my flogging hour at noon—
When I count up the boys that stay behind,
And class their bottoms in my cheerful mind!
I whipped <u>him</u> yesterday the <u>first</u>—today,
He's the <u>bonne bouche</u> with which to close the play,—

For nothing charms the true schoolmaster more
Than tickling up afresh the half-healed sore.
. . . Delightful sport! whose never failing charm
Makes young blood tingle and keeps old blood warm—
From you I have no fancy to repair
To where <u>unbottomed</u> cherubs haunt the air;
Rather methinks, I could with better grace
Present myself at some inferior place—
There offer, without salary, to pursue,
The business that on Earth I best could do—
Purpose to scourge the diabolic flesh,
For ever tortured, and forever fresh;
Cut up with red-hot wire adulterous Queens,
Man-burning bishops, Sodomizing Deans;
Punish with endless pain a moment's crime,
And whip the wicked out of space and time;
Nor if the "Eternal Schoolmaster" is stern,
And dooms me to correction in my turn,
Shall I Complain. When better hope is past,
Flog and be flogged—is no bad fate at last.

Swinburne Fondly Recalls Getting Flogged, 1863

His teacher called the freckled-face, frizzy haired future poet "pepper-bottom." Algernon Charles Swinburne (1837–1909), ever the enfant terrible, wrote poems about flogging and was obsessed with memories of it. He and porno collector Lord Houghton were flagellatory pen pals.

In a February 10, 1863, letter to Lord Houghton, Swinburne describes his former tutor:

His great idea was to inflict no pain elsewhere while the swishing proceeded. I should have been thankful for the diversion of a box on the ear. I have known him [to] perfume the flogging room (not with corduroy or onion) but with burnt scents or choose a sweet place out of doors with smell of firwood. This I call real delicate torment. Please tell me what you think. Once, before giving me a swishing that I had the marks of for more than a month (so fellows declared that I went to swim with) he let me saturate my face with eau-de-cologne. . . . He meant to stimulate and excite the senses by that preliminary pleasure so as to inflict the acuter pain afterwards on their awakened and intensified susceptibility.

Lord Houghton's commonplace book, November 1862:
Algernon Swinburne with a tutor who flogged him over the fallen trunk of a tree, till the grass was stained with his blood and another time when wet out of the water after bathing: the last much the more painful! His dreadful disappointment at seeing the big boys at Eton getting off with a few unimpressive switches. Tutor telling him he had no pleasure in flogging boys who were not gentlemen: the better the family the more he enjoyed it. The tutor once flogging him in three different positions till he was quite flayed. A.S. very fair, the tutor often flogging a very dark boy by way of contrast, making them hold each other. Using different rods—sometimes made of the lower twigs of fir with the buds on. Calling A.S. "Pepperbottom."

—LORD HOUGHTON

Slavery in America

One of the most degrading aspects of slavery was the forced sex and unpunished rape. Plantation owners, for the most part, could do what they wanted with slaves, and the legacy—at least physiologically—can be seen in the faces of millions of lighter-skinned African-Americans.

A Georgia Slave Girl Fights Off Her Master, *circa* 1860

The Federal Writers' Project tracked down former slaves in the 1930s and interviewed them. This verbatim "slave narrative" comes from Richmond County, Georgia:

In them times white men went with colored gals and women bold. Any time they saw one and wanted her, she had to go with him, and his wife didn't say nothin' 'bout it. Not only the men, but the women went with colored men too. That's why so many women slave owners wouldn't marry, 'cause they was goin' with one of their slaves. These things that's goin' on now ain't new, they been happenin'. That's why I say you just as well leave 'em alone cause they gwine to do what they want to anyhow. . . .

My young marster tried to go with me, and 'cause I wouldn't go with him he pretended I had done somethin' and beat me. I fought him back because he had no right to beat me for not goin' with him. His mother got mad at me for fightin' him back and I told her why he had beat me. Well then she sent me to the courthouse to be whipped for fightin' him. They had stocks there where most people would send their slaves to be whipped. These stocks was in the shape of a cross, and they would strap your clothes up around your waist and have nothin' but your naked part out to whip. They didn't care who saw your nakedness. Anyway they beat me that day till I couldn't sit down. When I went to bed I had to lie on my stomach to sleep. After they had finished whippin' me, I told them they needn't think they had done somethin' by stripping me in front of all them folk 'cause they had also stripped their mamas and sisters. God had made us all, and he had made us just alike.

They never carried me back home after that; they put me in the Nigger Trader's Office to be sold. About two days later I was sold to a man at McBean. When I went to his place everybody told me as soon as I got there how mean he was and they said his wife was still meaner. She was jealous of me because I was light; she said she didn't know what her husband wanted to bring that half white nigger there for, and if he didn't get rid of me pretty quick she was goin' to leave. Well he didn't get rid of me and she left about a month after I got there. When he saw she warn't comin' back 'til he got rid of me, he brought me back to the Nigger Trader's Office.

As long as you warn't sold, your marster was 'sponsible for you, so whenever they put on the market you had to praise yourself in order to be sold right away. If you didn't praise yourself you got a beatin'. I didn't stay in the market long. A "dissipated woman" [*a prostitute?*] bought me and I done laundry work for her and other "dissipated women" to pay my board 'til freedom come. They was all very nice to me.

Whenever you was sold your folk never knowed about it 'til afterwards, sometimes they never saw you again. They didn't even know who you was sold to or where they was carryin' you, unless you could write back and tell 'em.

The market was in the middle of Broad and Center Streets. They made a scaffold whenever they was goin' to sell anybody, and would put the person up on this so everybody could see 'em good. Then they would sell 'em to the highest bidder. Everybody wanted women who would have children fast. They would always ask you if you was a good breeder, and if so they would buy you at your word, but if you already had too many chillun, they would say you warn't much good. If you hadn't ever had any chillun, your marster would tell 'em you was strong, healthy and a fast worker. You had to have somethin' about you to be sold. Now sometimes, if you was a real pretty young gal, somebody would buy you without knowin' anythin' 'bout you, just for yourself. Before my old marster died, he had a pretty gal he was goin' with and he wouldn't let her work nowhere but in the house, and his wife nor nobody else didn't say nothin' 'bout it; they knowed better. She had three chillun for him and when he died his brother come and got the gal and the chillun.

One white lady that lived near us at McBean slipped in a colored gal's room and cut her baby's head clean off 'cause it belonged to her husband. He beat her 'bout it and started to kill her, but she begged so I reckon he got to feelin' sorry for her. But he kept goin' with the colored gal and they had more chillun.

—UNNAMED FORMER SLAVE

Portrait of a Southern Gentlemen, 1856

James Henry Hammond (1807–1864), the pro-slavery governor of South Carolina and an admitted womanizer, bought seamstress Sally Johnson and her daughter Louisa for $900 in 1838. About a decade later, his wife, Catherine, caught him having sex with one of them. When he refused to sell either, Catherine left him for more than a year.

In this letter to his son, Hammond tells how he wants the slaves taken care of:

February 19, 1856

In the last will I made I left to you . . . Sally Johnson the mother of Louisa & all the children of both. Sally says Henderson is my child. It is possible, but I do not believe it. Yet act on her's rather than my opinion. Louisa's first child <u>may</u> be mine. I think not. Her second I believe is mine. Take care of her & and her children who are both of <u>your</u> blood if not of mine & of Henderson. The services of the rest will I think compensate for indulgence to these. I cannot free these people and send them North. It would be cruelty to them. Nor would I like that any but my own blood should own as slaves my own blood or Louisa. I leave them to your charge, believing that you will best appreciate & most independently carry out my wishes in regard to them. Do not let Louisa or any of my children or possible children be the Slaves of Strangers. Slavery <u>in the family</u> will be their happiest earthly condition.

—JAMES HENRY HAMMOND

The Sexual Side of the Civil War, 1862–1867

Mention of the Civil War conjures up images of gaunt, gangly Lincoln, of unspeakable battlefield carnage, of sad-faced Southern boys writing poignant letters home. This conflict is the most written about event in the history of the United States, yet there's a giant piece of the puzzle left out: the accompanying flood tide of professional sex and venereal disease.

The very term "hooker" apparently came from General Joseph Hooker, who so loved to visit a row of bawdy houses in Washington, D.C., on Lafayette Square that it came to be known as "Hooker's Row." The song "Yellow Rose of Texas" was about an overweight madame of mixed-race origins who ran a boarding house in Galveston. At one point, records of the Union Medical Corps showed 202,000 cases of venereal disease among 531,000 soldiers examined; and they didn't all catch it from some outhouse seat. (Special thanks to the Kinsey Institute for Research in Sex, Gender and Reproduction for use of this rare material.)

Letters Home

Fall of 1864, Drewry's Bluff

Several nights a week our lonely post is visited by two sisters who are rentable for riding. They visit the boys at Brooks and Semes also, as they lived at Hatcher's. Amanda is about 15 and my favorite. She has never asked for more of me than a good poking, but does of the others, but her sister Carrie will ask pay for her accommodations to me, so you know which I choose.

Sometimes they bring a nigger with them and the gentlemen prefer her, but I have never had wealth enough to acquire such tastes.

—HARRIS LEVIN, COMPANY L OF THE 2ND VIRGINIA RESERVES

Rebel Party, Yankee Whiskey

On June 27, 1863, at Carlisle, Pennsylvania, a rebel regiment captured a large quantity of U.S. government whiskey and threw a party. A musician in the 14th N.C. Regimental Band writes:

Some of the Pennsylvania women, hearing the noise of the revel and the music, dared to come near to us. Soon they had formed the center of attention and joined the spirit of the doings. After much whiskey and dancing, they shed most of their garments and offered to us their bottoms. Each took on dozens of us, squealing in delight. For me it was hard come, easy go.

In Bed, Ready, Paid but Unused

A union scouting party chased a Confederate picket team away from White's Tavern in no-man's-land on Charles City Road, Virginia:

March 1865

We found we had interrupted a party in the side room. Our little Earnestine was left in bed, ready, paid but

unused—We were too much of the gentlemen to leave a
"lady" in so distressing a condition.

City of Whores: Tax Dollars at Work

*A young self-righteous worker on the U.S. Sanitary
Commission complained to his father about City Point, Virginia:*

Late 1864

This is a whole city of whores. Yes, father, a whole city.
They have laid out a village to the east of where the
railroad bends to the docks. Streets, signs, and even
corduroy sidewalks with drain gutters. Of course, it was
built with Army supplies and by the very men for free
from whom they have extracted their sinful wages.
These whores do pay negroes fair wages for whatever
work they do, but so much more than we can that the
blacks prefer to work for them to us. . . . I determined to
see the place myself and protest to General Grant in
person. There were three parallel streets about four
blocks each long. Each block there are about ten
structures on either side. They are for the most part one-
storied, northern log or clapboard make. The number of
rooms are different. . . . For the most part they do not
cook inside but have tents with negroes behind or on the
side of them, with pine or evergreen bows covering.
They, like the rebels, seem to separate the officers from
the men. They will not do double duty. To each their
own. Most of the officer ones have fine horse, saddles,

furniture, etc., all from our supply houses. The men ones have things in equality from the store house. At pay time, the lines before these houses are appalling and men often fight each other for a place. The average charge is $3 and on pay days some make as much as $250/$300. Though between pay periods, it is said they will take their time and do many special things and charge amountingly. Some of these hussies, during their indisposed periods, sell their services to the men to write letters for them to their loved ones back home. How foul. A mother, a wife or sweetheart receiving a mistle penned by these soiled hands. I have not yet been able to reach Grant to protest these matters. Though he has ordered our men not to rape the rebel women, under penalty of death, two have so been executed since I have been here. I have talked with Bowers and he tries to defend the village as necessary in view of that order. Think of it, father, he implies our devoted soldiers would become rapers and satyrs if not for these creatures.

Clara's Civil War Client List, 1862–1867

Clara A. was born in Richmond, Va. in 1848 and was 14 years old when she first became a prostitute. She operated in Locust Alley, near the Ballard and Exchange Hotels. She always worked alone, never having either pimps, partners or employees, and catering only to the finest carriage trade. She married well, into a prominent Richmond family, at the age of 40. Her wealth being such that it helped found one of the South's leading department stores. She died at the age of 79 in 1927, leaving an estate of over 3 1/4 million dollars.

(That's according to Kinsey Historian, Robert Waitt, Jr.)
Clara A. kept a notebook from 1862 to 1867, in which she catalogued the quirks of her clientele:

- J.B. liquor man—must be undressed on his arrival.
- General Limpy, the food fop—he must do the undressing. Shoes too.
- From the Patrick Henry: Bite his shoulders deeply.
- March 1864—From today on take no more Confederate or local money. Metals, greenbacks or barter goods. I must make no exceptions. I must make no exceptions.
- Whig—no clothes.
- the book man—no clothes.
- Big brass, big belly—since my rule he brings only Yankee money. Wonder where he gets it. Wonder what sourface would say if he knew one of his plate-lickers had so much yankee money. Should I tell him?
- The Maryland Governor? Do it bending over, bark sometimes.
- Dan the Railroad man—great for one, good for two, maybe for three, pay for all!!
- The noble defender—for gold, he stays all night.
- Bubblehead says the war will be over soon. Says Grant knows what they talk about before our own generals. Says there are spies everywhere. I bet big belly is one. Says one more push at Williamsburg Road or Petersburg and I will be servicing Grant or Meade. I wonder what a yankee will feel like.
- Lumberman—red wine and red clothes.
- Some country girls are now working in five or six hospitals.

Some of the doctors are pimping for them. It is all profit for them, as they eat and sleep at the hospital. Naomi says it is hurting her business. I am glad I don't service that low class of customer.

- Rednose Mayo had some of his bully police break in seven houses, around the corner last night. I sent S. $50 in metal this morning. Let them come here!
- War Talk—Four big generals last night came together. Red beard really has red hair all over. They brought two more barrels of wine and 20 blankets. They came back again tonight with more blankets. Must sell some of the blankets. Have too many.
- Red beard brought the hero. I wondered why he came here when he could get all he wanted free—all he can do is play.
- Christ! The praying general was brought in today by Preacher H. He is rough and brutal. After I serviced him, he dropped to his knees and asked God to forgive me for my sins!

—CLARA A.

Patriotic Pissing

War time calls for sacrifices but none quite as unusual as the Confederate wagon that trawled the streets asking the women to donate the pee from their chamber pots. The Confederate Mining and Nitre Bureau then distilled the liquid into nitre for gunpowder. The whole bizarre process inspired a poem by an anonymous Alabama soldier:

John Harralson! John Harralson! You are a wretched creature,
You've added to this bloody war a new and awful feature.
You'd have us think while every man is bound to be a fighter
That ladies, bless the dears, should save their pee for nitre.

John Harralson! John Harralson! Where did you get the notion
To send your barrel around the town to gather up the lotion?
We thought the girls had work enough making shirts and kissing,
But you have put the pretty dears to patriotic pissing.

John Harralson! John Harralson! Do pray invent a neater,
And somewhat more modest way of making your salt-petre;
But 'tis an awful idea, John, gunpowdery and cranky,
That when a lady lifts her skirts, she's killing off a yankee!

Rebuttal

Once the poem crossed over enemy lines, a Union soldier crafted a retaliatory version, which first appeared in an Ohio regiment newspaper:

John Harralson! John Harralson! We've read in song and story
How women's tears through all the years have moistened
    fields of glory,
But never was it told before amid such scenes of slaughter,
Your southern belles dried their tears and went to making water.

No wonder that your boys are brave, who wouldn't be a fighter,
If every time, he fired his gun, he used his sweetheart's nitre:
And vice versa, what would make a yankee soldier madder,
Than dodging bullets fired from a pretty woman's bladder?

They say there was a subtle smell that lingered in the powder,
And as the smoke grew thicker and the din of battle louder,
There was found to this compound one serious objection,
No soldier boy did sniff the stuff without having an erection!

Civil War Mail-Order Ads

*"Ormsby's New-York Mail Bag: A Journal of Wit, Humor
and Romance," which appeared monthly, was marketed to
soldiers and loaded with ads for condoms, love manuals, and
stereoscopic views of Paris.*

Condoms with Directions

September 1863

One of the greatest curses upon society in this
country, originates solely from the sad misfortune of
many married couples being pecuniarily unable to
support the children bestowed upon them by due
course of nature. . . . To remedy the evil, the
FRENCH SAFE (an article manufactured from the
finest skin, that has been long in use in the European
Cities), is the most reliable, and is recommended by
the leading physicians. It is simple in construction,
and can be relied upon in all cases as a sure
preventive against disease and pregnancy.

Having imported a large quantity—I can supply
same at the following prices:

One . . . 25 cts.
5 . . . $1.00
12 . . . $2.00

They can be sent in a sealed envelope, free from observation with full directions for use.

ALL COMMUNICATIONS CONFIDENTIAL
Address, THOMAS ORMSBY
Purchasing Agency, 86 Nassau St., N.Y.

Ormsby's Mail Bag also promoted literacy:

READ! READ!! READ!!!
WOMAN, & HER SECRET PASSIONS
containing an exact description of
The Female Organs of Generation . . .
Illustrated with five handsome plates, beautifully colored . . .
Price . . . 50 cts.
OVID'S ART OF LOVE
Complete and unabridged
This work contains the most exquisite love feast that ever regaled human taste. Price . . . $1.00

GAY & WITTY NOVELS
Confessions of a Voluptuous Young Lady of High
Rank . . . 25 cts.
Bertha, or the Adventures of a Spring Mattress . . . 25 cts.
The Private Looking Glass, or Secrets of Nature . . . 50 cts.
The Amours of a Quaker . . . 50 cts.

The Intrigues and Amours of Aaron Burr . . . 25 cts.
Confessions of a Boarding School Miss . . . 25 cts.

MARRIED WOMAN'S
PRIVATE MEDICAL COMPANION
For every female's private use. Price . . . $1

THE WEDDING NIGHT, or advice to timid
Bridegrooms
Coloured plates, neatly bound. Price . . . 50cts

MALE GENERATIVE ORGANS IN HEALTH
AND DISEASE
From Infancy to Old Age
A complete practical treatise on the anatomy and
physiology of the male generative system . . . By Dr.
Hollock. Price . . . $1

The Book Has Survived

*Ormsby misspelled the author's name, but here's a selection
from Dr. Frederick Hollick's book,* The Male Generative
Organs *(1853):*
[*To combat premature ejaculation*], the first requisite is to
remove all extraneous sources of irritation, and to attend to
the diet, clothing and general regimen, then the great point is
to harden the skin of the Glans, so that the nerves may be
more thickly covered, and their sensibility reduced. This must

be affected by the constant use of astringent washes, or caustics, and in certain cases by the use of Galvanism [*electricity*]. Every one is familiar with the effect of certain substances on the hands for instance in making them hard and destroying the delicacy of their touch, and it will be readily seen that the same means will deaden the sensibility of other parts. Lime-water is very good in some cases, and water saturated with iron rust in others, but the best agents are astringents, such as alum-water, solutions of tanin or white oak bark, or gum kino or catechu. These must be used every day, as washes, and the Glans kept covered with cotton soaked in them.

—DR. FREDERICK HOLLICK

Quack Sex Cures, 1848

Dr. William Earl of 26 Laight St., New York, self-published a pocket-sized sex manual/sales catalogue called "The Illustrated Silent Friend." He offered home remedies for everything from consumption to syphilis, impotence to gray hair:

The penis can not only be made <u>to erect but to grow when too small</u>. In like manner, the vagina can be either enlarged or opened in the female, and the cause of impotence in her can therefore be removed.

It would be impossible in a public work of this kind to point out my infallible method of restoring the genital organs, in either sex, to the <u>largest natural size</u> but that such is the fact scores of individuals who are now happily married with children can attest. Those who labor under deformities of any kind, by stating full particulars, and inclosing $10, will receive through mail, free of charge, such appliance means, etc. as will restore them to their natural size and appearance.

The method I pursue to bring about this desideratum is one of the simplest kind, being partly mechanical and partly medicinal. The mechanical consists of an instrument which I call the <u>congester</u>. This appliance induces the blood to flow freely in all the minute blood vessels of the organ, and produces distension of all its cavities which, when filled, is retained by the instrument. The medicinal consists of a lotion which acts upon the nutrition of the part, as the same principle that compost does to earth.

—DR. WILLIAM EARL

The "Personals" Column, *circa* 1860

The Women of New York—or The Underworld of the Great City, *by George Ellington, appeared in 1869, proclaiming itself a work of solid reporting:*

The "Personal" column of the morning paper was originally started to afford a means of making public inquiry for absent friends. But it very soon came to be abused, and before long served principally as a means for appointing assignations. . . . Take a copy of the morning "Herald" and run your eye down the personal column. There you will see . . . the dark lady desires the acquaintance of the blonde gentleman who rode up town in a Fifth Avenue stage and was eating peanuts. Andrew O'Rourke wants information about his long lost sister Bridget. . . .

Sometimes matrimonial prizes [*i.e.*, *people looking to find a wife*] are advertized for under the head of "Personals" in the morning paper.

A few months since, a girl living in a town in Massachusetts answered one of these advertisements, telling a pitiful story of abuse at home, inability to earn an honest living, a board-bill unpaid and her trunk in pawn and in the hands of her boarding house keeper. She wound up by saying in plain terms, after stating her age, that her friends considered her good-looking, that she didn't suppose the advertiser really wanted a wife, but that dis-satisfaction rendered her not unwilling to be his mistress. If the advertiser would send her enough money to pay her board-bill and fare to New York— say twenty dollars—she would meet him in New York. An investigation into the affair resulted in finding out that the young girl was a young man who made it a practice of answering advertisements in that way.

—George Ellington

Horatio Alger Gets Caught with His Pants Down, 1866

Horatio Alger (1832–1899) wrote extremely popular dime novels that helped define the rags-to-riches American Dream. He dedicated his life to helping homeless boys, but it turns out that his motives were sometimes more than philanthropic. Alger left the Unitarian Church of Brewster, Massachusetts, in 1866 under a cloud.

Report of a Brewster church committee:

That Horatio Alger, Jr. who has officiated as our Minister for about 15 months past has recently been charged with gross immorality and a most heinous crime, a crime of no less magnitude than the abominable and revolting crime of unnatural familiarity with <u>boys</u>. . . . Whereupon the committee sent for Alger and to him specified the charges and evidence of his guilt which he neither denied or attempted to extenuate but received it with apparent calmness of an old offender— and hastily left town on the very next train for parts unknown. . . .

Alger headed south to New York City, where he soon starting helping youngsters at the Newsboys' Lodging House and chronicling their lives in his pulp fiction. His first series of books was named after a young hero: Ragged Dick.

Walt Whitman and His Longtime Lover, Peter Doyle, 1869

Walt Whitman (1819–1892)—headstrong optimistic poet ("Leaves of Grass"), cataloguer of America's strengths—had many male lovers throughout his life, including ones during his long stint as a nurse during the Civil War. But Whitman, who so proudly sang of his joys, refused to acknowledge his homosexuality publicly (denying it, for instance, to British art critic J.A. Symonds). Whitman was obviously torn on some level because he had several bouts—recorded in his diary—of trying to "depress" his "adhesive" nature. Whitman especially liked to meet young trolley-car drivers, such as his longtime favorite, Peter Doyle.

Whitman's Lover Tells How They Met

Peter Doyle, born in Ireland in 1847, fought in the Confederate Army in the Civil War and later met Whitman in Washington, D.C. (It was actually Doyle—not Whitman—who attended the play at the Ford Theater the night Lincoln was shot. Whitman's account of it is famous.)

Doyle was interviewed in 1895 by Whitman's literary executors, three years after the poet's death:

You ask where I first met him? It is a curious story. We felt to each other at once. I was a conductor. The night was very stormy,—he had been over to see Burroughs before he came down to take the car—the storm was awful. Walt had his blanket—it was thrown round his shoulders—he seemed like an old sea-captain. He was the only passenger, it was a lonely night, so I thought I would go in and talk with him. Something in me made me do it and something in him drew me that way. He used to say there was something in me had the same effect on him. Anyway, I went into the car. We were familiar at once—I put my hand on his knee—we understood. He did not get out at the end of the trip—in fact went all the way back with me. I think the year of this was 1866. From that time on we were the biggest sort of friends. I stayed in Washington until 1872, when I went on the Pennsylvania Railroad. Walt was then in the Attorney-General's office. I would frequently go out to the Treasury to see Walt; Hubley Ashton was commonly there—he would be leaning familiarly on the desk where Walt would be writing. They were fast friends—talked a good deal together. Walt rode with me often—often at noon, always at night. He rode round with me on the last trip—sometimes rode for several trips. Everybody knew him. He had a way of taking the measure of the driver's hands—had calf-skin gloves made for them every winter in Georgetown—these gloves were his personal presents to the men. He saluted the men on the other cars as we passed—threw up his hand. They cried to him, "Hullo, Walt!" and he would reply, "Ah, there!" or something like. He was welcome always as the flowers in May. Everybody appreciated his attentions, he seemed to appreciate our attentions to him. Teach the boys to read, write or cipher? I never heard of, or saw that. There must be some mistake. He did not make much of what people call learning. But he gave us papers, books, and other such articles, too. In his habits he was very temperate. He did not smoke. People seemed to think it odd that he didn't, for everybody in Washington smoked. But he seemed to have a positive dislike for tobacco. He was a very moderate drinker. You might have thought something different, to see the ruddiness of his complexion—but his complexion had no whiskey in it. We might take a drink or two together occasionally—nothing more. It was our practice to go to a hotel on Washington Avenue after I was done with my car. I remember the place well—there on the corner. Like as not I would go to sleep—lay my head on my hands on the table. Walt would stay there, wait, watch, keep me undisturbed—would wake me when the hour of closing came. In his eating he was vigorous, had big appetite, but was simple in his tastes, not caring for any great dishes.

I never knew a case of Walt's being bothered up by a woman. In fact, he had nothing special to do with any woman except Mrs. O'Connor and Mrs. Burroughs. His disposition was different. Woman in that sense never came into his head. Walt was too clean, he hated anything which was not clean. No trace of any kind of dissipation in him. I ought to know about him those years—we were awful close together. In the afternoon I would go up to the Treasury building and wait for him to get through if he was busy. Then we'd stroll out together, often without any plan, going wherever we happened to get. This occurred days in and out, months running. Towards women generally Walt had a good way—he very easily attracted them. But he did that with men, too. And it was an irresistible attraction. I've had many tell me—men and women. He had an easy, gentle way—the same for all, no matter who they were or what their sex.

. . . Walt's manners were always perfectly simple. We would tackle the farmers who came into town, buy a water-melon, sit down on the cellar door of Bacon's grocery, Seventh and Pennsylvania Avenue, halve it and eat it. People would go by and laugh. Walt would only smile and say, "They can have the laugh—we have the melon."

My Darling Boy

This is how fifty-year-old Whitman closed his letter to twenty-two-year-old Peter Doyle, who had recently contemplated suicide because he thought he had VD:

August 21, 1869, Brooklyn

. . . Dear comrade, I think of you very often. My love for you is indestructible, & since that night & morning has returned more than before.

Dear Pete, dear son, my darling boy, my young & loving brother, don't let the devil put such thoughts in your mind again—wickedness unspeakable—death and disgrace here and hell's agonies hereafter—Then what would it be afterward to the mother? What to me?—

Pete, I send you some money, by Adam's Express—you use it, dearest son, & when it is gone, you shall have some more, for I have plenty. I will write again before long—give my love to Johnny Lee, my dear darling boy, I love him truly—(let him read these three last lines)—Dear Pete, <u>remember</u>—Walt.

Regret

Less than a year later, though, Whitman felt tormented by this relationship. He wrote about it in his notebook but employed code to camouflage his homosexuality. According to poet-scholar Charley Shively in Calamus Lovers, *Whitman disguises Peter Doyle as "16.4"—P is the sixteenth letter of the alphabet, D the fourth—and switches "him" to "her." He uses the word "adhesiveness" to refer to homosexuality.*

July, 15, 1870

Cheating, childish abandonment of myself, fancying what does not really exist in another, but is all the time in myself alone—utterly deluded & cheated by <u>myself</u>, & my own weakness—REMEMBER WHERE I AM MOST WEAK, & lacking. Yet always preserve a kind spirit & demeanor to 16 [*Peter*]. BUT PURSUE HER NO MORE.

A COOL, GENTLE, (LESS DEMONSTRATIVE) MORE UNIFORM DEMEANOR—give to poor—help any—be indulgent to the criminal & silly & to low persons generally & the ignorant, but SAY little—make no explanations—<u>give no</u>

<u>confidences</u>—never attempt puns, or plays upon words, or utter sarcastic comments, or (under circumstances) hold any discussions or arguments.

It is IMPERATIVE that I obviate & remove myself (& my orbit) <u>at all hazards</u>, from this incessant <u>enormous & abnormal</u>
PERTURBATION

TO GIVE UP ABSOLUTELY & for good from the present hour this FEVERISH, FLUCTUATING, <u>useless</u> UNDIGNIFIED PURSUIT OF 16.4—<u>too long, (much too long)</u> persevered in,—so humiliating—<u>it must come at last</u> & had better come now—<u>(It cannot possibly be a success)</u> LET THERE FROM THIS HOUR BE NO FALTERING, NO GETTING, <u>at all henceforth</u>, (NOT ONCE, UNDER <u>any circumstances</u>)—<u>avoid seeing her, or meeting her, or any talk or explanation</u>—or ANY MEETING WHATEVER, FROM
THIS HOUR FORTH, FOR LIFE

July 15 '70

Outline sketch of a superb calm character

his emotions &c are complete in himself, irrespective of whether his love, friendship &c are returned or not

He grows, blooms, like some perfect flower or tree, in Nature, whether viewed by admiring eyes, or in some wild or wood, entirely unknown

His analogy is as of the earth, complete in itself, enflooding in itself all processes of growth effusing life & power, for hidden purposes

Depress the adhesive nature/

It is in excess—making life a torment/

All this diseased, feverish disproportionate adhesiveness/

Remember Fred Vaughan/
Case of Jenny Bullard/
Sane Nature fit & full Rapport therewith/
Merlin strong & wise & beautiful at 100 years old.

Breaking the Vow Fast

Walt Whitman to Peter Doyle:

July 30, 1870 Brooklyn

Dear Pete,
Well here I am home again with my mother, writing to
you from Brooklyn once more. We parted there, you
know, at the corner of 7th st. Tuesday night. Pete, there
was something in that hour from 10 to 11 o'clock
(parting though it was) that has left me pleasure &
comfort for good—I never dreamed that you made so
much of having me with you, nor that you could feel so
downcast at losing me. I foolishly thought it was all on
the other side. But all I will say further on the subject is,
I now see clearly, that was all wrong. . . .
   Monday Aug. 1
   The carrier brought quite a bunch this forenoon for
the Whitman family but no letter from you. . . . There is
a cool breeze & the moon shining. I think every time of
you, & wish if we could only be together these evenings
at any rate.

—WALT WHITMAN

The Smell of His Male Lover

Victorian sex researcher Havelock Ellis was sent this letter, written by an Italian marquis:

Bonifazio stripped one evening to give me pleasure. He has the full rounded flesh and amber coloring which painters of the Giorgione school gave to their S. Sebastians. When he began to dress, I took up an old "fascia," or girdle of netted silk, which was lying under his breeches, and which still preserved the warmth of his body. I buried my face in it, and was half inebriated by its exquisite aroma of young manhood and fresh hay. He told me he had worn it for two years. No wonder it was redolent of him. I asked him to let me keep it as a souvenir. He smiled and said: "You like it because it has lain so long upon my "pancia."

"Yes, just so," I replied, "whenever I kiss it, thus and thus, it will bring you back to me." Sometimes I tie it around my naked waist before I go to bed. The smell of it is enough to cause me a powerful erection, and the contact of its fringes with my testicles and phallus has once or twice produced an involuntary emission.

—UNIDENTIFIED ITALIAN MARQUIS

Seduction by Chloroform

This British handbill, which has the ring of "reefer madness," was distributed in the mid-nineteenth century in England:

The Secret and Villainous Use Made of the power of a new and scientific discovery lately introduced BY CELEBRATED DOCTORS and used in the Hospitals as an antitode to pain, by its acting on the system, and RENDERING THE PERSON SENSELESS And entirely at the mercy of the Party who presents it; showing the whole mystery of THE DEVIL'S SECRET As applied in the most artful manner for SEDUCING FEMALES! Whereby they have no power to resist the wicked desires or inclinations of their seducers; also the tricks played to stupefy the senses and overcome virtuous FEMALE SERVANTS, and afterwards dragging them into secret places or private closets and finally the art PRACTISED BY UNFORTUNATE WOMEN in stupefying the Male Sex by the use of chloroform, to rob and plunder them.

. . . Read this book in time. This valuable Work has run through Eleven Editions in one year. . . . A copy of the above valuable Work will be sent to any address upon the receipt of 8 Postage Stamps to pre-pay postage. Please let your letter be addressed to MISS W. WILLIAMS, care of W.H. COOK, 5, Sims' Alley, Broadmead, Bristol.

Immaculate Conception and Chloroform

The book Les Mysteres du Confessional *features some vintage Catholic-bashing by anonymous Protestant authors. Are any of the charges true?*

In the month of July 1872, a young girl, Anna Dunzinger, appeared before Court of Assizes in Linz in Austria, to be interrogated about the facts reported by a newspaper, the "Tagespost," under the title: "Incident of Chloroformed Handkerchief." The young girl gave the following details: "The reverend father Gabriel, of the Carmelite order, my confessor, had many times made declarations of love to me, but I had always refused to yield myself to his desires. One day, he made me pass into the sacristy in order to hear me in the confession booth; there, was located a particularly secret confessional. I had barely sat down when the Carmelite father lifted the trellis, slipped his arm through the opening and held next to my face a handkerchief laden with an extremely penetrating odor. I felt myself growing dizzy, and almost immediately I lost consciousness. I have no idea whatsoever as to what happened from that moment until when I regained consciousness, and was able to get up, re-adjust my clothes and leave the confessional."

Here is what had taken place. The Carmelite had opened a movable partition which separated the two compartments of the confessional; he had abused the girl's inert body and accomplished a disgusting rape. The young girl was going to become a mother without even knowing that she had had sexual relations with a man.

—Les Mysteres du Confessional

The Lovely Golden Showers of Havelock Ellis

Havelock Ellis (1859–1939) was a pioneer sex researcher, a tireless scholar, and a tolerant Victorian who defended homosexuals' rights, as well as a woman's right to birth control. (He even had an affair with Margaret Sanger.) Maybe some of his tolerant attitudes sprang from Ellis' own predeliction for "golden showers," or "urolagnia."

The First Time—Mom's Golden Shower, 1871

Once at the age of twelve [*my mother*] took me to spend the day at the London Zoological Gardens. In the afternoon as we were walking side by side along a gravelled path in a solitary part of the Gardens, she stood still, and soon I heard a very audible stream falling to the ground. When she moved on I instinctively glanced behind at the pool on the path, and my mother, having evidently watched my movements, remarked shyly: "I did not mean you to see that."

Ellis came to realize that somehow he appreciated this act in his lovers:

Later my vision of this function became in some degree attached to my feeling of tenderness towards women—I was surprised how often women responded to it sympathetically—and to my conception of beauty, for it was never to me a vulgar interest, but, rather, an ideal interest, a part of the yet unrecognised loveliness of the world, which we already recognise in fountains, though fountains, it is now asserted, have here had their origin. It would be easy to over-rate the importance of this interest. But it is necessary to note it.°

Ellis supplied his own footnote:

The Genius Of Rembrandt

°I may be regarded as a pioneer in the recognition of the beauty of the natural act in women when carried out in the erect attitude. . . . But Rembrandt preceded me. There is a fine and admired picture of his in the National Gallery (No. 54) of a woman standing in a pool and holding up her smock, with parted legs, in an attitude which has always seemed to me undoubtedly to represent the act of urination. In recent years, I have learnt on good authority that so it really came from the artist's hands, but at some later date the falling stream was painted out. The picture is dated 1654, and experts now consider that it probably represents Hendrickje Stoffels, the charming and beloved figure whom, about that time, Rembrandt painted in various intimate situations. I should like to think that the indignation I feel at this sacrilegious distortion of a supreme artist's work will some day be generally shared.

Mixing Business and Pleasure

Ellis also undertook several serious studies of urine streams:

In a paper . . . published in the <u>American Journal of Dermatology</u> *(May 1902)*, I brought forward a systematic series of observations showing that the expulsive power of the bladder, when measured by the distance to which the stream can be expelled, is not only an index of individual energy but is subject to constant variations under the varying influences of daily life. . . . It was found [*in men*] that the energy of the bladder tends on the whole to rise during the day. No monthly curve was detected, but there was a weekly rhythm with a marked fall on Sundays, quickly recovering to a climax on Tuesdays. There was also a yearly curve, with a minimum in autumn, followed by a slow rise to a height maintained through the spring reaching a climax in August.

It was more difficult to make observations on women but one series on a nulliparous woman [*i.e., childless*] of 32, of entirely feminine conformation and disposition, made with the subject lying on her back with separated nymphae, showed as far as they went, concordant results [*with patterns for the male*]. The average distance of the jet was 48 inches (which agrees with that of some women in the erect position) and the maximum, with very full bladder and some general excitement, as much as 75 inches, which indicates an energy probably not often exceeded by the female bladder.

In Love: Watching American Poet Hilda Doolittle

Impressions and Comments, March 17, 1921:
The tall form languidly arose and stood erect, taut and massive it seemed now with the length of those straight adolescent legs still more ravishing in their unyielding pride, and the form before me seemed to become some adorable Olympian vase, and a large stream gushed afar in the glistening liquid arch, endlessly, it seemed to my wondering eyes, as I contemplated with enthralled gaze this prototypal statue of the Fountain of Life ... while on the firm austere lines of the face one read not pride, but a shy and diffident

smile, the fear lest to the merely human spectator that which is transcendent should be mistaken for what is gross.

—HAVELOCK ELLIS

The One and Only Original Masochist, 1873

Leopold von Sacher-Masoch (1836–1895) is now a forgotten German novelist, but his name (or at least part of it) will probably live on for centuries, thanks to psychologist Richard von Krafft-Ebing, who used it to coin the term "masochism."

In Sacher-Masoch's most notorious work, Venus in Furs *(1870), he explained:* "Nothing can intensify my passion more than the tyranny, cruelty and especially the faithlessness of a beautiful woman." *He also chose some unlikely role models:* "I envied King Gunther whom the mighty Brunhilde chained on their wedding night, and the poor troubadour whom his capricious mistress had sewn into the skins of wolves to have him hunted like game."

But those lines are from fiction. Leopold actually tried to live out his fantasies with his wife, Aurora, a fairly conventional bourgeois woman. And she records in her memoirs (1907) how he begged her to wear furs and whip him so as to create the proper home environment for him to pursue his writing career:

Leopold Wants His Wife to Beat Him

Very soon after Leopold and Aurora were married in 1873, this incident took place:

I had picked up at Graz a young servant, [*Marie*]. Daughter of a country surgeon, she thought herself well-educated because she knew how to say: "Je vous baise la main [*I kiss your hand*]." But she wasn't a dope and had a mind as lively as her body was well-proportioned and strong. In her village, she must have passed for a beauty, and Leopold used to go so far as to say there was something of the "Brunhilde" about her.

. . . The evenings were already long. To pass the time, Leopold made us play "brigands" [*i.e., highwaymen*]. The brigands were Marie and I, and we had to chase after him. I had to lend Marie one of my furs and wear one myself, without which we wouldn't have the aura of brigands. Throughout the entire house, there began a race, a mad chase, until we had captured our victim. Then we had to tie him with ropes to a tree, and decide his fate. He was condemned to death, of course, while we ignored his pleas for mercy.

To that point, it was only a game; but one fine day, Leopold gave the thing a more serious turn, and what for me was a more disturbing turn. He wanted to receive a <u>real</u> punishment, which would cause him <u>pain</u>, and since we couldn't kill him, he wanted at least to be beaten with ropes which he had prepared.

I refused point blank; but he did not give up. He found my refusal infantile and told me that if I would not beat him, he would have himself beaten by Marie; since he saw in her eyes that she had a taste for it.

To avoid that, I gave him a few light strokes. That didn't satisfy him, and since I assured that I <u>could</u> not hit him any harder, he said that he absolutely wanted to be beaten with <u>the most force possible</u>, and that Marie could handle that better than I.

I left the room. I thought thus to put an end to that scene. But I was wrong. Marie pounded him just as he wanted to be beaten, with all her strength; from the room next door I heard the thwack of her blows on his back.

The minutes seemed like centuries. Finally, the punishment stopped. He entered the room where I was waiting, as though nothing had happened and said to me:

"Alright! she has beaten me magnificently! My back must surely carry the scars! You have no idea of the strength that girl has in her arms. At each blow, I thought my skin was going to be ripped off."

I did not want to discuss the subject given his tone, so I kept my mouth shut. He looked at me and realized I was in no mood for banter.

"What's your problem?" he asked me. "Is there something wrong?"

"Yes, there is. It doesn't suit me for you to have yourself beaten by our servant."

"Come on! You see something wrong with that? Well, maybe something else is bothering you. . . . But how could I have ever imagined that you could be <u>jealous</u> of a girl as backward as Marie?"

"It is not proper for the servant to beat the master. It puts all three of us in a horribly false position. And don't expect Marie to keep this to herself, as boisterous as she is, she's going to tell everyone she meets about it. What are they going to think of us?"

"But we can forbid from speaking about it!"

"You can't forbid anything to a girl who has beaten you. That would do nothing but jumble things up. Marie must leave the house immediately. That way, we will end the scandal— here, at least."

"You are right. I didn't think of all that. Yes, send her back as soon as possible. Better that she leaves tonight."

Marie took the first train in the morning for Graz. I replaced her with a woman around forty years old, completely devoid of charm.

Aurora Agrees to Whip Him

Sacher-Masoch was criticized by a German book reviewer for creating the same evil dominatrix character over and over.

If that <u>cruel</u> woman were <u>in my life</u> . . . , she would not have to be <u>in my books</u>. She sneaks in there because my head is full of her. When I want to depict a woman, it's she who flows out of my pen; in spite of myself, it's she who I must describe endlessly; whenever I'm at it, it's like a drunken obsession; I can't stop myself before I have painted her in all her demonic beauty. . . . That winds up boring the readers, I have often feared that myself, but what can I do?

"Have there been women like that in your life?"

"You mean P–?"

"Her and others."

"Ah! they all wanted to be her, but they were too weak."

"That's very natural. How can you hope to find in real life a creature in all points similar to the one in your imagination? You're asking too much. You should not compromise your value as a writer. . . ." The German critic shouts "Watch out". . . make up your mind once and for all to throw this "horrid role model" into the sea.

He eyed me seriously.

"You're right. I must renounce her. You could help me a lot."

"How?"

"By wearing furs and wielding the whip."

"But I already wear furs!"

"But you don't want anyone to speak to you about whipping."

"The stakes are our future, which you must care about as much as I. If I make a sacrifice, you can also make one. It's a voluptuous pleasure for me to be abused by my wife. So, abuse me, and I promise you, on all that is most sacred, I give you my word of honor that from now on there will no longer be any cruel women in my books. Do you agree?"

I didn't mull it over for long. If he kept his word, which I didn't doubt, all would be well.

From that time, not a single day passed without my whipping my husband, without my holding up my end of the bargain. At first, my distaste was great; but after a while, I got used to it, although I did it only against my will and compelled by necessity.

Seeing that I was headed where he wished, he connived to make the thing as painful as possible. He commissioned whips to be made according to his specifications—among others a "knout" [*a brutal Russian variety*] with six lashes studded with sharp nails.

But he kept his promise and in the books he wrote from then on, he had no more furs, no more whips, no more tortures.

But Aurora did draw the line somewhere:

Not in Front of the Children

He had asked me several times to beat him in front of Sacha [*one of their two sons*], and once, joking around, I had struck him a light blow on the shoulder. The child grew pale, threw his arms around his father as though to defend him, and looked at me with terrified eyes. Leopold laughed, flattered and happy to be so loved. That was a joke and cruel game to play with the heart of a child. His vanity pushed him to start this game gain.

"You must not ask me to beat you in the presence of the children," I went on, "just as you have to stop telling me over and over how I am so cruel and heartless. By hearing that repeated over and over by their <u>father</u>, who should know what he's saying, they will end up inevitably believing it. Spare the children your twisted little games which they cannot understand; it will wind up costing you their esteem and me their love. Do you think it doesn't hurt me to see my children turn against me, and can you imagine a mother who could love them more? or who is ready to do more for them than I?"

—AURORA VON SACHER-MASOCH, *CONFESSION DE MA VIE*

Leopold kept upping the demands, going so far as to place newspaper ads looking for an "energetic" man for her to have an affair with, even though she was pregnant. Aurora finally left him in 1883.

Victorian Masturbation: Some Background

With prudery rampant, preachers and doctors in Europe and America railed against masturbation, claiming that this demon practice of self-abuse was literally killing thousands of young people and turning entire generations into feeble, pale, drooling idiots.

A Factory Worker Livens Up Her Day, 1880

Thésée Pouillet, a doctor specializing in self-abuse, searched everywhere for the evils of masturbation for his book The Onanism of Women *(1877).*

During a visit I once paid to a manufactory of military clothing, I witnessed the following scene. In the midst of the uniform sound produced by some thirty sewing machines, I suddenly heard one of the machines working with much more velocity than the others. I looked at the person who was working it, a brunette of 18 or 20. While she was automatically occupied with the trousers she was making on the machine, her face became animated, her mouth opened slightly, her nostrils dilated, her feet moved the pedals with constantly increasing rapidity. Soon I saw a convulsive look in her eyes, her eyelids were lowered, her face turned pale and was thrown backward; her hands and legs stopped and became extended; a suffocated cry, followed by a long sigh, was lost in the noise of the workroom. The girl remained motionless a few seconds, drew out her handkerchief to wipe away the pearls of sweat from her forehead, and, after casting a timid and ashamed glance at her companions, resumed her work. The forewoman, who acted as my guide, having observed the direction of my gaze, took me up to the girl, who blushed, lowered her face, and murmured some incoherent words before the forewoman had opened her mouth, to advise her to sit fully on the chair, and not on its edge.

As I was leaving I heard another machine at another part of the room in accelerated movement. The forewoman smiled at me, and remarked that that was so frequent that it attracted no notice. It was specially observed, she told me, in the case of young work-girls, apprentices, and those who sat on the edge of their seats, thus much facilitating friction of the labia.

—THÉSÉE POUILLET

Kellogg's Founder Performs Surgery to Stop Masturbation, *circa* 1880

Dr. John Harvey Kellogg (1852–1943) ran an immensely successful health clinic in Battle Creek, Michigan, which eventually spawned—against the doctor's wishes—the family's billion-dollar cereal empire. This tireless Victorian do-gooder, who liked to wear white suits, tried to whip America into shape by preaching exercise, vegetarianism, and chastity, especially to young women. He harangued against novel-reading, honeymoons, and the waltz. While some of his advice has proven well grounded medically, he went a bit off the deep end on the dangers of masturbation, especially in his Ladies' Guide in Health and Disease *(1883).*

The Dangers of Holding It In

Mothers ought to . . . instruct their daughters respecting the importance of regularly relieving the bowels and bladder at certain times each day. The call of nature should never be resisted or delayed a moment when such delay can be avoided. The inactive condition of the bowels and the irritable state of the bladder which often result from violation of this simple rule of health are not infrequently the means of inducing abnormal excitement in the genital organs which may result in the formation of habits [*i.e., masturbation*] most deplorable in their character and consequence.

Widespread Problem of Female Masturbation

Within the last ten years we have examined and treated for various local ailments the cases of several thousand women of various ages, and more often than we have dared to declare have we found convincing evidence that the foundation of the disease from which the patient was suffering had been laid in vicious habits acquired in early childhood. . . .

Kellogg laid out twelve signs of self-abuse in girls:

1) A sudden marked decline in health . . .
2) A marked change in disposition . . .
3) Loss of memory and of the love for study . . .
4) Unnatural baldness . . .
5) A forward or loose manner in company with boys . . .
6) Languor and lassitude . . .
7) An unnatural appetite . . . excessive fondness for mustard, pepper, vinegar, spices and other stimulating condiments . . .
8) Presence of leucorrhea [*whitish discharge*], accompanied by a relaxed condition of the vagina . . .
9) Ulceration about the roots of the nails, especially affecting one or both of the first two fingers of the hand, usually the right . . .
10) Biting the finger nails . . .
11) Blank dull lustreless expressionless eye surrounded by a dark ring . . .
12) Palpitation of the heart, hysteria, nervousness . . .

Cures, Including Surgery

Kellogg recommended giving the girl a fire-and-brimstone speech, then watching her like a hawk and making sure she did lots of exercise. But he warns that sometimes more drastic measures are needed:

In obstinant cases, very severe means must be sometimes adopted. We were once obliged after every other measure had failed, to perform a surgical operation before we were able to break the habit in the case of a young girl of eight or ten years who had become addicted to the vice to a most extraordinary degree.

Almost four hundred pages later in his Ladies' Guide, *Kellogg explains what that surgical procedure was. He is listing the proper care for nymphomaniacs:*

Treatment: Cool sitz baths; the cool enema; a spare diet; the application of blisters and other irritants to the sensitive parts of the sexual organs, the removal of the clitoris and nymphae, constitute the most proper treatment.

The same measures of treatment are indicated in the cases in which the disposition to practice self-abuse is uncontrollable by other means. In an extreme case of this kind brought to us for treatment a few years ago, we were compelled to adopt the last mentioned method of treatment before the patient could be cured.

—JOHN HARVEY KELLOGG

In 1896 Dr. Kellogg invented a breakfast cereal as a bland dietary alternative which, among other benefits, would help patients keep their hands off their genitals: the product was called "corn flakes." And if the cereal didn't work taken by mouth, it could also be administered as an enema.

Mark Twain Delivers a Speech on Masturbation, 1879

Amid all this mass hysteria over masturbation, Mark Twain (1835–1910) delivered a wiseguy speech on the Science of Onanism *at the Stomach Club in Paris in 1879. (This Twain selection is routinely excluded from collections of the famed humorist's work.)*

My gifted predecessor has warned you against the "social evil—adultery." In his able paper he exhausted that subject. He left absolutely nothing more to be said on it. But I will continue his good work in the cause of morality by cautioning you against that species of recreation called self-abuse, to which I perceive you are too much addicted.

All great writers upon health and morals, both ancient and modern, have struggled with this stately subject. This shows its dignity and importance. Some of these writers have taken one side, some the other.

Homer, in the second book of the <u>Iliad</u>, says with fine enthusiasm, "Give me masturbation or give me death!" Caesar, in his <u>Commentaries</u>, says, "To the lonely it is company. To the forsaken it is a friend. To the aged and impotent it is a benefactor. They that be penniless are yet rich in that they still have this majestic diversion." In another place this excellent observer has said, "There are times when I prefer it to sodomy."

Robinson Crusoe says, "I cannot describe what I owe to this gentle art." Queen Elizabeth said, "It is the bulwark of virginity." Cetewayo, the Zulu hero, remarked that "a jerk in the hand is worth two in the bush." The immortal Franklin has said, "Masturbation is the best policy."

Michelangelo and all the other Old Masters—Old Masters, I will remark, is an abbreviation, a contraction—have used similar language. Michelangelo said to Pope Julius II, "Self-negation is noble. Self-culture is beneficent. Self-possession is manly. But to the truly great and inspiring soul they are poor and tame compared to self-abuse."

Mr. Brown, here, in one of his latest and most graceful poems refers to it in an eloquent line which is destined to live to the end of time—"None know it but to love it, None name it but to praise."

Such are the utterances of the most illustrious masters of this renowned science and apologists for it. The names of those who decry it and oppose it are legion. They have made strong arguments and uttered bitter speeches against it. But there is not room to repeat them here in much detail.

Brigham Young, an expert of incontestable authority, said, "As compared with the other thing, it is the difference between the lightning bug and the lightning."

Solomon said, "There is nothing to recommend it but its cheapness."

Galen said, "It is shameful to degrade to such bestial use that grand limb, that formidable member, which we votaries of science dub the 'Major Maxillary'—when they dub it at all—which is seldom. It would be better to decapitate the Major than to use him so. It would be better to amputate the <u>os frontis</u> [*i.e., front bone*] than to put it to such a use."

The great statistician, Smith, in his report to Parliament says, "In my opinion more children have been wasted in this way than any other."

It cannot be denied that the high authority of this art entitles it to our respect. But at the same time I think that its harmfulness demands our condemnation. Mr. Darwin was grieved to feel obliged to give up his theory that the monkey was the connecting link between man and the lower animals. I think he was too hasty. The monkey is the only animal except man that practices this science. Hence he is our brother. There is a bond of sympathy and relationship between us. Give this ingenious animal an audience of the proper kind and he will straightaway put aside his other affairs and take a whet. And you will see by the contortions and his ecstatic expression that he takes an intelligent and human interest in his performance.

The signs of excessive indulgence in this destructive pastime are easily detectable. They are these. A disposition to eat, to drink, to smoke, to meet together convivially, to laugh, to joke and tell indelicate stories—and mainly a yearning to paint pictures. The results of the habit are: loss of memory, loss of virility, loss of cheerfulness, loss of hopefulness, loss of character and loss of progeny. Of all the various kinds of sexual intercourse this has the least to recommend it.

As an amusement it is too fleeting. As an occupation it is too wearing. As a public exhibition there is no money in it. It is unsuited to the drawing room. And in the most cultured society it has long been banished from the social board. It has at last, in our day of progress and improvement, been degraded to brotherhood with flatulence. Among the best bred these two arts are indulged only in private. Though by consent of the whole company, when only males are present, it is still permissible in good society to remove the embargo upon the fundamental sigh.

My illustrious predecessor has taught you that all forms of the "social evil" are bad. I would teach you that some of those forms are more to be avoided than others. So in concluding I say, "If you must gamble away your lives sexually, don't play a Lone Hand too much." When you feel a revolutionary uprising in your system get your Vendôme Column down some other way—don't jerk it down.

—MARK TWAIN

Victorian Sexual Ignorance

Writer Samuel Butler tells this story:
A little boy and a little girl were looking at a picture of Adam and Eve. "Which one is Adam and which is Eve?" said one. "I do not know," said the other, "but I could tell if they had their clothes on." *Probably not an exaggeration.*

Victorian sexual ignorance, especially among women, was truly astounding; the birds and the bees were the birds and the bees. "Girls are not even prepared in many cases for the appearance of the pubic hair," *wrote Victorian sex researcher Havelock Ellis.* "The unexpected growth of hair frequently causes young girls much secret worry and often they carefully cut it off."

Throughout British society, which during this era produced flagellation parlors and Jack the Ripper, was a sense that sex and the naked body were unspeakably dirty. And Victorian doctors came up with theories to match. "I should say that the majority of women (happily for society) are not very much troubled with sexual feeling of any kind," *opined Dr. William Acton, the most influential family doctor of his generation and the man who inspired lots of prudery in America. As for marriage, here is what Thackeray wrote about what British men sought in a wife:* "An exquisite slave is what we want for the most part: a humble, flattering, smiling, tea-making, pianoforte-playing being, who laughs at our jokes however old they may be, coaxes us and wheedles us in our humours and . . . fondly lies to us through life."

Lewis Carroll's Nude Photography, 1879

In the early days of photography, when it was still a rare and expensive hobby, Lewis Carroll (1832–1898), author of Alice's Adventures in Wonderland, *liked to have little girls over to his studio for unchaperoned nude modeling sessions. His letters requesting permission from the parents are prototypes of delicate diplomacy. Bathing drawers only? Nude back view only?*

Was Lewis Carroll a saintly virgin bachelor, or was there a darker side? Were his so-called sins simply in the eyes of the Victorian mothers who couldn't understand Carroll's genuinely innocent adoration of the naked prepubescent female form?

Lewis Carroll (real name, Charles Lutwidge Dodgson) was a clergyman and mathematics don at Oxford who preferred the company of little girls and entertained them with stories, puzzles, and games:

We are but older children, dear,
Who fret to find our bedtime near.

And maybe also fret to find others questioning our motives.

Lewis Carroll had become friends with the children of fellow Oxford professor Anthony Mayhew. He had begun photographing them clothed and was hoping to do some nudes. (Scrutinize the ages of the three girls.)

Asking Permission

May 26, 1879, Christ Church, Oxford

Dear Mrs. Mayhew,

. . . Now your Ethel [*age eleven*] is beautiful, both in face and form; and is also a perfectly simple-minded child of Nature, who would have no sort of objection to serving as model for a friend she knows as well as she does me. So my humble petition is, that you will bring the 3 girls, and that you will allow me to try some groupings of Ethel and Janet [*age six*] (I fear there is no use naming Ruth [*age thirteen*] as well, at her age, though I should have no objection!) without any drapery or suggestion of it.

I need hardly say that the pictures should be such as you might if you liked frame and hang up in your drawing-room. On no account would I do a picture which I should be unwilling to show to all the world—or at least the artistic world.

If I did not believe I could take such pictures without any lower motive than a pure love of Art, I would not ask it: and if I thought there was any fear of lessening <u>their</u> beautiful simplicity of character, I would not ask it.

I print all such pictures <u>myself</u>, and of course would not let anyone see them without your permission. . . .

Sincerely,

C.L. Dodgson

Mrs. Mayhew's note has not survived, but we can piece it out from Carroll's reply to Mr. Mayhew:

May 27, 1879, Christ Church, Oxford

Dear Mr. Mayhew,

. . . As to the photography, I am heartily obliged to Mrs. Mayhew for her kind note. It gives more than I had ventured to hope for, and does not extinguish the hope that I may yet get <u>all</u> I asked. You will think me very sanguine in saying this: but I will make it plain.

First, the permission to go as far as bathing-drawers

[*i.e., bottoms*] is very charming, I presume it includes
Ethel as well as Janet (otherwise there would be no
meaning in bringing more than Janet) though I hardly
dare hope that it includes Ruth. I can make some
charming groups of Ethel and Janet in bathing-drawers,
though I cannot exaggerate how much better they would
look without. Also the bathing-drawers would enable me
to do a full front view of Ethel, which of course could
not be done without them: but why should you object to
my doing a back view of her without them? It would be
a perfectly presentable picture, and far more artistic
than with them. As to Janet, at her age they are surely
unnecessary, whatever view were taken.

Now comes my reason for hoping you and Mrs.
Mayhew will after all give carte blanche as to dress—at
any rate for Ethel and Janet. It is that I pay Mrs.
Mayhew the compliment of believing that she states her
real reason for objecting to the entire absence of
drapery. Oh the trouble I have sometimes had with
ladies, who will give fictitious reasons for things, and
when those break down, invent others, till at last they
are driven to speak the truth! But I don't believe this of
Mrs. Mayhew. I feel pretty sure that neither she nor you
would have admired, as you have done, all those studies
of naked children (which of course were done from live
children), if you had objected on general principles to
children being pictured in that condition. And therefore
I was really pleased to read in Mrs. Mayhew's note that
her reason for objecting to absolute undress was because
she felt "sure that the children themselves would
decidedly object." Those words were very welcome

reading, because I happen to feel sure, and for good
reasons, that they would not only not "decidedly" object,
but they wouldn't object at all. For I had told them (I
hope there is no harm in doing so) of the pictures I
wished to take, but had said that of course Mrs. Mayhew
must give leave before I could do them. Both Ruth and
Ethel seemed quite sure that Janet wouldn't object in
the least to being done naked, and Ethel, when I asked
her if she would object, said in the most simple and
natural way, that she wouldn't object at all. I didn't ask
Ruth, as I felt no hope of leave being given by the higher
powers in her case.

Now don't crush all my hopes, by telling me that all
Mrs. Mayhew said was merely facon de parler, and that
all the time you and Mrs. Mayhew object absolutely to
the thing, however much the children themselves would
like it!

At any rate, I trust you will let me do some pictures of
Janet naked: at her age, it seems almost absurd to even
suggest any scruple about dress.

My great hope, I confess, is about Ethel, who is
(artistically) worth ten Janets. Do consider her case in
reference to the fact that she herself is quite indifferent
about dress.

If worst comes to the worst, and you won't concede
any nudities at all, I think you ought to allow all three to
be done in bathing drawers, to make up for my
disappointment!

Sincerely yours,

C.L. Dodgson

P.S. I hope Mrs. Mayhew won't mind my suggesting that I never photograph well when a large party come. If Ruth and Ethel bring Janet, there is really no need for her to come as well—that is if you can trust me to keep my promise of abiding strictly by the limits laid down. If you can't trust my word, then please never bring or send any of the children again! I should certainly prefer, in that case, to drop the acquaintance. I get on pretty well with three people on the premises: better, usually, with two: what I like best of all is to have two hours of leisure-time before me, one child to photograph, and no restrictions as to costume! (It is a descending Arithmetical Series—2, 1, 0.)

Christ Church, Oxford, May 28, 1879

Dear Mrs. Mayhew,

Thanks for the letter. After my last had gone, I wished to recall it, and take out the sentence in which I had quite gratuitously suggested the possibility that you might be unwilling to trust me to photograph the children by themselves in undress. And now I am more than ever sorry I wrote it, as it has accidentally led to your telling me what I would gladly have remained ignorant of. For I hope you won't think me very fanciful in saying I should have no pleasure in doing any such pictures, now that I know I am only permitted such a privilege on condition of being under chaperonage. I had rather do no more pictures of your children except in full dress: please forgive all the trouble I have given you about it. . . .

    Sincerely yours,

C.L. Dodgson

Carroll faced more headaches, especially after he kissed a seventeen-year-old girl, Atty Owen, who he thought was fourteen. Carroll gave up photography entirely by the following summer.

Another Kiss, circa 1885

Was clergyman Dodgson on the edge of the abyss? One Isa Bowman described—without casting any blame—this scene in her brief memoir about her friendship with Lewis Carroll:

I had an idle trick of drawing caricatures when I was a child, and one day when he was writing some letters I began to make a picture of him on the back of an envelope. I quite forget what the drawing was like—probably it was an abominable libel— but suddenly he turned round and saw what I was doing. He got up from his seat and turned very red, frightening me very much. Then he took my poor little drawing, and tearing it into small pieces threw it into the fire without a word. Afterwards he came suddenly to me, and saying nothing, caught me up in his arms and kissed me passionately. I was only ten or eleven years of age at the time but now the incident comes back to me very clearly, and I can see it as if it happened but yesterday— the sudden snatching of my picture, the hurried striding across the room, and then the tender light in his face as he caught me up to him and kissed me.

—ISA BOWMAN

Hermaphrodite on Tour, 1882

Henry Spencer Ashbee (1834–1900), a Victorian collector of pornography, bequeathed his collection of rare Don Quixote editions to the British Museum on the condition that after his death they also house his enormous erotic library. The museum reluctantly agreed, but for almost three-quarters of a century it followed its standard procedure for erotica and refused to enter the eight thousand or so titles into its card catalogue, making them just a bit difficult to find.

Ashbee, in his bibliography of erotica, added the following story as a personal footnote:

I visited Madame H. Balzac, for so she called herself, on the 2nd February 1882. She was travelling to gain money by showing the peculiarity of her conformation, and has, I believe, been described in The Lancet. She was about 20 years of age, rather pretty and quite womanly, with beautiful blue eyes, a good complexion, and fair hair; her nose was rather masculine, and her mouth rough and large, with bad teeth; her chest was expansive and her breasts well developed; the lower part of her legs slightly bowed and masculine. She possessed in appearance at least, the organs of both sexes, but neither perfect: a small penis, as in a lad of 12 or 14 years, and testicles apparently developed; the yard was however not perforated. Underneath the testicles was what seemed to be a perfect female vestibule, of which the opening was however only large enough to allow her to pass her water, but not to receive a man, or even to admit the insertion of the end of a quill. She told me she was born in Paris; that she had no monthly flow, but felt nevertheless a periodical indisposition; that she experienced pleasure in the embraces of both sexes and had even an erection when with a sympathetic female. She could not of course satisfy her desires.

Ashbee—under the pen name Pisanus Fraxi—wrote the definitive three-part bibliography to pornography, beginning with "Index Librorum Prohibitorum," and he displayed a knack for selecting just the wickedest story to illustrate the nature of a particular book, such as the following:

Erection and Resurrection

This piece—called "The Priest" and written by an unidentified doctor of the Sorbonne in 1802—comes from a volume called Uncertainties in Identifying Signs of Death:

A younger brother was forced against his will to enter into a religious order. Once while travelling, he stops at an inn, which he finds in deep mourning. The innkeeper's only daughter, who was remarkably beautiful, had just died. They ask the monk to perform a wake over her; he agrees and during the night, curious to see the features of a young girl who he was told was so lovely, he uncovers her face, and, spurred by the demon of lust, he violates her and then departs the next morning. The following day, while they were putting the coffin in the ground, someone heard some movement; the bier is opened; the young girl is put back in bed and soon nursed back to health. A little while later, the symptoms of pregnancy appear, and at the end of nine months, she gives birth to a baby, all the while protesting her virginity. A few years later when the monk's older brother died, he renounced his vows. His business took him back to that same inn where he found the deceased to be alive and a mother. Charmed by her beauty, he confessed his crime and expiated it by marrying her.

—INDEX LIBRORUM PROHIBITORUM

Virgins for Sale in London, 1885

Just three years before Jack the Ripper stalked the prostitutes of London, W.T. Stead (1849–1912)—a crusading journalist, a fireworks-for-God type of reporter—decided he would prowl those same streets, try to buy a virgin, and write about it.

Stead's thirty-thousand-plus word, four-part series, "The Maiden Tribute of Modern Babylon," ranks among the most "sensational" in British journalism history. Lewis Carroll was so disturbed by the graphic descriptions of child sex crimes that he tried to have the newspaper shut down.

The Violation of Virgins

July 6, 1885, Pall Mall Gazette

Before beginning this inquiry I had a confidential interview with one of the most experienced officers who for many years was in a position to possess an intimate acquaintance with all phases of London crime. I asked him, "Is it or is it not a fact that, at this moment, if I were to go to the proper houses, well introduced, the keeper would, in return for money down, supply me in due time with a maid—a genuine article, I mean, not a mere prostitute tricked out as a virgin, but a girl who had never been seduced?"

"Certainly," he replied, without a moment's hesitation.

"At what price?" I continued.

"That is a difficult question," he said. "I remember one case which came under my official cognizance in Scotland-yard in which the price agreed upon was stated to be £20. Some parties in Lambeth undertook to deliver a maid for that sum to a house of ill fame, and I have no doubt it is frequently done all over London."

"But," I continued, "are these maids willing or unwilling parties to the transaction—that is, are they really maiden, not merely in being each a 'virgo intacta' in the physical sense, but as being chaste girls who are not consenting parties to their seduction?"

He looked surprised at my question, and then replied emphatically: "Of course they are rarely willing, and as a rule they do not know what they are coming for."

"But," I said in amazement, "then do you mean to tell that in very truth actual rapes, in the legal sense of the word, are constantly being perpetrated in London on unwilling virgins, purveyed and procured to rich men at so much a head by keepers of brothels?"

"Certainly," said he, "there is not a doubt of it."

Among the many cases cited, the following was among the more disturbing:

A Child of Thirteen Bought for £5

I can personally vouch for every fact in the narrative. . . .

Lily was her own daughter, a bright, fresh-looking little girl, who was thirteen years old last Christmas. . . . The brothel-keeper offered her a sovereign for her daughter. The woman was poor, dissolute, and indifferent to everything but drink. The father, who was also a drunken man, was told his daughter was going to a situation. He received the news with indifference, without even inquiring where she was going to. The brothel-keeper having thus secured possession of the child, then sold her to the procuress . . . for £5—£3 paid down and the remaining £2 after her virginity had been professionally certified. The little girl, all unsuspecting the purpose for which she was destined, was told that she must go with this strange woman to a situation. The procuress, who was well up to her work, took her away, washed her, dressed her up neatly, and sent her to bid her parents good-bye. The mother was so drunk she hardly recognized her daughter. The father was hardly less indifferent. The child left her home, and was taken to the woman's lodging in A——street.

The first step had been thus taken. But it was necessary to procure the certification of her virginity—a somewhat difficult task, as the child was absolutely ignorant of the nature of the transaction which had transferred her from home to the keeping of this strange but apparently kind-hearted woman. Lily was a little cockney child, one of those who by the thousand annually develop into the servants of the poorer middle-class. She had been at school, could read and write, and although her spelling was extraordinary, she was able to express herself with much force and decision. Her experience of the world was limited to the London quarter in which she had been born. With the exception of two school trips to Richmond and one to Epping Forest, she had never been in the country in her life, nor had she ever seen the Thames excepting at Richmond. She was an industrious warm-hearted little thing, a hardy English child, slightly coarse in texture, with dark black eyes, and short sturdy figure. Her education was slight. She spelled write "right" for instance, and her grammar was very shaky. But she was a loving affectionate child, who kindly feeling for the drunken mother who sold her into nameless infamy was very touching to behold. In a little letter of hers which I once saw, plentifully garlanded with kisses, there was the following ill-spelled childish verse:—

> As I was in bed
> Some little forths (thoughts) gave (came) in my head.
> I forth (thought) of one, I forth (thought) of two;
> But first of all I forth (thought) of you.

The poor child was full of delight at going to her new situation and clung affectionately to the keeper who was taking her away—where she knew not.

The first thing to be done after the child was fairly severed from the home was to secure the certificate of virginity without which the rest of the purchase money would not be forthcoming. In order to avoid trouble she was taken in a cab to the house of midwife [*a Madame Mourez*], whose skill in pronouncing upon the physical evidences of virginity is generally recognized in the profession. The examination was very brief and completely satisfactory. But the youth, the complete innocence of the girl, extorted pity even from the hardened heart of the old abortionist. "The poor little thing," she exclaimed. "She is so small, her pain will be extreme. I hope you will not be too cruel with her"—as if to lust when fully roused the very acme of agony on the part of the victim has not a fierce delight. To quiet the old lady the agent of the purchaser asked if she could supply anything to dull the pain. She produced a small phial of chloroform. "This," she said, "is the best. My clients find it the most effective." The keeper took the bottle, but unaccustomed to anything but drugging by the administration of sleeping potions, she would infallibly have poisoned the girl had she discovered by experiment that the liquid burned the mouth when an attempt was made to swallow it. £1 1s was paid for the certificate of virginity— which was verbal and not written—while £1 10s more was charged for the chloroform, the net value of which was probably less than a shilling. An arrangement was made that if the child was badly injured, Madame would patch it up to the best of her ability, and then the party left the house.

From the midwife's the innocent girl was taken to a house of ill fame, No.—, P– street, Regent-street, where, not-withstanding her extreme youth, she was admitted without question. She was taken upstairs, undressed, and put to bed, the woman who brought her putting her to sleep. She was rather restless, but under the influence of chloroform she soon went over. Then the woman withdrew. All was quiet and still. A few moments later the door opened, and the purchaser entered the bedroom. He closed and locked the door. There was a brief silence. And then there rose a wild and piteous cry—not a loud shriek, but a helpless startled scream like the bleat of a frightened lamb. And the child's voice was heard crying, in accents of terror, "There's a man in the room! Take me home; oh, take me home!"

And then all once more was still.

That was but one case among many, and by no means the worst. It only differs from the rest because I have been able to verify the facts. Many a similar cry will be raised this very night in the brothels of London, unheeded by man, but not unheard by the pitying ear of Heaven.

—W.T. STEAD

Surprising Aftermath

The articles unleashed a tabloid war, and a rival paper discovered Lily's mother, a Mrs. Armstrong, and found out from her that Stead had fudged many details. Lily was indeed her daughter Eliza, and was actually thirteen years old, but the client was not some anonymous stranger but rather Stead himself. And that final brutal rape scene never took place, because the crusading journalist stopped far short of having sex with the girl. After their encounter, though, he sent Eliza to France for safekeeping until publication, without ever asking her mother's permission.

Ironically, Stead was convicted of one of the crimes he was investigating: of exporting a minor without parental consent. He was sentenced to three months in jail.

On the flip side, his series of articles led directly to the passage of the Criminal Law Amendment of 1885, raising the age of consent from thirteen to sixteen, making procuring a crime, and increasing the penalties for assaulting a girl under thirteen. Stead, who always had a flair for the dramatic, died on the Titanic in 1912.

Van Gogh Loses an Ear, 1888

The ear. The notorious ear. The image is of a mad, passionate Dutchman giving a "token of his esteem" to his beloved. The truth is, he gave it to a prostitute, and the incident probably had more to do with his relations with his temperamental house mate Paul Gauguin than with the girl.

December 30, 1888

Last Sunday [*December 23*], at 11:30 p.m., one Vincent Vangogh [*sic*], a painter born in Holland, arrived at the House of Tolerance [*brothel*] No. 1, asked for one Rachel, and handed her his ear, saying, "Keep this and treasure it." Then he disappeared. Informed of this action, which could only be that of a poor lunatic, the police went to the man's address the next morning and found him lying in bed and giving almost no sign of life. The unfortunate was admitted to hospital as an emergency case.

—LE FORUM REPUBLICAIN, ARLES

Alone with the Hairy Ainu: Love Bites, 1890

A. H. Savage Landor (1865–1924) visited the Japanese-controlled Kurile Islands where the locals—both men and women—were noted for having hair all over their bodies and faces. The young writer had an unusual little romance:

At Tobuts, a small village of a few huts, situated at the mouth of the Saruma lagoon, I halted for the night. There was a change in my diet that day, and I was entertained, or rather I entertained myself to an oyster supper. They were enormous oysters, similar to those found at Akkeshi, but not very palatable. However, I was in luck that day, and not only did I have this oyster supper, but I actually was the hero of a tender little idyll. In this country surprises never come alone, and while I was sketching in the twilight to pass away the time, a tall slim figure of a girl came out of one of the huts. She had slipped her arms out of her robe, leaving the latter to hang from the girdle, and her breasts, arms and lower half of her legs were uncovered. She was pretty and quaint with her tattooed arms and a semicircular black spot on her upper lip. She walked a few steps forward, and when she saw me she stopped. She looked at me and I looked at her. Hers, with her soft eyes, was one of those looks which a man feels right through his body, notwithstanding all the self-control he may possess. There she stood, a graceful silhouette, with a bucket made of tree-bark in one hand and a vine-tree rope in the other, her supple figure almost motionless, and her eyes fixed on me. She was the most lovely Ainu girl I had ever come across, and not nearly so hairy as most of them. In, in that soft twilight, and her wavy long hair blown by the fresh breeze, she was a perfect dream.

"Wakka!" ("Water!") cried an angry old voice from inside the hut, interrupting the beginning of our romance, and she sadly went to the brook, filled her bucket with water and took it into the hut. It was only a few seconds before she reappeared, and came closer, and I finished the sketch somewhat hurriedly.

"Let me see the tattoo on your arm," I asked her, and to my surprise the pretty maid took my hand in both her own, gave me one of those looks that I shall never forget, and her head fell on my shoulder. She clutched my hand tightly, and pressed it to my chest, and a force stronger than myself brought her and myself to the neighbouring forest. There we wandered and wandered till it grew very dark; we sat down, we chatted, we made love to each other; then we returned. I would not have mentioned this small episode if her ways of flirting had not been so extraordinary and funny. Loving and biting went together with her. She could not do the one without doing the other. As we sat on a stone in the semi-darkness, she began by gently biting my fingers, without hurting me, as affectionate dogs often do to their masters; she then bit my arm, then my shoulder and when she had worked herself up into a passion she put her arms round my neck and bit my cheeks. It was undoubtedly a curious way of making love, and when I had been bitten all over, and was pretty tired of the new sensation, we retired to our respective homes.

In the evening, as I was writing my diary by the light of one of the oyster-shell primitive lamps, somebody noiselessly crept by my side. I turned my head round. It was she! She grew more and more sentimental as it grew later, and she bestowed on me caresses and bites in profusion. Kissing, apparently, was an unknown art to her. The old woman, in whose house I was, slept soundly through all this, as old women generally do on such occasions. By the mysterious light of the dying wick, casting heavy shadows, which marked her features strongly, with her jet-black wild hair fading away into the black background, with her passionate eyes and her round statue-like arms, the girl was more like a strange fairy than a human being.

I sketched her twice in pencil, and the wick—that wretched wick!—grew feeble, and for the lack of oil, began to dwindle away. I persuaded her to return to her hut, and with a few "bites" my hairy maid and I parted.

The next morning, Landor continued on his thirty-eight-hundred-mile trek, never to see her again.

Toulouse Lautrec Adores Redheads, 1890s

The world remembers his posters; his friends remember his penis. Henri de Toulouse-Lautrec (1864–1901)—five-feet-tall, quick-witted, crippled painter—captured in posters such as the one for the Moulin Rouge nightclub the joyful carousing and the sadness of the Gay Nineties in Paris. He drank a lot, lived in brothels, loved fondling women, and more than one friend noted in his memoirs about his disproportionately large member.

Thadée Nathanson, friend of the artist, wrote Un Henri de Toulouse-Lautrec.

Redheads

Lautrec was crazy about redheads, but only redheads born redheads, who are "the blonds of the gods." The hair dressers are going to multiply the troops of redheads, but no chemistry will ever succeed in counterfeiting the quality of the whiteness of their skin. It's even less possible for artifice to imitate the skin of those whose blood glows through, which gives it a bluish tint.

"When a woman is a redhead," he used to say in his halting manner, "redhead! but there redhead!"—in a phrase there was always one word that resounded—"redhead! . . . tek-nik of the Venetians!"

Even though that skin-tone had tarnished, though blemishes had surfaced and the copper of the hair had been unraveled by gray strands, Lautrec would still voluptuously inhale the flesh just beginning to grow old.

His eyes shut, he would seek out the memory of their

splendor, tasting the power which preserved the odor strongly marking their bodies; above all, the skinniest ones.

Tech . . . nique of the armpit!

The Man Who Loved Women

Women, there was not a single one who didn't fascinate him.

Whatever girls passed by, that one dangling a package at the end of a ribbon. That other one whose basket of linen forces her to arch her bust to maintain her balance. Even those carrying only their unchanged attitude across the sidewalk.

Everywhere, almost at every step, some other aspect of the magnificence of the statues of women rivet the little man. From below, where he contemplated them, their bodies have their own dimensions.

Clothed or unclothed, their breasts have the same insolence. If they hang down, they have their form as well. The models, even those who had long ago forgotten the shame of their debuts, as soon as they make an effort, there's a blush of blood that he sees spreading across their skin. When he contemplates them, naked from their tip of their toes to the sheen of their forehead, he scarcely dares to touch anywhere.

Too Fine For . . .

"A woman's body," explains Lautrec, "a beautiful woman's body, you see . . . it's not made for love-making . . . it's too fine, isn't it? To make love . . . requires just any body . . . any body's suffices—he pronounced it 'tuffit'—any body. . . ."

Lautrec Swan Dives into Their Cleavage

He loved women's bodies. The bodies of all women. Their hats enchanted him as much they did Renoir; their muffs and their dresses which he couldn't stop himself from stroking them as though they were living beings. He used to get drunk off their hands. How many times have I seen him plunge into their bosoms! He delighted in caressing women. More from friendship than from love. Moreover at the same time with the ingenuousness of a fawn and the devotion of learned amateur.

The Artist's Tool

Henri de Toulouse-Lautrec was very short, very dark. He resembled a dwarf in that his chest, which was that of a grown man, seemed with its weight and that of his big head to have crushed the tiny legs that appeared below. . . .

Anyone who saw him naked stored the memory of his manhood, and understood how someone could have called it "verge à pattes" [*a walking penis*].

—THADÉE NATHANSON

The Sodomy Trial of Oscar Wilde, 1895

It was the tabloid trial of the century: Oscar Wilde (1854–1900) up for sodomy. Here are the circumstances: Oscar Wilde—poet, playwright (The Importance of Being Earnest), *novelist* (The Picture of Dorian Gray), *poseur, conversationalist, married man—played mentor and probably more to a petulant scholar-athlete-aristocrat Alfred Douglas.*

The fellow's father, the marquess of Queensberry, a rough carousing sportsman, stalked and bad-mouthed Wilde in the name of trying to save his son. Queensberry accused Wilde of being a "posing Somdomite" [sic]. Wilde—tired of the harassment and goaded by members of Douglas' own family— sued the marquess for libel. Not only did Wilde lose—names of ten boys he propositioned were eventually produced in court— but the British government went on to charge him with sodomy and indecency.

Libel Trial: Wilde's Letter to Alfred Douglas

My own boy,

Your sonnet is quite lovely, it is a marvel that those red rose-leaf lips of yours should have been made no less for music of song than for madness of kisses. Your slim gilt soul walks between passion and poetry. I know Hyacinthus, whom Apollo loved so madly, was you in Greek days.

Why are you alone in London, and when do you go to Salisbury? Do go there to cool your hands in the grey twilight of Gothic things, and come here whenever you like. It is a lovely place—it only lacks you; but go to Salisbury first.

Always, with undying love,

Oscar

Wilde's lawyer tried to reverse the spin:
The words of that letter, gentlemen, may appear extravagant to those in the habit of writing commercial correspondence

(Laughter) . . . but Mr. Wilde is a poet, and the letter is considered by him as a prose sonnet, and one of which he is in no way ashamed and is prepared to produce anywhere as the expression of true poetic feeling, and with no relation whatever to the hateful and repulsive suggestions put to it in the plea in this case.

Young Men

Later, Wilde is confronted with the testimony of several young men, whom he is accused of paying for sex.
Mr. Carson (Queensberry's lawyer): Did you know that one Parker was a gentleman's valet, and the other a groom?
Wilde: I did not know it, but if I had I should not have cared. I didn't care twopence what they were. I liked them. I have a passion to civilize the community.
Mr. Carson: What enjoyment was it to you to entertain grooms and coachmen?
Wilde: The pleasure to me was being with those who are young, bright, happy, careless and free. I do not like the sensible and I do not like the old.

Sodomy Trial

The government proceeded with sodomy charges against Wilde, and provided room, board, clothing, and money to a handful of young male witnesses for the prosecution, according to Oscar Wilde, *by Richard Ellman:*
Frederick Atkins, examined by Mr. Avory.
Mr. Avory: How old are you?
Atkins: I am twenty years old.

Mr. Avory: What is your business?

Atkins: I have been a billiard marker. I have also been a bookmaker's clerk and a comedian.

You are doing nothing now?

No.

Who introduced you to the prisoners?

I was introduced to Taylor by a young fellow named Schwabe in November, 1892, and afterwards by Taylor to Mr. Wilde.

Have you met Lord Alfred Douglas?

I have. I dined with him and Mr. Wilde at the Florence.

What happened at the dinner?

Mr. Wilde kissed the waiter.

Did he ask you to go with him to Paris?

Yes. We were seated at the table, and he put his arm round me and said he liked me. I arranged to meet him two days afterward at Victoria Station, and went to Paris with him as his private secretary. We stayed at 29 Boulevard des Capucines. We had two rooms there—a bed-sitting room and a bedroom, one leading into the other. The day after we got to Paris I did some writing for him. Afterwards I lunched at the Cafe Julien with him. We went for a drive in the afternoon. Next day we went to a hairdresser's, and I had my hair cut.

Did you tell him to curl it?

No he did it on his own account.

Wilde was there?

Yes, he was having his hair cut, and was talking to the man in French all the time. After dinner on the second day we were in Paris I went to the Moulin Rouge. Mr. Wilde told me not go there but I went. I had to pay to go in. I had some money Mr. Wilde had given me. . . . Mr. Wilde told me not to go see those women, as women were the ruin of young fellows. Mr. Wilde spoke several times about the same subject, and always to the same effect. I got back to the rooms very late. Mr. Wilde was in bed. I went into his room and had something to drink. A man about twenty-two years of age was in bed with Mr. Wilde. It was Schwabe. I went to bed by myself. Before I got out of bed in the morning Mr. Wilde came into my room. That was about nine o'clock. He talked about the Moulin Rouge, and I told him that I had enjoyed myself. Mr. Wilde then said to me, "Shall I come into bed with you?" I replied that it was time to get up. Mr. Wilde did not get into bed with me. A waiter came into the room with the breakfast, and after drinking a cup of coffee I got up. I returned to London with Mr. Wilde, who gave me money and a silver cigarette case.

Sentence

Wilde was convicted of indecency and sodomy. On May 25, 1895, Justice Arthur Charles sentenced Wilde to two years' hard labor:

And that you, Wilde, have been the centre of a circle of extensive corruption of the most hideous kind among young men, it is equally impossible to doubt.

I shall under the circumstances be expected to pass the severest sentence that the law allows. In my judgement, it is totally inadequate for a such a case as this.

Evidence suggests Wilde, like many of the ancient Greeks, preferred teenage boys and had a brief physical relationship with Alfred Douglas, before graduating to being his mentor. (However, after his conviction, Wilde harshly denounced Douglas.)

A Final Defense by Alfred Douglas

Alfred Douglas wrote a passionate reply to an antihomosexual editorial written by crusading journalist W. T. Stead:

Rouen, 28th July, 1895

. . . Why on earth in the name of liberty and common sense a man cannot be allowed to love a boy, rather than a woman when his nature and his instinct tell him to do so, and when he has before him the example of such a number of noble and gifted men who have had similar tastes (such as Shakespeare, Marlowe, Michael Angelo, Frederick the Great, and a host of others), is another question and one to which I should like to hear a satisfactory answer. Certain it is that persecution will no more kill this instinct in a man who has it, than it killed the faith of the Christian martyrs. I am not pleading for prostitution, but I think if a man who affects female prostitutes is unmolested it is disgraceful that a man who prefers male prostitutes should be thus barbarously punished. The only difference is that the man who brings bastards into the world, who seduces girls or commits adultery does an immense amount of harm, as you yourself have pointed out, whereas the paederast does absolutely no harm to anyone.

While on this point, sir, may I ask you if it ever occurred to you to consider the relative desserts of Mr. Oscar Wilde and the man who ruined him, my father, Lord Queensberry? Mr. Oscar Wilde seduced no one, he did no one any harm, he was a kind, generous and astoundingly gifted man, utterly incapable of meanness or cruelty. Lord Queensberry was divorced from my mother after, for twelve years, she had silently endured the most horrible suffering at his hands.

He broke her heart, ruined her health and took away all joy from her life, and after his divorce till the present day he has not ceased to persecute her with every fiendish ingenuity of cruelty and meanness that a man could devise. Hardly a week passes without her receiving some letter from him containing some horrible insult, he has been to beat on the door of her house when she was nearly dying upstairs, and he has taken away from her every penny of money that as an honourable man he should have given her, and left her only that which he is forced to give by the Scotch law which is so hard on a woman who divorces her husband. In the meanwhile he flaunts about with prostitutes and kept women and spends on them the money he should give to his children, for he has cut off all money supplies from my brother, myself and my sister.

Last year he induced a girl of seventeen to marry him in a registry office against the wish of her people. On the following day, he deserted her and has since been divorced for the second time. Not content with practising fornication and adultery, he has written pamphlets advocating what he calls a "sort of polygamy" which is neither more nor less than free love. This is the man who has been made into a hero by the English people and the press, who is cheered in the streets by the mob, and who has crowned his career by dishonouring and driving out of England his son who now writes to you.

I am, sir, your obedient servant,

ALFRED DOUGLAS

Oscar Wilde was released from prison in 1897 and died in Paris in 1900. He never really recovered from his stint in Reading Gaol.

Freud: Travel Anxiety and Seeing Mom . . . , 1897

Sigmund Freud (1856-1939) pioneered self-analysis on himself, especially when business was slow. To help with the process, he wrote letters to Dr. Wilhelm Fliess, who acted as a sounding board. Here, Freud is convinced he has made something of a breakthrough, and a key part dates back to Mother, to seeing MOTHER . . . (Freud coyly refers to her in Latin as "matrem.")

October 3, 1897

. . . There is still very little happening to me externally, but internally something very interesting. For the last four days my self-analysis, which I consider indispensable for the clarification of the whole problem, has continued in dreams and has presented me with the most valuable elucidations and clues.

. . . (Between two and two and a half years) my libido towards <u>matrem</u> was awakened, namely, on that occasion of a journey with her from Leipzig to Vienna, during which we must have spent the night together and there must have been an opportunity of seeing her <u>nudam</u> [*i.e., nude*] (you inferred the consequences of this for your son long ago, as a remark revealed to me). . . . You yourself have seen my travel anxiety at its height. . . .

Business is still very poor. I fear if it gets better, it might prove an obstacle to my self-analysis. . . .

—SIGMUND FREUD

A French Doctor Catalogues Sex Organs, 1898

A nineteenth-century French army doctor, who wrote under the pseudonym of Dr. Jacobus X., dedicated twenty-eight years of his life to examining and measuring the genitals of "semi-civilized" people around the world, from Africa to South America. While he failed to win many converts to his anthropological theory, called the "Genital Sense," he did amass an astounding amount of eyewitness and anecdotal information about Third World genitalia, from the twelve-incher he handled in Mali to the priapism he treated in Guyana.

(A handwritten note in the card catalogue at the Kinsey Institute library identified Dr. X. as one Louis Jacolliot.)

African

In no branch of the human race are the male organs more developed than in the African Negro. I am speaking of the penis and not of the testicles, which are often smaller than those of the majority of Europeans.

The genital organ of the male is in proper proportion as regards size, to the dimensions of the female organ. In fact, with the exception of the Arab, who runs him very close in this respect, the Negro of Senegal possesses the largest genital organ of all the races of mankind. . . .

The Negro is a real "man-stallion," and nothing can give a better idea (both as to colour and size) of the organ of the Negro, when erect, than the tool of a little African donkey. The absence of hair on the pubes—which the Negroes remove—makes the resemblance more complete. Nor is it confined merely to the colour and size for the penis of the Negro even when in complete erection, is still soft like that of the donkey, and when pressed by the hands feels like a thick india-rubber tube full of liquid. Even when flabby, the Negro's penis still retains a size and consistence that are greater than that of the European, whose organ shrivels up and becomes limp. The average size of the penis generally appeared to me to be about 7 3/4 to 8 inches in length, by two inches in diameter. Except with the young lads, just arrived at the age of puberty, the penis is rarely less than 6 1/2 inches in length by 1 3/4 inches in diameter. I took these measurements from the Sharpshooters, amongst whom I met specimens of most of the races of Senegal and the Upper Niger. I often came across a penis of 9 3/4 to 10 inches, by 2 1/4 inches, and once, in a young Bambara [*Mali*], barely twenty years of age, found a monstrous organ 11 3/4 inches long by 2.6 inches in diameter at the circumcision mark. . . . This was a terrific machine, and except for a slight difference in length, was more like the penis of a donkey than that of a man. This unfortunate Sharpshooter who possessed this "spike" could not find a Negress large enough to receive him with pleasure, and he was an object of terror to all the feminine sex.

India

Dr. Jacobus compared historical data with his eyewitness evaluations:

The Kama Sutra does not give the dimensions of the "lingam" but this omission is repaired by the Ananga Ranga, written in the 16th century of our era, whilst the previous work dates from the 5th century. The Ananga Ranga gives, for dimensions of the penis of the "hare-man," a length of six fingers broad; for the "bull-man," nine; for the "man stallion" twelve. It should be remarked that the finger of the Hindoo, being thin and delicate, is not more than 0.6 of an inch in breadth and these measures would correspond to 3.6 inches, 5.4 inches and 7.2 inches. The result of my personal observations is, that the great bulk of Hindoo coolies may be classed as "hare-men," only a small number as "bull-men" and a smaller number still "stallion-men."

Arabs

The Arabs I examined, and who for the most part had been sentenced for rapes or sodomy committed upon children of either sex, in the proportions of their genital members considerably surpassed the fair average of the Negroes. In the bodies of many Arabs I dissected, the penis, instead of being drawn up and reduced to a small volume, like that of the European, still showed a considerable development.

In its usual condition, their penis, instead of being quite limp, still maintains a certain consistency and feels to the hand like hollow india-rubber, or like the penis of the Negro. The gland is of a normal form, well developed and of a dirty red brown, lighter however than that of the Mulatto, but not so red as that of the Quadroon. It is, in proportion, smaller than the shaft of the penis, which is swollen a little underneath; the maximum diameter is found where the foreskin is cut in circumcising. This part of the penis sometimes swells out like a sort of external pad. According to the measurements I made, the penis of the Arab has an average length, when in erection of 7.2 to 7.6 inches by 1.6 to 2.0 inches in diameter; but I have found often a penis measuring 8 to 10 inches in length, by 2.0 or 2.4 in diameter. The organ then becomes a sort of pole which only a Negress could accommodate while a Hindoo woman of the class called "hare-women," would shrink from it in terror, and it would produce mischief in the rectum of any poor wretch who consented to suffer its terrible attacks. With such a weapon does the Arab seek for anal copulation. He is not particular in his choice, and age or sex makes no difference to him. At the hulks, he finds among other convicts, Blacks or Hindoos, or even whites, the scum of the great cities, upon whom he can satisfy his miserable lust.

Shipwrecked in North Africa

The Arab tribes of the coasts of Algeria and Morocco, it is well-known, take by force the unfortunate wretches who are wrecked on their shores. A little time before the Algerian expedition, a French ship of war, a brig called the Silenus, was thrown on the African coast, and all the crew had to pass under the "Caudine Forks," whether they liked it or not. Among them was a young naval officer, who suffered the same fate as the others. One day—some years after the taking of Algiers—in a drawing room in Paris, a lady who was known to be rather "fast" and very free-spoken, asked him, with an air half-serious, half-jesting, if he had really been–"forked."

"Madame," he replied coolly, "imagine yourself for a moment in my place. If there was before you a sabre ready to cut your head off, and behind you a big tool, what would you do? I went backwards, and I think you would have done the same."

The Death of an Arab Child Bride, 1869

A fellow medical officer, M. Prospero Albert, stationed in Algeria, relayed this information to Dr. Jacobus:

On the 25th of September, 1869, in the village of El-Mesloub, the young Aini-Ntamrant, of the Beni-Raten tribe, aged twelve and married since about thirty days to El Haoussin or Ali, a youth of from 15 to 16 years old, died suddenly.

Public rumour, from the very next morning, accused the husband of having killed his wife by premature and forced conjugal approach. The Amyn or judge of the tribe thought it his duty to have the body sent to the Bureau Arabe, and we were charged to proceed to a post-mortem examination of it. The following was the result.

The body is that of a quite young girl not yet developed. She is thin, and the mammae are not yet elevated above the surface of the breast, nor is there yet any hair on the pubis, which is merely covered with down. The vulva is but imperfectly developed and the girl had never been nubile. Her conformation and her exterior genital organs were those of a child. A close examination showed that the fork was torn vertically downwards for a distance of three tenths of an inch; the rent extends through the "navicular fossa" into the vagina.

There is no trace of the hymen left, but in its place red excoriations. On further examination, the vagina was found to be extremely short, measuring not more than 1¼ inch in depth, and at its inner extremity there was an opening through which the finger could penetrate right into the abdomen.

The uterus is that of a child and weighs only three grams. All these facts show positively that Aini-Ntamrant was quite unfit for marriage, and her husband must have used the utmost violence to have caused the lesions we noticed. The examination of the brain showed the death was owing to intense cerebral congestion.

We caused the young husband of the victim to appear before us. He is a lad of 15 or 16 years old, of middle height, well constituted but thin. He has no beard and but little hair on the pubis, which besides is shaved. His genital organs are greatly developed for his age. His testicles are voluminous. From the tip of the gland to its insertion in the pubis the penis measures three inches and one sixth in length; its average circumference is 4⅓ inches.

Is it necessary to draw attention to the enormous disproportion between the volume and length of the penis of the young man, when in a state of erection, and the opening of the vulva and length of the vagina of his wife.

From his own admission, we gleaned the following: the marriage took place a month ago, but the first conjugal approaches were so painful to her that the girl wanted to go back to her mother. But he refused to let her do so, promising however to have patience. Unfortunately, he could not contain himself and the extreme violence he used, notwithstanding the supplications of his wife, ruptured the vagina, the walls of which we had besides noticed to be very thin.

This unfortunately is one of the examples of the disadvantages of the Koran, which omits to assign an inferior limit of age to marriage between young people.

Eggplant Penis Enlarger

Dr. Jacobus observed this practice in Guyana:

For this method of enlarging the member, an eggplant, of an appropriate size, is taken and split lengthwise. In each half is hollowed out a deep groove capable of containing the member when erect. Then a paste is made with flour, and water, in which has been boiled some "bois bandé" or "tightening wood" [*the bark of a variety of "nux vomica" tree*], some phosphorescent matches (six to twelve), two or three small pimentos, a dozen peppercorns, and as many cloves, with one or two vanilla beans to give it perfume. The foreskin is drawn back, and the penis and gland covered with this paste, and then enclosed in the eggplant. The plaster is left on for some minutes, and at once produces intense phlogosis [*inflammation*]. To allay this, the penis is bathed with a luke warm decoction of mallow, and then is rubbed with soap suds, which are allowed to dry. If these various operations are performed in the morning, eight or ten hours before copulating, it will be found that the penis really has increased in size. It is hot and inflamed, springs into an almost permanent erection at the least touch, and copulation produces a sharp feeling, almost painful. If the eggplant is kept on too long, priapism or cystitis will ensue.

A young lieutenant of the Marines, a neighbor of mine, tried the experiment one day. He was a fair man, of lymphatic temperament, with genital organs rather below the average size, and, moreover, suffering from a disagreeable phimosis [*tight foreskin*]. I was called to see him one morning, and found him in bed, complaining greatly of an intense priapism; the penis, which was triple the usual size, was red and inflamed, the head was enormous and in the form of a pear, being strangled by the foreskin. The patient also complained of a pain in the bladder. I was obliged to cut the foreskin, and then stopped the inflammation by suitable treatment. The patient swore—but rather too late in the day—that he would never try the process again.

—Dr. Jacobus X

8

Early
Twentieth
Century

Guide to Storyville of New Orleans, 1906

New Orleans, with its French roots, became Sodom-by-the-sea, offering more and kinkier sex for sale than any other U.S. city. In 1897, with a reform movement gathering steam, Alderman Sidney Story proposed cordoning off a huge red-light district. Thirty-eight square blocks wound up in "Storyville" and lasted as a mecca of regulated vice and Jazz piano until the U.S. Navy with a large base nearby forced its closing in 1917 during World War I.

The Blue Book *was a tourist guide/directory to the parlors of Storyville:*

Introduction to the 1906 Edition

To know a thing or two, and know it direct, go through this little book and read it carefully, and then when you go on a "lark" you'll know "who is who" and the best place to spend time and money.

Read all the "Ads." as all the best houses are described in special write-ups, and are known as the "Cream of Society."

Names in capitals are Landladies. "W" in front of name means White; "C" stands for Colored; "Oct." for Octoroon [*very light-skinned, i.e., one eighth-part African*]; the "J" means Jewess; and the Star for French.

The contents of this book are facts, and not dreams from a "hop joint."

You will find the boundary of the Tenderloin District, commonly called Anderson County or Storyville: North side Customhouse Street to South side St. Louis, and East side North Basin to West side North Robertson Streets.

This is the boundary in which the lewd women are compelled to live according to law.

Yours,
BILLY NEWS

Miss Lulu White

Nowhere in this country will you find a more popular personage than Madam White, who is noted as being the handsomest octoroon in America, and aside from her beauty, she has the distinction of possessing the largest collection of diamonds, pearls and other rare gems in this part of the country.

To see her at night, is like witnessing the electrical display on the Cascade, at the late St. Louis Exposition.

Aside from her handsome women, her mansion possesses some of the most costly oil paintings in the Southern country. Her mirror parlor is also a dream.

There's always something new at Lulu White's that will interest you. "Good time" is her motto.

There are always ten entertainers, who recently arrived from the "east," some being well known to the "profession" who get paid to do nothing but sing and dance.

PHONES MAIN 1102 AND 1331.

—THE BLUE BOOK

U.S. Army Doctor Witnesses Auto-Fellatio

Dr. J. Richardson Parke, acting assistant surgeon in the U.S. Army, noted an unusual case in his book, Human Sexuality *(1908):*

The most remarkable and interesting case of auto-stupration by the mouth I have ever met with, was that of a neurasthenic boy of fifteen, who, by years of training, had succeeded in making his spinal column so flexible that he was enabled to suck his own penis. From his nervousness, emaciation, and osteomalacious condition, I was led to suspect the truth, when his mother brought him to me for treatment; and boldly charging him with the act, at a later visit, when his mother was absent, obtained not only a complete confession, but, far more interesting, a practical illustration of the act itself. In order to convince myself that the thing was possible I asked him to put his penis into his mouth. He did not hesitate to do so, apparently regarding the act as of little consequence; but seemingly by instinct, when he did so the old passion revived, and absorbed him irresistibly; and whether the reader regard the part played by me as morally culpable, or professionally justifiable, I at least had the novel experience of witnessing an act of mouth-stupration by a boy—self-performed—in my own private consulting room. He lay on a couch; and as the climax of the orgasm approached, apparently forgetting my presence, and every other consideration, he resigned himself with utmost abandonment to the delirium of his pleasure, rolling, gasping, writhing, and resembling nothing so much as some sort of animal, curled up in a ball, enduring its death agony. He was afterward committed to a sanitarium for the treatment of such cases.

—Dr. J. Richardson Parke

Accused Irish Spy Charts His Male Lovers, 1910

Roger Casement was an Irish-born British diplomat who was hung for treason in 1916 for going to Berlin to try to win arms and aid for the Irish independence movement. His appeal of the sentence was quashed, in some measure because of the discovery of the so-called Black Diaries, which recounted homosexual meetings. His defenders claimed they were fakes produced by the British government, but scholars are now pretty much agreed on their authenticity. In them, we get glimpses of Casement's love life in Brazil, and his obsession with size:

February 28, 1910
Deep screw & to hilt. X "poquino"; Mario in Rio 8 1/2 + 6" $40. Hospedaria, rue do Hospicio, $3 only. ANE room shut window lovely young 18 and glorious. Biggest since Lisbon July 1904. Perfectly huge. 'Nunca veio maior!' Nunca.

March 2nd

arr. S. Paulo. Antonio 10$ Rua Direita. Dark followed and hard. Teatro Municipal. Breathed and quick, enormous push. Loved mightily, to hilt deep X.

May 26th

In Dublin. 'See it coming.' To Belfast, John McGonegal, huge and curved up by Cregagh Road, met by chance near clock tower and off on tram. It was huge and curved and he awfully keen. X 4/6.

May 28th

Left for Warrenpoint with Millar. Heated and huge enjoyment both enjoyed. He came to lunch at G. Central Hotel. Turned in together at 10.30 to 11—after watching billiards. Not a word said till—'Wait till I untie it' and then 'Grand.' Told many tales and pulled it off on top grandly. First time after so many years and so deep mutual longing. Rode gloriously, splendid steed. Huge, told of many. 'Grand.'

May 29th

At Warrenpoint and Rostrevor. Enormous over 7½ I think. 1 back. Asked after friend repeatedly. Millar again. First time he turned his back, 'Grand' back voluntarily.

—Roger Casement

Lawrence of Arabia Is Captured, 1917

Unlike Peter O'Toole, the real Lawrence of Arabia (1888–1935) was a very short (five-foot-five), very driven man

*who was quite confused about his sexuality. In an auto-
biographical work,* The Mint, *he writes:* "At Oxford, the select
preacher, speaking of venery, said, 'And let me implore you,
my young friends, not to imperil your immortal soul upon a
pleasure, so I am credibly informed, lasts less than one and
three-quarter minutes.' Of direct experience, I cannot boast,
never having been tempted to peril my immortal soul."
Lawrence made that claim at age forty.

Winston Churchill called him "one of the greatest beings
alive in our time." *Thomas Edward Lawrence—bastard son,
archaeologist—played an astounding role in World War I
unifying the Arabs to fight the Turks.* "Bedouin ways were
hard even for those brought up to them, and for strangers
terrible: a death in life," *he wrote in* Seven Pillars of Wisdom.

*On November 20, 1917, Lawrence, needing advance
information on the enemy in Deraa, Syria, posed as a
Circassian peasant to explore the town. He was captured by
the Turks and discovered a dark side of himself, a sensual
appreciation of pain:*

They led me into a guard-room, mostly taken up by large
wooden cribs, on which lay or sat a dozen men in untidy
uniforms. They took away my belt, and my knife, made me
wash myself carefully, and fed me. I passed the long day there.
They would not let me go on any terms but tried to reassure
me. A soldier's life was not all bad. To-morrow, perhaps, leave
would be permitted, if I fulfilled the Bey's pleasure this
evening. The Bey seemed to be Nahi, the Governor. If he was
angry, they said, I would be drafted for infantry training to the
depot in Baalbek. I tried to look as though, to my mind, there
was nothing worse in the world than that.

Soon after dark three men came for me. It had seemed a

chance to get away, but one held me all the time. I cursed my littleness. Our march crossed the railway, where were six tracks, besides the sidings of the engine-shop. We went through a side gate, down a street, past a square, to a detached, two-storied house. There was a sentry outside, and a glimpse of others lolling in the dark entry. They took me upstairs to the Bey's room; or to his bedroom, rather. He was another bulky man, a Circassian himself, perhaps, and sat on the bed in a night-gown, trembling and sweating as though with fever. When I was pushed in he kept his head down, and waved the guard out. In a breathless voice he told me to sit on the floor in front of him, and after that was dumb; while I gazed at the top of his great head, on which bristling hair stood up, no longer than the dark stubble on his cheeks and chin. At last he looked me over, and told me to stand up: then to turn round. I obeyed; he flung himself back on the bed, and dragged me down with him in his arms. When I saw what he wanted I twisted round and up again, glad to find myself equal to him, at any rate in wrestling.

He began to fawn on me, saying how white and fresh I was, how fine my hands and feet, and how he would let me off drills and duties, make me his orderly, even pay me wages, if I would love him.

I was obdurate, so he changed his tone, and sharply ordered me to take off my drawers. When I hesitated, he snatched at me; and I pushed him back. He clapped his hands for the sentry, who hurried in and pinioned me. The Bey cursed me with horrible threats: and made the man holding me tear my clothes away, bit by bit. His eyes rounded at the half-healed places where the bullets had flicked through my skin a little while ago. Finally he lumbered to his feet, with a glitter in his look, and began to paw me over. I bore it for a little, till he got too beastly; and then jerked my knee into him.

He staggered to his bed, squeezing himself together and groaning with pain, while the soldier shouted for the corporal and the other three men to grip me hand and foot. As soon as I was helpless the Governor regained courage, and spat at me, swearing he would make me ask pardon. He took off his slipper, and hit me repeatedly with it in the face, while the corporal braced my head back by the hair to receive the blows. He leaned forward, fixed his teeth in my neck and bit till the blood came. Then he kissed me. Afterwards he drew one of the men's bayonets. I thought he was going to kill me, and was sorry; but he only pulled up a fold of flesh over my ribs, worked the point through, after considerable trouble, and gave the blade a half-turn. This hurt, and I winced, while the blood wavered down my side, and dripped to the front of my thigh. He looked pleased and dabbled it over my stomach with his finger-tips.

In my despair I spoke. His face changed and he stood still, then controlled his voice with an effort, to say significantly, "You must understand that I know: and it will be easier if you do as I wish." I was dumbfounded, and we stared silently at one another, while the men who felt an inner meaning beyond their experience, shifted uncomfortably. But it was evidently a chance shot, by which he himself did not, or would not, mean what I feared. I could not again trust my twitching mouth, which faltered always in emergencies, so at last threw up my chin, which was the sign of "No" in the East; then he sat down, and half-whispered to the corporal to take me out and teach me everything.

They kicked me to the head of the stairs, and stretched me over a guard bench pommelling me. Two knelt on my ankles, bearing down on the back of my knees, while two more twisted my wrists till they cracked, and then crushed them and my neck against the wood. The corporal had run downstairs; and now came back with a whip of the Circassian sort, a thong of supple black hide, rounded, and tapering from the thickness of a thumb at the grip (which was wrapped in silver) down to a hard point finer than a pencil.

He saw me shivering, partly I think, with cold and made it whistle over my head, taunting me that before the tenth cut I would howl for mercy, and at the twentieth beg for the caresses of the Bey; and then he began to lash me madly across and across with all his might, while I locked my teeth to endure this thing which lapped itself like flaming wire about my body.

To keep my mind in control I numbered the blows, but after twenty lost count, and could feel only the shapeless weight of pain, not tearing claws, for which I had prepared but a gradual cracking apart of my whole being by some too-great force whose waves rolled up my spine till they were pent within my brain, to clash terribly together. Somewhere in the place a cheap clock ticked loudly, and it distressed me that their beating was not in its time. I writhed and twisted, but was held so tightly that my struggles were useless. After the corporal ceased, the men took up, very deliberately giving me so many, and then an interval, during which they would squabble for the next turn, ease themselves, and play unspeakably with me. This was repeated often, for what may have been no more than ten minutes. Always for the first of every new series, my head would be pulled around, to see how a hard white ridge, like a railway, darkening slowly into crimson, leaped over my skin at the instant of each stroke, with a bead of blood where two ridges crossed. As the punishment proceeded the whip fell more and more upon existing weals, biting blacker and more wet, till my flesh quivered with accumulated pain, and with terror of the next blow coming. They soon conquered my determination not to cry, but while my will ruled my lips I used only Arabic, and before the end a merciful sickness choked my utterance.

At last when I was completely broken they seemed satisfied. Somehow I found myself off the bench, lying on my back on the dirty floor, where I snuggled down, dazed, panting for breath, but vaguely comfortable. I had strung myself to learn all pain until I died, and no longer actor, but spectator, thought not to care how my body jerked and squealed. Yet I knew or imagined what passed about me.

I remembered the corporal kicking me with his nailed boot to get me up; and this was true, for next day my right side was dark and lacerated, and a damaged rib made each breath stab me sharply. I remembered smiling idly at him, for a delicious warmth, probably sexual, was swelling through me; and then that he flung up his arm and hacked with the full length of his whip into my groin. This doubled me half-over, screaming, or, rather, trying impotently to scream, only shuddering through my open mouth. One giggled with amusement. A voice cried, "Shame, you've killed him," Another slash followed. A roaring, and my eyes went black; while within me the core of life seemed to heave slowly up through the rending nerves, expelled from its body by this last indescribable pang.

By the bruises perhaps they beat me further; but I next

knew that I was being dragged about by two men, each disputing over a leg as though to split me apart; while a third man rode me astride. It was momently better than more flogging. Then Nahi called. They splashed water in my face, wiped off some of the filth, and lifted me between them, retching and sobbing for mercy, to where he lay; but he now rejected me in haste, as a thing too torn and bloody for his bed, blaming their excess of zeal which had spoilt me; whereas no doubt they had laid into me much as usual, and the fault rested mainly upon my indoor skin, which gave way more than an Arab's.

So the crestfallen corporal, as the youngest and best-looking of the guard, had to stay behind, while the others carried me down the narrow stair to the street. The coolness of the night on my burning flesh, and the unmoved shining of the stars after the horror of the past hour, made me cry again. The soldiers, now free to speak, warned me that men must suffer their officers' wishes or pay for it, as I had just done, with greater suffering.

They took me over an open space, deserted and dark, and behind the Government house to a lean-to wooden room, in which were many dusty quilts. An Armenian dresser appeared, to wash and bandage me in sleepy haste. Then all went away, the last soldier delaying by my side a moment to whisper in his Druse accent that the door into the next room was not locked.

—LAWRENCE OF ARABIA

Lawrence was hooked; later in life, he hired a strong young man to beat him.

President Harding in the White House Coat Closet, 1921

Tall, handsome, easy-going, Warren Harding (1865–1923) during his administration was at the center of several scandals, including the Teapot Dome affair. But it was after his death that an equally large scandal erupted. Nan Britton published The President's Daughter *in 1927, contending that Harding started secretly seeing her when she was sixteen and that, while as a senator, he fathered her child in 1919. Names, dates, details—but she had burnt his letters and had no photographs.*

In June of that spring, 1921, I made my first trip to Washington. . . .

As soon as I reached Washington I connected with Tim on the phone. It seems to me he told me my appointment with Mr. Harding had already been arranged. In any event, Tim called for me at my hotel and escorted me to the White House.

Needless to say, I "took in" everything I could on that first visit. We entered the executive offices through the main office entrance, which is the entrance on the right of the White House portico, and passed through the hall leading to the Cabinet Room. Here we waited for Mr. Harding.

While we waited, I observed the Cabinet Room with less awe, I guess, than natural curiosity. There was a long table around which stood the substantial chairs of the twelve men who met there every Tuesday morning and every Friday morning, each chair having the name of the particular Cabinet member engraved upon a little metal plaque which was fastened on the back. A fireplace, a clock on the mantelpiece, and a few pictures completed the furnishings. Mr. Harding's chair at the head of the table interested me most, and I stroked the back of it and sipped stale water from a partially filled glass which stood on the table in front of the President's chair. So this was where sat the leaders of the greatest nation in the world! I recalled articles I had read about this awesome office. One had recently appeared in the New York Times and was entitled, "At the Keyhole of the Cabinet Room." But I was not at the keyhole. I was on the really and truly <u>inside</u>!

We had been waiting only a very few minutes when Mr. Harding opened the door, a door immediately behind and opposite his Cabinet Room chair. He greeted me cordially and instructed Tim to remain in the Cabinet Room. Then I preceded him into a very small adjoining room, a room with one window. He explained to me that this was the ante-room, and crossed over to another door which led into his own private office.

Once in there, he turned and took me in his arms and told me what I could see in his face—that he was delighted to see me. Not more delighted, however, than I was to see him.

There were windows along one side of the room which looked out upon the green of the White House grounds, and outside, stalking up and down, face rigidly to the front, moved the President's armed guard. But in spite of this apparent obliviousness on the part of the guard, we were both skeptical and Mr. Harding said to me that people seemed to have eyes in the sides of their heads down there and so we must be very circumspect. Whereupon he introduced me to the one place where, he said, he thought we <u>might</u> share kisses in safety. This was a small closet in the ante-room, evidently a place for hats and coats, but entirely empty most of the times we used it, for we repaired there many times in the course of my visits to the White House, and in the darkness of a space not more than five feet square the President of the United States and his adoring sweetheart made love.

—NAN BRITTON

* * * * * * *

Acknowledgments

I want to acknowledge my debt to all the translators who tackled these passages before me, and I also want to thank all the historians who paved the way, especially Joyce Salisbury, who wrote a brilliant bibliography on medieval sexuality.

I hired two translators—Andy Meadows of Oxford University and Jeri Fogel of Columbia University—to help with the Latin, and they produced wonderfully fluid, readable prose.

This book would have been impossible without the unsung heroes: librarians and permissions editors. Special thanks goes out to the New York Public Library, the University of Michigan's Hatcher and Clements Libraries, the Kinsey Institute (Margaret Harter especially), Columbia University Butler Library and its Rare Book Room, and Indiana University's Lilly Library.

And more thanks to my editor, Craig Nelson, my agent, Esther Newberg, and Dorothea Herrey, Gordon Kato, Heather Schroeder, Sloan Harris, JTL Hitt, Jim Lyons, Jeff Kaye, Lauren Marino, and Vincent Morgenstern. Above all, thanks go to my super supportive wife, Kris Dahl, who even gave her blessing to my spending two weeks at the Kinsey Institute.

I sent out more than 150 letters requesting permission to excerpt passages, and every effort has been made to track down the copyright holders of the material quoted. If, however, there have been any accidental omissions, I (along with HarperCollins) would be more than happy to correct these in future editions.

Copyright
Acknowledgments

Genuine thanks go out to the following publishers and rights holders for kind permission to reprint excerpts from their works:

Academy Chicago Publishers: *Flaubert in Egypt,* trans. Francis Steegmuller (Bodley Head, 1972).

Anderson, Emily, estate of: *Letters of Mozart and His Family,* trans. Emily Anderson (New York: Macmillan/St. Martin's Press, 1966). Permission granted by Elisabeth Ingles.

AP Watt Ltd.: *The Twelve Caesars: Suetonius,* trans. Robert Graves (New York: Penguin, 1989). By permission of AP Watt Ltd. on behalf of the Robert Graves Copyright Trust.

Associated University Presses: *Laughter for the Devil: The Trials of Gilles de Rais,* Reginald Hyatte (Rutherford, 1984).

Augsburg Fortress: *Luther's Works,* vol. 54, ed. Theodore G. Tappert. Copyright © 1967 Fortress Press. Used by permission of Augsburg Fortress.

Burns & Oates: *Summa Theologica,* Thomas Aquinas (London, 1922).

Cailler: *Un Henri de Toulouse-Lautrec* (Geneva: Pierre Cailler, 1951). Permission granted by Nane Cailler.

Carol Publishing: *Demonolatry,* Nicolas Remy, trans. E. A. Ashwin (University Books, 1974). Copyright © 1974 University Books. Reprinted by arrangement with Carol Publishing Group.

Carol Publishing: *The Three Trials of Oscar Wilde,* ed. H. Montgomery Hyde. (University Books, 1956) Copyright, 1956. Used by arrangment with Carol Publishing.

Catholic University of America Press: *Rules for the Monastery at Compludo,* Fathers of the Church, Vol. 63 (1969).

Center for Medieval and Early Renaissance Studies: *The Chronicle of Salimbene de Adam,* trans. Joseph L. Baird et al., *Medieval & Renaissance Texts & Studies,* vol. 40 (Binghamton, N.Y., 1986), pp. 56, 365–369, 412–413; *Albert the Great: Man and the Beasts,* trans. James J. Scanlan, M.D., *Medieval & Renaissance Texts & Studies,* vol. 47 (Binghamton, N.Y., 1987), p. 60; *Witches, Devils, and Doctors in the Renaissance: Johann Weyer,* ed. George Mora, M.D., et al., *Medieval & Renaissance Texts & Studies,* vol. 73 (Binghamton, N.Y., 1991), pp. 310–311, 334–335, 393, 464. Copyright © 1986, 1987, 1991, respectively, Center for Medieval and Early Renaissance Studies, SUNY Binghamton.

Chatto & Windus: *Trial by Impotence,* Pierre Darmon (London, 1985).

Continuum Publishing: *The Art of Courtly Love,* Andreas Capellanus, trans. John Jay Perry (New York, 1985). Copyright © 1957, 1985 Frederick Ungar Publishing Co. Reprinted by permission of Continuum Publishing Co.

Doubleday: *Seven Pillars of Wisdom,* T. E. Lawrence (New York: Doubleday, 1935). Permission granted by Doubleday.

Duckworth: *The English Vice,* Ian Gibson (London, 1978). Used by permission of Duckworth.

Edinburgh and Yale: *London Journal,* James Boswell, ed. Frederick Pottle (Folio Society, 1985); *Boswell on the Grand Tour,* ed. Frank Brady and Frederick Pottle (New York, 1955). Permission granted by Edinburgh University Press and Yale Editions of the Private Papers of James Boswell.

Editions du Seuil: *Le Tribunal de l'Impuissance,* Pierre Darmon (Paris, 1979). Copyright © 1979 Editions du Seuil.

Ellis, Havelock, estate of: *Studies in the Psychology of Sex,* Havelock Ellis; *Impressions and Comments,* Havelock Ellis. Permission granted by Prof. F. Lafitte, executor of the estate of Havelock Ellis.

Grove Press: *The Black Diaries: An Account of Roger Casement's Life and Times...,* Maurice Girodias and Peter Singleton-Gates (Grove Press, 1959).

Sources

* * * * * * *

(When a source is responsible for *more* than one item, a brief subject reference has been added in parentheses for the sake of clarity. Publishers are cited for more recent editions.)

Abelard, Peter. *The Story of Abelard's Adversities,* trans. J. T. Muckle (Pontifical Institute of Medieval Studies, 1964), pp. 26–32, 37–39.

Aelred of Rievaulx. *De Sanctimoniali de Wattun* (Latin Fathers, vol. 195/Migne) (translation of excerpt by Jeri Fogel). Also, see *Aelred of Rievaulx and the Nun of Watton,* Giles Constable, in *Medieval Women,* ed. Derek Baker (Oxford University Press, 1978).

Albert of Aachen. *History of the Crusades,* in *Collections des memoires relatifs a l'histoire de France* (Paris, 1824), p. 160 (translation of excerpt by Richard Zacks).

Albert the Great (on fear and position). Quoted in *Sexuality and Medicine in the Middle Ages,* Danielle Jacquart and Claude Thomasset (Princeton University Press, 1988), pp. 82, 135 (translation of excerpt by Matthew Adamson).

———(mental). *De Animalibus, Man,* 3: *Albert the Great: Man and the Beasts,* trans. James J. Scanlan, M.D. (Medieval & Renaissance Texts & Studies, 1987), p. 60.

———(on virginity). *Le sixième sens,* Augustin Cabanes, trans. Robert Meadows (London, 1914), p. 16.

Alexis. Quoted in Athenaius's *Deipnosophistae* book 13 section 568b (translation of excerpt by Richard Zacks).

Alvarotto, Jules. Quoted in *Histoires d'amour de l'histoire de France,* Guy Breton (Paris, 1955–1965), vol. 2, pp. 232–233.

Ancillon, Charles. *Eunuchism Display'd. . . ,* (London, 1718), p. 42 (Edited).

Anonymous (on chloroform). *Les mysteres du confessional* (Paris, 1850), p. 126.

——— (on Anne Boleyn). *Chronicle of King Henry VIII of England,* trans. Martin Sharp Hume (London, 1889), pp. 55–58.

Aretino, Pietro. *Il Primo Libro delle Lettere,* ed. Fausto Nicolini (Bari, 1913), pp. 199–201, 397–398 (translation of excerpt by Richard Zacks).

Arnauld de Villanova. *Breviarum Practice,* quoted in Jacquart and Thomasset, *Sexuality and Medicine in the Middle Ages,* p. 147.

Arnault, A. V. *Souvenirs d'un sexaginaire* (Paris, 1833), pp. 31–35.

Ashbee, Henry Spencer. *Index Librorum Prohibitorum* (London, 1877), pp. xxxiv–xxxv, xliii–xlv, 328–332, 380–381, 400, 413.

——— (on memories). *Centuria Librorum Absconditorum* (London, 1879), pp. 458–459.

——— (on hermaphrodite). *Catena Librorum Tacendorum* (London, 1885) p. xv. Also, see modern editions: *Bibliography of Prohibited Books* (Jack Brussel, 1962), *Forbidden Books of the Victorians,* ed. Peter Fryer (Odyssey, 1970).

Assyrian Law Tablet. *Ancient Near Eastern Texts Relating to the Old Testament,* ed. James Pritchard (Princeton University Press, 1969), pp. 181, 185.

Athenaius (on Phryne). *Deipnosophistae* book 13, section 590e (translation of excerpt by Richard Zacks).

Aubrey, John. *Brief Lives,* ed. Oliver Lawson Dick (University of Michigan Press, 1957).

Avicenna. *Canon,* book 3, section 20, 21. Quoted in Jacquart and Thomasset, *Sexuality and Medicine in the Middle Ages,* pp. 130–131.

Bachaumont, M. *Memoires secrets* (London, 1777), vol. 6, pp. 196–197 (translation of excerpt by Richard Zacks).

The Blue Book: A Bibliographical Attempt. . . . pp. 56–61 (1936).

Bonaparte, Napoleon. *Lettres d'amour* (Paris, 1928), pp. 51–53, 65, 88–89, 123–124 (translation of excerpt by Richard Zacks).

Boswell, James. *London Journal,* ed. Frederick Pottle (Folio Society, 1985), vol. 1, pp. 230–231, 263–264, vol. 2, p. 229; *Boswell on the Grand Tour*, ed. Frank Brady and Frederick Pottle (McGraw-Hill, 1955), pp. 261, 277–281.

Bowman, Isa. *The Story of Lewis Carroll Told for Young People by the Real Alice in Wonderland* (New York, 1899).

Bradford, William. *History of Plymouth Plantation 1620–1647* (Massachusetts Historical Society, 1912), pp. 328–329.

Brantôme, Le Seigneur de. *Vies des dames gallantes*.

Breton, Guy. *Histoires d'amour de l'histoire de France* (Paris, 1955–1965).

———. *Napoleon and His Ladies*, trans. Frederick Holt (Coward-McCann, 1966), p. 32.

British handbill (on chloroform). Lilly Library, University of Indiana (1840s).

Britton, Nan. *The President's Daughter* (Elizabeth Ann Guild, 1927), pp. 170–173.

Burchard, Johann. *Diarium 1483-1506*, ed. L. Thuasne (Paris, 1884) (translation of excerpt by Jeri Fogel and others). Also, see *At the Court of the Borgia*, Geoffrey Parker (Folio Society, 1963).

Burchard of Worms. *Decreta* (Latin Fathers, Migne, 140), book 19, chap. 5 (translation of excerpt by A. R. Meadows).

Burns, Robert. *Burns Chronicle and Club Directory* 2 (1893), p. 56.

Burton, Sir Richard Francis (on Hankey). Quoted in *The Worm in the Bud*, Ronald Pearsall (Penguin, 1969), p. 385.

———. *Book of the Thousand Nights and a Night*, vol. 1, p. 6; vol. 4, p. 227; vol. 5, p. 76; vol. 10, pp. 205, 235-236, 239 (Benares ed., 1885).

Bussy-Rabutin, Roger de. *Histoire amoureuse des Gaules* (Paris, 1695/1829), pp. 197–205 (translation of excerpt by Richard Zacks).

Cadillac, Lamothe. Quoted in *Harlots, Whores & Hookers*, Hilary Evans (Dorset, 1979), p. 166.

Martyrology of Aengus. trans. Whitley Stokes in *Calender of Oengus* (Dublin, 1871), p. 32 (Edited).

Callender, James T. see *Richmond Recorder*.

Cantemir, Demetrius. *History of the Growth and Decay of the Ottoman Empire* (London, 1734), p. 254.

Capellanus, Andreas. *The Art of Courtly Love*, trans. John Jay Perry (Continuum, 1985), pp. 17, 23, 24.

Carey, John. *Eyewitness to History* (Avon, 1990).

Carroll, Lewis. *The Letters of Lewis Carroll* (Oxford University Press, 1979), pp. 337–341.

Casanova, Giacomo. *Mémoires de J. Casanova de Seingalt* (Paris, 1910), vol. 1, pp. 104–112 (translation of excerpt by Richard Zacks).

Casement, Roger. Quoted in *The Black Diaries: An Account of Roger Casement's Life and Times with a Collection of His Diaries and Public Writings*, Peter Singleton-Gates and Maurice Girodias (Grove, 1959), pp. 207, 211.

Catherine II of Russia. *Lettres d'amour de Catharine II à Potemkine* (Paris, 1934), pp. 39, 150. See also *Potemkin*, George Soloveytchik (Butterworth, 1938).

Cellini, Benvenuto. *La Vita* (Milano, 1811), vol. 2, pp. 113–120, 153–154 (translation of Italian excerpt by Richard Zacks).

Cibber, Theophilus. *Lives of the Poets* (London, 1753), pp. 289–290.

Civil War. All quotations from *A Kinsey Report on the Civil War*, Robert Waitt, Jr. (1963).

Clement of Alexandria. *Pedagogus*, book 3, chap. 3, in *The Ante-Nicene Fathers*, ed. Rev. Alexander Roberts and James Donaldson (Scribners, 1913).

Conti, Nicolo de. Quoted in *Sexual Relations of Mankind*, Paolo Mantegazza (New York, 1917), p. 76.

Corberon, Chevalier de. *Un diplomate Francais à la cour de Catherine II* (Paris, 1901), vol. 2, pp. 137, 151–152.

Corio, Bernadino. *Storia di Milano* (1510).

Court records ("A Sinful Error"). *Reports of Cases in the Courts of Star Chamber and High Commission*, ed. S. R. Gardiner (Camden Society, 1886), p. 296.

——— (on wife selling). *Oxfordshire Record Society* 10 (1928), p. 184.

——— (on Wilde). *The Trials of Oscar Wilde*, ed. H. Montgomery

Hyde (W. Hodge, 1948), in *Notable British Trial Series*, pp. 112, 143, 206, 361.

———. Quoted in *The Case of Sodomy in the Trial of Mervin Lord Audley . . .* (London, 1708).

Cuneo, Michele de. Quoted in *Journals and Other Documents on the Life and Voyages of Christopher Columbus*, trans. Samuel Eliot Morison (Heritage Press, 1963), pp. 209–212.

Dallam, Thomas. *Early Voyages and Travels in the Levant* (Hakluyt Society, 1893), pp. 74–75.

Damiani, Peter. *Book of Gomorrah: An Eleventh Century Treatise against Clerical Homosexual Practices. . .* , trans. Pierre J. Payer (Wilfrid Laurier University Press, 1982), p. 62.

Darmon, Pierre. *Le tribunal de l'impuissance* (Editions du Seuil, 1979), pp. 38–39, 190–191, 215–216 (translation of excerpt by Richard Zacks).

da Vinci, Leonardo. *The Literary Works of Leonardo da Vinci*, trans. J. P. Richter, ed. Carlo Peretti (Phaidon Press, 1977), pp. 112, 272.

Deffand, Madame du. *Lettres de la Marquise du Deffand à Horace Walpole* (London, 1912), pp. 247–253 (translation of excerpt by Richard Zacks).

Defoe, Daniel. *Conjugal Lewdness* (London, 1727), pp. 366–367.

Dens, Pierre. Quoted in *Confessional Unmasked*, C. B. (London, 1851), pp. 54–59.

Douglas, Sylvester. *The Journals of Sylvester Douglas, Lord Glenbervie* (New York, 1928), pp. 76–77.

Doyle, Peter. Interviewed in *Calamus: A Series of Letters Written during the Years 1868–1880 . . .* (Boston, 1897), pp. 23–31.

Dulaure, Jean Jacques. Quoted in *Human Ordure and Human Urine*, John Bourke (Washington, D.C., 1888), p. 21 (translation of excerpt by Richard Zacks).

Earl, William. *The Illustrated Silent Friend* (New York, 1848), pp. 113–114.

Egyptian victory monument. *Keeper of the Bed*, Charles Humana (Arlington, 1973), p. 20.

Ellington, George. *The Women of New York—or The Underworld of the Great City* (New York, 1869), pp. 475–476.

Ellis, Havelock. *My Life* (Neville Spearman, 1939), pp. 67–69.

———. *Impressions and Comments* (Houghton Miflin, 1930), p. 61.

———. *Studies in the Psychology of Sex* (Philadelphia, 1901–1928), vol. 1, pp. 171–172, 176–177; vol. 4, p. 89; vol. 7, pp. 380–381. *Sexual Selection in Man, Undinism.*

Eusebius. Quoted in *Witches, Devils, Doctors in the Renaissance: Johann Weyer*, ed. George Mora, M.D., et al. (Medieval & Renaissance Texts & Studies, 1991), p. 247.

Flaubert, Gustave. In *Flaubert in Egypt*, trans. Francis Steegmuller (Bodley Head, 1972), pp. 84–86, 113–120.

Forberg, Frederich. *Manual of Classical Erotology* (Manchester, 1884) (leads for Ancient Greece and Rome).

Formulae Liturgicae. Quoted in *Select Historical Documents of the Middle Ages,* trans. Ernest Henderson (London, 1925), pp. 314–315.

Fournier, Jacques. *Le registre d'inquisition de Jacques Fournier, eveque de Pamiers, 1318–1325* (Privat, 1965), vol. 1, p. 302; vol. 2, pp. 243–244; vol. 3, pp. 31, 39. (Translation of excerpt by A. R. Meadows.)

Franklin, Benjamin. Curious and Facetious Letters of Benjamin Franklin Hitherto Unpublished (1898), pp. 1–3.

Freud, Sigmund. *The Complete Letters of Sigmund Freud to Wilhelm Fliess 1887–1904*, trans. Jeffrey M. Masson (Belknap Press/Harvard University Press, 1985), pp. 268–269.

Fulcher of Chartres. *Historia Hierosolymitana,* ed. Heinrich Hagenmeyer (Heidelberg, 1913), p. 257 (translation of excerpt by Richard Zacks). Cited in *Prostitution, Miscegenation and Sexual Purity in the First Crusade*, James Brundage.

Galen. *Preservation of Health*, section 3.

Gilbert, Arthur. "Buggery and the British Navy," *Journal of Social History* 10, pp. 72–98.

Gilles de Rais (trial records of). *Laughter for the Devil: The Trials of*

Gilles de Rais, Reginald Hyatte (Associated University Presses, 1984), pp. 93–96.

Goncourt, Edmond and Jules de. *Journal des Goncourt* (Paris, 1891–1907), vol. 2, pp. 26–29 (translation of excerpt by Richard Zacks).

Gowdie, Isabel. Recorded in *Criminal Trials in Scotland*, ed. Robert Pitcairn (Edinburgh, 1833), vol. 3, app. 7, pp. 596–616.

Graham, Sylvester. *Lecture to Young Men* (New York, 1848), pp. 83, 208–209.

Guibert of Nogent. *Memoirs*, book 3, chap. 17. Quoted in *Self and Society in Medieval France,* trans. C. C. Swinton Bland (University of Toronto Press, 1984).

Hair, Paul. *Before the Bawdy Court* (Paul Elek Books, 1972).

Hakluyt Society Records. Quoted in *Sexual Relations of Mankind*, Paolo Mantegazza (New York, 1917), pp. 75–76.

Hallé, Jean Noel. Letter of April 21, 1807, quoted in *Napoleon Intime*, Arthur Levy (Paris, 1893), pp. 317–319.

Hammond, James Henry. *James Henry Hammond and the Old South: A Design for Mastery*, Drew G. Faust (Louisiana State University Press, 1982), p. 87.

Heloise. *The Letters of Abelard and Heloise*, trans. Betty Radice (Penguin, 1974), pp. 114, 119, 133.

Henry VII. *Historia Regis Henrici Septimi*, ed. James Gairdner (London, 1858), pp. 223–239.

Herodotus (on necrophilia). *History*, book 2, section 89 (translation of excerpt by Richard Zacks).

———. (on temple). *History*, book 1, section 199 (translation of excerpt by Richard Zacks).

Hippocrates. *On Generation*, section 4 (translation of excerpt by Richard Zacks).

Hittite law tablet. *Ancient Near Eastern Texts Relating to the Old Testament*, ed. James Pritchard (Princeton University Press, 1969), pp. 196–197.

Hollick, Frederick. *The Male Generative Organs* (New York, 1853), p. 217.

Holloway (Vere Street Coterie). Quoted in *Index Librorum Prohibitorum*, Henry Spencer Ashbee (1877), pp. 328-332.

Houghton, Lord (conversation and on Swinburne). Quoted in *The English Vice*, Ian Gibson (Duckworth, 1978), pp. 125, 242–243.

Ibn Fadlan. *Ibn Fadlan's Account of Scandinavian Merchants on the Volga in 922*, trans. Albert Cook (1923), quoted in *Journal of English and Germanic Philology* 22, pp. 54–63.

Imad ad Din. Quoted in *Arab Historians of the Crusades: Selected and Translated from the Arabic Sources*, Francesco Gabrieli, trans. from the Italian by E. J. Costello (University of California Press, 1969), pp. 204–206.

James I. *Letters of King James I & VI*, ed. G. P. V. Akrigg (University of California Press, 1984), pp. 337–339. Also, see *Royal Family, Royal Lovers: King James of England and Scotland*, David M. Bergeron (University of Missouri Press, 1991).

Jefferson, Thomas (on sodomy). *The Papers of Thomas Jefferson*, ed. Julian Boyd (Princeton University Press, 1950), vol. 2, p. 497.

Joan of Arc (court records). *Procès de condamnation et de rehabilitation de Jeanne d'Arc dite la Pucelle*, ed. Jules Quicherat (Paris, 1845), vol. 3, pp. 63, 89, 121, 147–149, 155, 163 (translation of excerpt by A. R. Meadows). Also, see *Joan of Arc: The Legend and the Reality*, Frances Gies (Harper & Row, 1981).

Johanna I of Naples. *Brothel Rules*, quoted in *History of Prostitution*, Paul LaCroix (Chicago, 1926), pp. 876–879.

Jones, John Paul (police). Quoted in *John Paul Jones: A Sailor's Biography*, Samuel Eliot Morison (Little, Brown/Naval Institute, 1989), pp. 459—460.

——— (Potemkin). *Life and Correspondence of John Paul Jones* (New York, 1830), p. 478.

Juvenal (on Messalina). *Satires*, book 6 (translation of excerpt by Richard Zacks).

——— (proverb). *Satires*, book 9, line 32 (translation of excerpt by Richard Zacks).

Katz, Jonathan. *Gay American History* (Crowell, 1976) (leads on Puritans, Horatio Alger, Jefferson).

Kellogg, John Harvey. *Ladies Guide in Health and Disease* (Battle Creek, Mich.: Health Publishing Company, 1883), pp. 144, 145, 150–153, 165, 546–547.

Kramer, Heinrich (and James Sprenger). *Malleus Maleficarum*, trans. Montague Summers (Hogarth Press, 1971), pp. 262–268.

Ladurie, Emmanuel Le Roy. *Montaillou, the Promised Land of Error*, trans. Barbara Bray (G. Braziller, 1978).

Lampridius. *Life of Heliogabulus*, chap. 5, 31 (translation of excerpt by Richard Zacks).

Landor, A. H. Savage. *Alone with the Hairy Ainu* (London, 1893), pp. 139–141.

Lassels, Richard. Quoted in *La femme Italienne*, Emmanuel Rodocanachi (Paris, 1907), pp. 173–174 (translation of excerpt by Richard Zacks).

La Tour-Landry, Chevalier de. *The Book of the Knight of La Tour-Landry*, ed. G. S. Taylor (London, 1906), p. 72 (Edited).

Lawner, Lynne. *Lives of the Courtesans* (Rizzoli, 1987).

Lawrence, T. E. *Seven Pillars of Wisdom* (Doubeday, 1935), pp. 441–447.

L'Estoile, Pierre de (on St. Bartholomew). *Mémoires relatif à l'histoire de France*, ed. MM. Michaud (Paris, 1854), vol. 14, pp. 25–26 (translation of excerpt by Richard Zacks).

Liguori, Alfonso. Quoted in *Confessional Unmasked*, C. B. (London, 1851), pp. 54–59.

Lincoln, Abraham. *Letters and Addresses of Abraham Lincoln* (New York, 1903), pp. 21–24.

Loeb Classical Library (Harvard University Press).

Lucian (on eunuchs). *The Gods of Syria*, trans. Sir James George Frazer in *The Golden Bough* (London, 1911), p. 50.

——— (on shaved heads). *The Gods of Syria*, chap. 6 (translation of excerpt by Richard Zacks).

Lucretius. *On the Nature of Things*, book 4, line 1263 (translation of excerpt by Richard Zacks).

Luther, Martin. *Werke, Briefwechsel* (Weimar, 1883), vol. 3, pp. 634–635 (translation of excerpt by Jeri Fogel).

———— (table talk). Reprinted from *Luther's Works*, vol. 54, ed. Theodore G. Tappert (Fortress Press, 1967), pp. 8, 161.

Maimonides, Moses. *Treatise on Cohabitation*, in *Maimonides' Medical Writings*, trans. Fred Rosner, M.D. (Haifa: Maimonides Research Institute, 1984).

Mairobert, Pidanzat de. *L'Espion Anglois; on Correspondence Secrete Entre Milord All'Eye et Milord All'Ear* (London, 1779) pp. 352ff (translation of excerpt by Richard Zacks).

Marie-Antoinette (and Comte de Creutz, Count Fersen). Quoted in *Histoires d'amour de l'histoire de France* (Paris, 1955–1965) vol. 5, pp. 202–203; vol. 6, pp. 231–232, 237.

Martial (on depilation). *Epigrams*, book 2, epigram #62; book 9, epigram #28.

Marx, Karl. Quoted in *Karl Marx: An Intimate Biography*, Saul Padover (McGraw-Hill, 1980), pp. 469–470.

Masoch, Aurora (Wanda) von Sacher. *Confession de ma vie*, serialized in *Mercure de France* (1907), January 15, pp. 257–259; February 1, pp. 433–436; March 15, pp. 288–289 (translation of excerpt by Richard Zacks).

Masson, Charles. *Memoirs of the Court of St. Petersburg* (Philadelphia, 1898), pp. 99–101.

McCall, Andrew (on street names). *The Medieval Underworld* (Dorset, 1979), p. 191.

McCartney, George. *McCartney's Commentary on Russia in 1786*, in Osborne Collection at Yale University; quoted in *Catherine the Great: Life and Legend*, John T. Alexander (Oxford University Press, 1989), pp. 215–216.

Menefee, Samuel. *Wives for Sale* (Oxford University Press, 1988), pp. 68, 75.

Mirabeau, Comte de. *Erotika Biblion* (Paris, 1783) (translation of excerpt by Richard Zacks).

Montagu, Lady Mary. *Letters from the Levant* (London, 1838), pp. 106–108, 225–226.

Montgomery, Janet Livingston. *Reminiscences*, reprinted in *Dutchess Co. Historical Society Year Book* (1930), p. 61.

More, Sir Thomas. *Utopia*, trans. Gilbert Burnet (Oxford, 1751) (Edited).

Mozart, Wolfgang A. *Letters of Mozart and His Family*, trans. Emily Anderson (Macmillan/St. Martin's Press, 1966), pp. 372, 782–784.

Nathanson, Thadée. *Un Henri de Toulouse-Lautrec* (Geneva: Pierre Cailler, 1951), pp. 52–53, 57, 286, 290.

Ordericus Vitalis. *Ecclesiastical History*, trans. Marjorie Chibnall (Clarendon Press, 1972), pp. 219, 221.

Ormsby's New York Mail Bag. September, 1863. Clements Library, University of Michigan.

Ortzen, Len. *Imperial Venus* (Constable, 1974). Also, see *Pauline Bonaparte: La fidèle infidèle*, Genevieve Chastenet (JC Lattes, 1986).

Pabrol. Quoted in *Aphrodisiacs and Anti-Aphrodisiacs*, John Davenport (London, 1869), p. 97 (translation of excerpt by Richard Zacks).

Parke, J. Richardson. *Human Sexuality* (Philadelphia, 1908), p. 285.

Parkinson, John. *A Tour of Russia, Siberia and the Crimea, 1792–1794* (London, 1971), quoted in *Catherine the Great: Life and Legend*, John T. Alexander (Oxford University Press, 1988), pp. 215–216.

Pausanius. *Description of Greece*, book 5, section 6 (translation of excerpt by Richard Zacks).

Pepys, Samuel. *Diary of Samuel Pepys*, ed. Robert Latham and William Matthews (University of California Press, 1974), May 15, 1663; July 1, 1663.

Platina, Bartolomeo. *Lives of the Popes*, trans. Paul Rycaut (London, 1688), p. 165 (Edited).

Plazzoni, Dr. Francesco. *De Partibus Generatoni Inserventibus* (1621), book 2, chap. 13 (translation of excerpt by Jeri Fogel).

Plutarch (on beheading). *Marcus Cato*, section 17 (translation of excerpt by Richard Zacks).

—— (on Cleopatra). *Life of Marc Antony*, section 26, 29 (translation of excerpt by Richard Zacks).

—— (on boy love). *Dialogue on Love*, section 752A (translation of excerpt by Richard Zacks).

Poe, Edgar Allan. *Letters of Edgar Allan Poe*, ed. John Ward Ostrow (Harvard University Press, 1948), pp. 400–403.

Polo, Marco (on Kublai Khan's beauty contest). *Travels*, trans. William Marsden (London, 1854), pp. 171–174; other passages from *The Travels of Marco Polo*, trans. Ronald Latham (Penguin, 1958), pp. 143–144, 168.

Porte, Pierre de la. *Memoires de Pierre de la Porte*, in *Mémoires relatif à l'histoire de France*, ed. M. Michaud (Paris, 1854), vol. 8, p. 19.

Pouillet, Thésée. *Etude médico-psychologique sur l'onanisme chez la femme*, quoted in *Studies in the Psychology of Sex, Auto-Eroticism*, Havelock Ellis, vol. 4, p. 89.

Priapeia. Trans. Richard Zacks, consulted *Priapea: Poems for a Phallic God*, W. H. Parker (Croom Helm, 1988), pp. 35, 56, 69.

Procopius (on Theodora). *Secret History*, chap. 9, section 7ff (translation of excerpt by Richard Zacks).

—— (on retirement). *Buildings*, book 1, chap. 9, sections 1–10; *Secret History*, chap. 17, section 5 (translation of excerpt by Richard Zacks).

Records of the Colony and Plantation of New Haven from 1638 to 1649, ed. Charles Hoadly (Hartford, 1857), pp. 295–296.

Rémy, Nicolas. *Demonolatry*, trans. E. A. Ashwin (University Books, 1974), p. 14.

Report of a Brewster Church Committee, Records of the Unitarian Church (Brewster, Mass., 1866), quoted in *The American Idea of Success*, Richard Huber (McGraw-Hill, 1971), pp. 45–46.

Restif de la Bretonne. *Mon calendrier* (Paris, 1932), p. 10 (translation of excerpt by Richard Zacks).

Richards, John. Quoted in *Harem*, N. Penzer (London, 1936), p. 224.

Richmond Recorder. All quotes taken from microfilm of original editions of the *Richmond Recorder*, Virginia State Archives. Also, see *The Jefferson Scandals: A Rebuttal*, Virginius Dabney (Dodd Mead, 1981).

Robbins, Rossell. *The Encyclopedia of Witchcraft and Demonology* (Crown, 1959).

Robertson, George. *The Discovery of Tahiti. . .* , ed. Hugh Carrington (Hakluyt Society, 1948), pp. 207–209.

Rodiad. Private edition, *circa* 1880s.

Roger of Wendover. *Flowers of History*, trans. J. A. Giles (London, 1849), p. 314 (Edited).

Rousseau, Jean-Jacques. *Les confessions* (Paris, 1913), vol. 1, pp. 22–28, 140–144, 174, 319 (translation of excerpt by Richard Zacks).

Ruggiero, Guido. *The Boundaries of Eros: Sex Crime and Sexuality in Renaissance Venice* (Oxford University Press, 1985), pp. 114–115, 117–119, 185.

Rules for the Monastery at Compludo. Fathers of the Church, 63 (Catholic University of America Press, 1969), p. 169.

Rycaut, Paul. *History of the Turkish Empire* (London, 1680), p. 19.

———. *The State of the Ottoman Empire* (London, 1668), pp. 39–40.

Sade, Marquis de. *Selected Letters*, trans. W. J. Strachan (Peter Owen, 1965), Letters of Feb. 20, 1781, April 17, 1782.

St. Athanasius. *Apology for His Flight*, section 26 (translation of excerpt by Richard Zacks).

St. Augustine. *City of God*, book 6, chap. 9; book 7, chap. 24 (translation of excerpt by Richard Zacks).

St. Basil. *Sermo de Renunciatione Saeculi* (Greek Fathers, vol. 31, Migne) p. 638 (wiseguy translation of excerpt by Richard Zacks).

St. Jerome (on marriage). Quoted by Thomas Aquinas in *Summa*

Theologica (Burns Oates & Washbourne, 1922), suppl. Q. 154, art. 7.

———— (on menstruation). Quoted by Thomas Aquinas in *Summa Theologica* (Burns Oates & Washbourne, 1922), suppl. Q. 64, art. 3.

Saint-Foix, Poullain de. *Essais Historiques Sur Paris* (Paris, 1766), pp. 22–24 (translation of excerpt by Richard Zacks).

Salimbene de Adam. *The Chronicle of Salimbene de Adam*, trans. Joseph L. Baird et al. (Medieval & Renaissance Texts & Studies, 1986), pp. 56, 365–369, 412–413.

Salisbury, Joyce. *Medieval Sexuality: A Research Guide* (Garland, 1990).

Ségur, Comte de. *Mémoires* (Paris, 1879), pp. 166–167 (translation of excerpt by Richard Zacks).

Sellon, Edward. *The Ups and Downs of Life*, quoted in *Index Librorum Prohibitorum*, Henry Spencer Ashbee (1877), pp. 380–381.

Selmuth, Henry. *Rerum Memorabilium*, Guido Pancirolli (London, 1631), book 2, tit. 10 (translation of excerpt by A. R. Meadows) (Edited).

Seneca (on mirrors). *Natural Questions*, book 1, section 16 (translation of excerpt by Richard Zacks).

———— (on see-through blouses). *On Benefits*, book 7, section 9 (translation of excerpt by Richard Zacks).

Servin, Louis. See Darmon, Pierre.

Slave narratives. Compiled by Federal Writers Project, 1936–1938, Works Progress Administration. Available at Library of Congress (Georgia narratives, pt. 3) or: *The American Slave: A Composite Autobiography*, ed. George Rawick (Greenwood, 1972).

Sonnini, C. S. *Travels in Upper and Lower Egypt*, trans. Henry Hunter (London, 1799), pp. 209–210, 258–259.

Soranos. *The Diseases of Women* book 1, section 5, 20 (translation of excerpt by Richard Zacks).

Speed, Joshua. *Reminiscences of Abraham Lincoln* (Louisville, 1896), pp. 21–22.

Speke, John Hanning. *Journal of the Discovery of the Source of the Nile* (Edinburgh, 1864), pp. 209–210, 231.

Statutes of Treviso. Quoted in *The Myth of Lesbian Impunity: Capital Laws from 1270–1791*, Louis Crompton, *Journal of Homosexuality* 6, p. 18.

Stead, W. T. *Pall Mall Gazette*, July 6, 1885. Lilly Library, Indiana University. Also, see *The Worm in the Bud*, Ronald Pearsall (Penguin, 1969), pp. 296–306.

Stendhal. *Vie de Henry Brulard*, in *Oeuvres completes de Stendhal* (Paris, 1913), vol. 1, pp. 38–40 (translation of excerpt by Richard Zacks).

———. *Journal* (Paris, 1937), *Oeuvres*, vol. 71, pp. 33–34, August 1, 1801 (translation of excerpt by Richard Zacks).

Strabo (on Cretans). *Geography*, book 10, section 483f (translation of excerpt by Richard Zacks).

——— (on sandals). *Geography*, book 6, section 259 (translation of excerpt by Richard Zacks).

Suetonius. *The Twelve Caesars*, trans. Robert Graves, rev. Michael Grant (Penguin, 1989): Julius Caesar, chap. 45, 49, 51, 52; Tiberius, chap. 43, 44, 45; Caligula, chap. 24, 36, 50; Nero, chap. 28, 29.

——— (on loop-hole). *Lives of the Caesars*: Tiberius, chap. 35 (translation of excerpt by Richard Zacks).

——— (on Cleopatra). *Lives of the Caesars*: Augustus, chap. 69 (translation of excerpt by Richard Zacks).

Swinburne, Charles Algernon. *The Swinburne Letters*, ed. Cecil Lang (Yale University Press, 1959), p.78.

Tacitus (on loop-hole). *Annals*, book 2, section 85 (translation of excerpt by Richard Zacks).

Tagereau, Vincent. See Darmon, Pierre.

Tannahill, Reay. *Sex in History* (Stein & Day, 1982).

Tanner, John. *A Narrative of the Captivity and Adventures of John Tanner* (London, 1830), pp. 105–106.

Tardieu, Ambroise. Quoted in *Medico-legal Moral Offenses*, Leon Thoinot, trans. Arthur Weysse (Philadelphia, 1911), pp. 449–457.

Terry, Edward. *A Voyage to East India* (London, 1777), p. 387.

Theopompus. Quoted in Athenaius's *Deipnosophistae*, book 12, section 517d (translation of excerpt by Richard Zacks).

Thomas, Abbot, of Burton. *Chronicle of Méaux*, quoted in *From St. Francis to Dante: Translations from the Chronicle of the Franciscan Salimbene, 1221–1288,* ed. Edward Peters (University of Pennsylvania Press, 1972), pp. 426–427.

Times of London. July 6, 1863, quoted in *The English Vice*, Ian Gibson (Duckworth, 1978), p. 248.

Tournefort, M. *A Voyage into the Levant* (London, 1718), vol. 2, p. 49.

Trotula. *Medieval Woman's Guide to Health*, trans. Beryl Rowland (Kent State University Press, 1981), p. 157.

Twain, Mark. *Science of Onanism*, from *The Outrageous Mark Twain*, ed. Charles Neider (Doubleday, 1987), pp. 58–60.

Usama ibn Manqidh. Quoted in *Arab Historians of the Crusades: Selected and Translated from the Arabic Sources*, Francesco Gabrieli, trans. from the Italian by E. J. Costello (University of California Press, 1969), p. 78.

Vallentin, Antonina. *Leonardo da Vinci: The Tragic Pursuit of Perfection* (Viking, 1938).

Van Gogh, Vincent. *Le forum républicain*, December 30, 1888.

Venette, Dr. Nicolas. *La génération de l'homme; ou tableau de l'amour conjugale considéré dans l'état du marriage* (London, 1779), pp. 3–8, 34–48 (translation of excerpt by Richard Zacks).

Vespucci, Amerigo. *Amerigo Vespucci: Letter to Piero Soderini*, trans. George Northrup (Princeton University Press, 1916), pp. 7–9; *Mundus Novus*, trans. George Northrop (Princeton University Press, 1916), pp. 5–6 (Edited to include "Lizard").

Villamont, Seigneur de. Quoted in *La femme Italienne*, Emmanuel Rodocanachi (Paris, 1907), pp. 173–174 (translation of excerpt by Richard Zacks).

Voltaire. *Dictionaire philosophique*, "Onan/Onanisme" and "Verge. Baguette Divinatoire" (Paris, 1829) (translation of excerpt by Richard Zacks); "Cuissage" (London, 1824).

Waitt, Robert, Jr. *A Kinsey Report on the Civil War* (1963).

Wallis, Capt. Samuel. *An Account of the Voyages. . .* , ed. John Hawkesworth (London, 1773), pp. 438ff.

Weyer, Dr. Johann. *Witches, Devils, and Doctors in the Renaissance: Johann Weyer*, ed. George Mora, M.D. et al. (Medieval & Renaissance Texts and Studies, 1991), pp. 310–311, 334–335, 393, 464.

The White Book of the City of London. Ed. Henry Riley (London, 1841), book 3, pt. 4, pp. 394–395.

Whitman, Walt. *Calamus: A Series of Letters Written during the Years 1868–1880. . .* (Boston, 1897), pp. 23–31, 53–55, 61–62. Also, see *Calamus Lovers: Walt Whitman's Working Class Camerados*, Charlie Shively (Gay Sunshine Press, S.F., 1987).

Wilde, Oscar. *The Three Trials of Oscar Wilde*, ed. H. Montgomery Hyde (W. Hodge, 1948), pp. 112, 143, 206–207, 361–362.

Wilmot, John, Earl of Rochester. *Poems* (from secondary sources). For a scholarly edition, see *The Complete Poems of John Wilmot, Earl of Rochester* (Yale University Press, 1968).

Wilson, Mary. *Venus Schoolmistress*, quoted in *Index Librorum Prohibitorum*, Henry Spencer Ashbee (1877), pp. xliii–xlv, 400.

Winthrop, John. *The History of New England from 1630 to 1649*, ed. James Savage (Boston, 1853), vol. 2, pp. 59–60. See also *Things Fearful to Name*, Robert Oaks, *Journal of Social History* 12, no. 3.

Woodhull, Victoria. *Tried as by Fire* (New York, 1874).

X, Dr. Jacobus. *Untrodden Fields of Anthropology* (Paris, 1898), pp. 72–74, 76, 190, 258–260, 284–285, 295–296, 299–300.

Xenarchus. Quoted in Athenaius's *Deipnosophistae*, book 13, section 569b (translation of excerpt by Richard Zacks).

Yves of Chartres. *Epistolae*, 205 (Latin Fathers, vol. 162, Migne) (translation of excerpt by Richard Zacks).

Index